MW00608241

THE LAWFUL AND THE PROHIBITED IN ISLAM
AL-HALAL WAL-HARAM FIL ISLAM

By: Yusuf al-Qaradawi

Translators:
Kamal El-Helbawy
M. Moinuddin Siddiqui
Syed Shukry

Translation Reviewed by: Ahmad Zaki Hammad

Copyright © American Trust Publications, 1994
All Rights Reserved
American Trust Publications
2622 East Main Street
Plainfield, Indiana 46168
Library of Congress Catalog No. 80-81562
ISBN 0-89259-016-5
January 1999

TABLE OF CONTENTS

CHAPTER ONE:
THE ISLAMIC PRINCIPLES PERTAINING TO
HALAL AND *HARAM*

CHAPTER TWO
THE *HALAL* AND THE *HARAM*
IN THE PRIVATE LIFE OF THE MUSLIM

CHAPTER THREE
THE *HALAL* AND THE *HARAM* IN MARRIAGE AND FAMILY LIFE

viii

CHAPTER FOUR
THE *HALAL* AND THE *HARAM*
IN THE DAILY LIFE OF THE MUSLIM

ix

In the name of Allah, the Compassionate, the Merciful

INTRODUCTION

The General Institute of Islamic Culture of al-Azhar University has requested me to participate in an academic project of writing easily understandable books or pamphlets which, when translated into the English language, would introduce Islam and its teachings to Europe and America, educating the Muslims who reside there and attracting the non-Muslims toward Islam.

Assuredly this project of producing books and pamphlets has both a lofty aim and a broad scope. It should have been initiated long ago, since many Muslims in Europe and America have very little knowledge of Islam, and even that little has not remained safe from distortion and confusion. Recently a friend from al-Azhar who was sent to one of the states in the United States of America wrote to us, saying,"Many Muslims in this state run bars and earn their living through the sale of liquor, not even knowing that this is a major sin in Islam." He adds, "Muslim men marry Christian, Jewish and sometimes *mushrik*[1] women, passing over the Muslim women, who remain unmarried and have to fend for themselves."

If this is the state of the Muslims, what can be said of the non-Muslims? People in the West have a very distorted and ugly picture of Islam, its Prophet (may Allah's peace and blessings be on him), and its followers, a picture painted by Christian missionaries and the representatives of the imperialist powers. They have used all means of propaganda at their disposal to malign Islam and to prejudice the minds of people against it,while we, at the same time, have been heedless and neglectful of combating this malicious propaganda.

It is indeed high time to launch an educational project in order to remedy this situation, to inform people about the truth of Islam, and to invite them toward it. We welcome this blessed step, commending these devoted people of al-Azhar; we request them to redouble their

---

[1]Ascribing partners, or associating others, with Allah. (Trans.)

1

efforts in this direction, and pray to Allah to bless and help them always.

The Institute of Islamic Culture assigned me the task of writing on the subject of the lawful (*al-halal*) and the prohibited *(al-haram)* in Islam, requesting that I present the subject in a simple and easily understandable manner which was also to include a comparison with other religions and cultures.

At first glance the subject of the lawful and the prohibited may seem easy to write about, but it is, in fact, extremely difficult. No previous author, either early or modern, has compiled a book dealing specifically with this topic. The student will find material pertaining to this subject scattered throughout various chapters in books on Islamic jurisprudence *(fiqh)*, and between the lines in the commentries on the Qur'an and in books of the Prophet's *ahadith*.

Such a subject, moreover, compels the writer to be definitive concerning many matters about which earlier scholars have differed and contemporary scholars are confused. Consequently, to prefer one opinion over another in matters relating to the *halal* and the *haram* in Islam requires patience, thoroughness in research, and intellectual exertion on the part of the researcher — all this after he has purified his heart from all desires except to please Allah Subhanahu wa Ta'ala and to seek the truth.

It is my observation that most contemporary researchers and writers about Islam fall into one of two groups. The vision of one group has been blinded by the glamor of Western civilization. Overawed by this great idol, they worship it, approach it imploringly, and stand before it humbly, with downcast eyes, accepting Western principles and customs as unassailable and proven beyond doubt. Accordingly, if some aspect of Islam agrees with these principles and customs, they praise and extol it, while if some aspect opposes them, they try to find similarities and agreements, offer excuses and apologies, or resort to far fetched explanations and distortions, as if Islam had no choice except to surrender to the philosophy and customs of Western civilization. When we examine their views, we find that they permit things which Islam has prohibited, such as statues, lotteries, interest, being in privacy with a non-*mahrem* woman, a man's wearing gold and silk, and so on. They frown upon things which Islam has

2

permitted, such as divorce and plurality of wives, as if, in their view, whatever is legal in the West is *halal* and what is illegal is *haram.* They forget that Islam is the word of Allah and that His word is always uppermost. Islam came to be followed, not to follow; to be dominant, not subordinate. How can the Lord of men follow men and how can the Creator submit to the whims of His creatures?

> If the reality had been in accord with their desires, the heavens and the earth, and whosoever is therein, would have been in corruption...(Holy Qur'an 23:71)[1]
> Say: Is there among your partners (whom you associate with Allah) any who guides to the truth? Say: Allah guides to the truth. Then does He Who guides to the truth have more right to be obeyed, or the one who is not guided unless he receives guidance? Then what is wrong with you all? How do you judge? (10:35)

The other group is frozen in its fixed opinions concerning questions about the *halal* and the *haram,* following a statement in a text which they assume to be Islam. They do not budge a hair's breadth from their position, nor do they try to weigh their opinion against the arguments of others, and to arrive at the truth after a comparison and critical evaluation of all opinions. If one of them were to be asked his opinion concerning music, singing, chess, women's education, a woman's showing her face and hands, and similar matters, the most likely word to issue from his tongue would be *Haram.* This group has forgotten the caution exercised by our righteous forebearers in such matters, who never applied the word *haram* to anything unless they knew it to be definitely prohibited. If there were the slightest doubt concerning the matter they would only say, "We disapprove of it" or "We do not like it," or some other similarly mild statement.

I have endeavored not to be in either of these two groups. I cannot compromise my religion by taking the West as my god after accepting Allah as the Lord, Islam as the religion, and Muhammad (peace be on him) as the Messenger.   At the same time, I cannot

---

[1]The numbering of Qur'anic chapters and verses used throughout this book is the standard numbering used in all editions of the Qur'an. The sole exception is in relation to *Surah al-Maidah,* the fifth *Surah,* the numbering of which differs slightly between the translations of A. Yusuf 'Ali and those of other translators. Where verses from this *surah* are cited, the numbering used by Yusuf 'Ali is given first and the numbering used by such translators as Pickthall, Maududi, M. Asad and others is given in brackets immediately following it. (Trans.)

3

compromise my intellect by following one particular school of jurisprudence in all its judgements, whether right or wrong, suspending my own faculty of reasoning and discernment. "A blind follower," in the words of Ibn al-Jawzi, "does not have any trust in what he follows. To imitate is to suspend the use of the intellect, whereas the intellect is created for thinking and reasoning. It is stupidity when a person is given a light to show him the way, he should extinguish it and walk in darkness."[1]

This is why I have not confined myself to any one of the several schools of jurisprudence (*madhahib*, singular *madhab*) prevalent in the Islamic world, for the truth is not the monopoly of any one school. The leading scholars of these schools never claimed that they were infallible; they were, in fact, researchers who sought to know the truth. If they erred in a ruling they will have a reward, while if they were correct, their reward will be twice as great.

Said Imam Malik, "The word of any person other than the Prophet (peace be on him) is sometimes accepted and sometimes rejected. " And Imam Shafi'i commented, "My opinion is correct with the possibility of its being in error. An opinion different from mine is in error with the possibility of its being correct."

While it is not worthy of a Muslim scholar who is capable of comparing and choosing to tie himself to a single school of jurisprudence or to submit to the opinion of a particular jurist, he must give weight to arguments and proofs. The jurist with strong arguments and a valid proof deserves to be followed, while the one with weak arguments and incorrect proofs should be rejected, regardless of who he is. On this point, Imam 'Ali says, "Truth is not to be learned on the basis of authorities. Learn the truth and then you will know who the truthful ones are."

I have tried, to the best of my ability, to follow the guidelines of the Institute of Islamic Culture. Thus I have presented the material supported by arguments, proofs, and comparisons, utilizing the latest scientific ideas and contemporary knowledge. *Alhamdulillah,* Islam is like the radiant sun, whose light bears the proof that it is an eternal religion for all mankind.

> The hue imparted by Allah - and who is better than
> Allah in imparting a hue?   (Holy Qur'an 2:138)

---

[1] *Talbis Iblis,* p. 81.

4

The concept of the lawful and the prohibited has been known to every people since ancient times. However, people have differed in defining the scope, variety, and causes of taboos and prohibitions, most of which were a product of their primitive beliefs, superstititions, and myths. Then came the divinely-revealed religions,[1] with their laws and injunctions concerning the *halal* and the *haram,* uplifting the human being from the level of superstition, myth, and tribalism to the level of dignity which befits a human being.

However, in the religions revealed prior to Islam there were some prohibitions and permissions which were legislated for a temporary period, in relation to the specific conditions of the people and their environments. For example, Allah prohibited some good things to the Children of Israel as a punishment for their rebellious attitude; thereafter, Jesus (peace be on him) told the people that he had come

> ...confirming the truth of what was before me of the
> *Taurat*[2] and to make lawful to you some of what was
> prohibited to you... (3:50)

Finally, when mankind had reached the stage of intellectual maturity and was ready to receive the last message from Allah Subhanahu wa Ta'ala, Islam came with its complete, comprehensive, and eternal *Shari'ah* (law) for the whole of mankind. Concerning this, after mentioning what He has prohibited as food, Allah says,

> ...This day I have perfected your religion for you and
> have completed My favor upon you, and have chosen
> Islam for you as the religion... (5:4)(3)

The Islamic view of the *halal* and the *haram* is very simple and clear. It is a part of that great trust which Allah offered to the heavens, the earth, and the mountains, which they declined but

---

[1]According to the Qur'an there has been only one true, authentic faith, Al-Islam. Islam means the attainment of peace through conscientious and loving submission to the Will and Guidance of Allah. This was the mission of all Prophets and Messengers in human history. It is the same fundamental faith which was revealed to Moses, Jesus, and Muhammad (peace be upon them). The original revelations given to Moses and Jesus are no longer available in their complete, original, and unadulterated form. The Qur'an is the only divine revelation which was meticulously preserved in it's complete, original, and unadulterated form. As such, it is to be used as the criterion to judge the authenticity of the present forms of previous revelations.

[2]*Taurat* refers to the original scripture revealed to the Prophet Moses by God.

which man accepted. This trust requires man to carry out the duties placed on him by Allah as His viceregent on earth and to assume accountability concerning them. This responsibility is the basis on which the human individual will be judged by Allah and given his reward or punishment. Because of this trust, Allah gave man intellect, will power, and freedom of choice; because of this, He sent His messengers and revealed His Books. It is not for man to ask, "Why is there *halal* and *haram*? Why am I not left free to do as I please?" for this is precisely the test of his freedom of choice and action. Moreover, man is neither a purely spiritual being like the angels nor simply a creature of instinct like the animals. Rather he occupies a position between the two: he can attain or even surpass the spiritual heights of the angels, or he can sink to the level of the beasts, or even lower.

From another perspective, the *halal* and *haram* are part of the total legal system of Islam, its *Shari'ah*, a system whose primary objective is the good of mankind. The Islamic *Shari'ah* removes from human beings harmful, burdensome customs and superstitions, aiming to simplify and ease the business of day-to-day living. Its principles are designed to protect man from evil and to benefit him in all aspects of his life. And they are designed to benefit everyone in the community — the rich and the poor, the rulers and the ruled, the men and the women — as well as to benefit the whole of humanity throughout the earth in various countries and climes, with its multitude of groupings, and in every period of time throughout succeeding generations.

This religion came as a mercy from Allah to include all His servants in the final stage among the various stages of man. Concerning His Messenger (peace be on him) Allah says,

> And We have not sent thee except as a mercy for all the worlds. (21:107),

and the Prophet (peace be on him) himself said,

> "I am a merciful gift".[1]

One aspect of this mercy is that Allah removed from the Muslim *ummah* (nation or community) all traces of fanaticism and zealotry, as well as all the means of declaring things to be *halal* and *haram* ;

---

[1]Reported by al-Hakim on the authority of Abu Hurairah; al-Dhahabi classifies this *hadith* as authentic.

contrary to the case of the idolators and the People of the Book (Jews and Christians), whose priests had prohibited the good things and permitted the foul. Allah says:

...My mercy embraces all things. Thus I shall ordain it for those who are conscious (of Me) and who give the purifying alms (*zakat*), and those who believe in Our revelations.(7:156)

The Islamic criteria with regard to the *halal* and *haram* are embodied in the following two verses, which we have placed at the beginning of this book:

Say: Who has forbidden the adornment of Allah which He has brought forth for His servants, and the good things of His providing? Say: They are, on the Day of Ressurection, exclusively for those who believed during the life of this world. Thus do We explain the signs for those who know. Say: What my Lord has indeed prohibited are shameful deeds, whether open or secret, and sin and rebellion without just cause, and that you associate with Allah that for which He has sent down no authority, and that you say concerning Allah that about which you do not know.   (7:32-33)

In view of the fact that the *halal* and *haram* constitute such an important subject, I believe that this book, in spite of its modest size, will fill a gap in the library of the contemporary Muslim; that it will solve many problems which he faces in his personal, family, and social life; and that it will answer many questions of this kind: What is permitted to me? What is prohibited to me? And what is the reason for permitting this and prohibiting that?

In bringing this introduction to a close, I would like to express my thanks to the scholars of al-Azhar and the Institute of Islamic Culture for placing their trust in me to deal with such a vital subject. I hope I have proved worthy of their trust and have achieved their objective.

I pray to Allah Subhanahu wa Ta'ala to benefit those people who read this book, to give us truthfulness in what we say and do, to keep our thoughts and our pens from abberations, and to guide us in all our affairs. It is He alone Who listens to supplications.

Dr. Yusuf al-Qaradawi
Safar 1380/August 1960

7

REVIEWER'S NOTE

The methodology of this book is unique in dealing with the many subjects it covers. In fact, Sheikh Yusuf al-Qaradawi is a pioneer, the first to handle this subject using this particular approach. He has attempted, with considerable success in the Arabic original, to collect and summarize the issues from both ancient and modern Islamic references. Being himself a recognized Islamic scholar, he has had to make a judgement in selecting those points of view which he strongly felt meet the needs of Muslims in reference to the changing circumstances of this time.

However, this by no means presents all dimensions of the discussion relating to each issue, which it is impossible to cover in a book of this modest size. Although the present volume is very useful, it cannot by itself fill the gaps, meet the challenges, or answer the multitude of questions which face Muslim communities living in the Western world. It is time that sincere and qualified Muslim scholars who have lived in the West, and who possess mastery of the Islamic *fiqh,* introduce into English a *fiqh* which will meet our Islamic needs in this part of the world, one which will demonstrate the ability of Islam, as Allah's final message to mankind, to meet the changing requirements of human society. We hope that this call to our brothers and sisters will not be lost, and that the Muslims in North America will carry out the responsibilities which confront them in a forceful and dynamic fashion. *Insha'Allah* the day will not be far off when the major reference works available in the Islamic languages - Arabic, Urdu, Persian, Turkish, etc. - will be accurately translated into English, giving the English-speaking Muslims the privilege of drawing their own conclusions concerning the many issues which confront them today.

We pray that Allah will forgive us, and that He will bless our work and make it useful for the Muslims of the English-speaking world.

Sheikh Ahmad Zaki Hammad

Say: Who has forbidden the adornment of Allah which He has brought forth for His servants, and the good things of His providing? Say: They are, on the Day of Ressurection, exclusively for those who believed during the life of this world. Thus do We explain the signs for those who know. Say: What my Lord has indeed prohibited are shameful deeds, whether open or secret, and sin and rebellion without just cause, and that you associate with Allah that for which He has sent down no authority, and that you say concerning Allah that about which you do not know.(7:32-33)

DEFINITIONS

Al-Halal (the lawful):   That which is permitted, with respect to which no restriction exists, and the doing of which the Law-Giver, Allah, has allowed.

Al-Haram (the prohibited or unlawful): That which the Law-Giver has absolutely prohibited; anyone who engages in it is liable to incur the punishment of Allah in the Hereafter as well as a legal punishment in this world.

Al-Makruh (the detested):   That which is disapproved by the Law-Giver but not very strongly. The *makruh* is less in degree than the *haram*, and the punishment for *makruh* acts is less than for those that are *haram*, except when done to excess and in a manner which leads an individual toward what is *haram*.

CHAPTER ONE
THE ISLAMIC PRINCIPLES PERTAINING TO *HALAL* AND *HARAM*

- The basic *asl*[1] is the permissibility of things.
- To make lawful and to prohibit is the right of Allah alone.
- Prohibiting the *halal* and permitting the *haram* is similar to commiting *shirk*[2].
- The prohibition of things is due to their impurity and harmfulness.
- What is *halal* is sufficient, while what is *haram* is superfluous.
- Whatever is conducive to the *haram* is itself *haram*.
- Falsely representing the *haram* as *halal* is prohibited.
- Good intentions do not make the *haram* acceptable.
- Doubtful things are to be avoided.
- The *haram* is prohibited to everyone alike.
- Necessity dictates exceptions.

---

[1]*Asl*, plural *usul*, denotes origin, source, foundation, basis, fundamental or principle. (Trans.)

[2]Ascribing partners, or associating others, with Allah. (Trans.)

11

The question of what ought to be *halal* (lawful) and *haram* (prohibited) was one of the matters concerning which, prior to the advent of Islam, the peoples of the world had gone very far astray and were utterly confused, permitting many impure and harmful things and prohibiting many things that were good and pure.

They erred grievously, going either far to the right or far to the left. On the extreme right was the ascetic Brahmanism of India and the self-denying monasticism of Christianity. In addition to these two, there were other religions which were based on the principles of the mortification of the flesh, abstention from good food, and avoidance of other enjoyments of life which Allah has provided for human beings. Christian monasticism attained its peak during the Middle Ages when the avoidance of good and pure things among the monks, thousands in number, reached the point at which washing one's feet was considered a sin and entering a bath was something to regret and repent. On the extreme left, the Mazdak philosophy emerged in Persia, advocating absolute freedom and allowing people to take whatever they wanted and do whatever they pleased, even exhorting them to violate what is naturally held inviolable by human beings.

The Arabs of the pre-Islamic era provide a noteworthy example of utter confusion regarding the criteria for making lawful or prohibiting things and actions. They permitted the drinking of alcohol, the taking of usury at exorbitant rates, the torturing and secluding of women, and many similar practices. Those who had diabolical minds made alluring to many of them the killing of their own children, until, suppressing their natural paternal feelings, they obeyed them. As Allah Subhanahu wa Ta'ala says:

> Thus have their partners made alluring to many of the
> idolaters the killing of their children, in order to destroy
> them and to confuse for them their religion. (6:137)

These "partners" from among the guardians of the idols had devised many impressive arguments to persuade fathers to kill their children; among them were the fear of actual or anticipated poverty, the impending shame in case of a daughter, and the closeness to the gods to be attained by the sacrifice of a son.

It is strange that these same people who permitted the killing of their children by cutting their throats or burying them alive had

12

prohibited to themselves the eating of certain argricultural produce and the flesh of cattle. Stranger still is that they considered such prohibitions as part of their religion, attributing them to Allah's command.[1] But Allah rejected their false claim:

> And they say, 'These cattle and crops are sacred; none shall eat of them except those whom we wish', — so they assert — 'and cattle whose backs are prohibited (to burden), as well as cattle on which (at slaughter) the name of Allah is not mentioned' a forgery against Him. He will assuredly recompense them for what they have forged. (6:138)

Moreover, the Qur'an exposed the error of those who made *halal* what should have been prohibited and made *haram* what should have been permitted:

> Lost are those who kill their children in folly, without knowledge and prohibited what Allah has provided them, forging (lies) against Allah. They have indeed gone astray and are without guidance. (6:140)

When Islam came, the errors, confusions, and deviations with respect to the question of *halal* and *haram* were very widespread. One of Islam's initial accomplishments was, therefore, to establish certain legal principles and measures for rectifying this important matter; these principles were then made the determining criteria on which the questions of what is *halal* and what is *haram* were to be based. Thus this vital aspect was determined according to the correct perspective, and rules related to matters of *halal* and *haram* were established on the basis of principles of justice. The *ummah* (nation) of Islam thus became an *ummah* occupying a position between the extremist deviations to the right and left, which Allah Ta'ala describes as a "middle *ummah*, the best *ummah* that has ever been brought forth for mankind." (3:110)

---

[1]It should be noted that while worshipping and ascribing powers to numerous male and female deities, the pagan Arabs of the pre-Islamic era possessed the concept of a supreme Deity, Allah, ascribing to Him many false attributes and laws. (Trans.)

1. The Basic *Asl¹* Refers to the Permissibility of Things

The first *asl,* or principle, established by Islam is that the things which Allah has created and the benefits derived from them are essentially for man's use, and hence are permissible. Nothing is *haram* except what is prohibited by a sound and explicit *nas²* from the Law-Giver, Allah Subhanahu wa Ta'ala. If the *nas* is not sound, as for example in the case of a weak *hadith,* or if it is not explicit in stating the prohibition, the original principle of permissibility applies.

The scholars of Islam have derived this principle of the natural usability and permissibility of things from the clear verses of the Qur'an. For example, Allah says:

> It is He who created all that is in the earth for you....(2:29)

> He has subjected to you, from Himself, all that is in the heavens and all that is on the earth....(45:13)

> Do you not see that Allah has subjected to you whatever is in the heavens and what is on earth, and has showered upon you His favors, both apparent and unseen? (31:20)

It cannot be that Allah, may He be glorified, would create all these things, give man control over them, count them as His favors upon him, and subsequently inform him that their use is prohibited; how could this be when He created all this for man's use and benefit? Indeed, He has prohibited only a few things for specific reasons, the wisdom of which will be discussed later.

In Islam the sphere of prohibited things is very small, while that of permissible things is extremely vast. There is only a small number of sound and explicit texts concerning prohibitions, while whatever is not mentioned in a *nas* as being lawful or prohibited falls under the general principle of the permissibility of things and

---

¹*Asl,* plural *usul,* denotes origin, source, foundation, basis, fundamental or principle. (Trans.)
²*Nas* denotes either a verse of the Qur'an or a clear, authentic, and explicit *sunnah* (practice or saying) of Prophet Muhammad. These are the two main sources of Islamic law, i.e., its *Shari'ah.* (Trans.)

within the domain of Allah's favor. In this regard the Prophet (peace be on him) said:

> What Allah has made lawful in His Book is *halal* and what He has forbidden is *haram*, and that concerning which He is silent is allowed as His favor. So accept from Allah His favor, for Allah is not forgetful of anything. He then recited, "And thy Lord is not forgetful." (19:64)[1]

Salman al-Farsi reported that when the Mesenger of Allah (peace be on him) was asked about animal fat, cheese, and fur, he replied,

> The *halal* is that which Allah has made lawful in His Book and the *haram* is that which He has forbidden , and that concerning which He is silent He has permitted as a favor to you.[2]

Thus, rather than giving specific answers to what the questioner had asked, the Prophet (peace be on him) referred to the general criterion for determining the *halal* and the *haram*. Accordingly, it is sufficient for us to know what Allah has made *haram*, since what is not included in it is pure and permissible. The Prophet (peace be on him) also said:

> Allah has prescribed certain obligations for you, so do not neglect them; He has defined certain limits, so do not transgress them; He has prohibited certain things, so do not do them; and He has kept silent concerning other things out of mercy for you and not because of forgetfulness, so do not ask questions concerning them.[3]

I would like to emphasize here that the principle of natural permissibility is not only limited to things and objects but also includes all human actions and behavior not related to acts of worship, which may be termed living habits or day-to-day affairs. Here again, the principle is that these are allowed without restriction, with the exception of a small number of things which are

---

[1]This *hadith* was reported by al-Hakim, classified as *sahih* (sound), and quoted by al-Bazzar.
[2]Reported by al-Tirmidhi and Ibn Majah.
[3]Reported by al-Darqutni and classified as *hasan* (good) by al-Nawawi.

definitely prohibited by the Law-Giver, Allah Subhanahu wa Ta'ala, Who says:

> ...He (Allah) has explained to you what He has made *haram* for you.... (6:119)

including both objects and actions.

The case is different, however, in relation to acts of worship. These are purely religious acts which can be taken only from what Allah Himself reveals. Concerning this we have a sound *hadith*:

> "Any innovation in our matter (worship) which is not a part of it must be rejected."[1]

Anyone who invents or originates a form of worship on his own has gone astray and must be repudiated, for only the Law-Giver Himself has the right to originate acts of worship through which human beings may seek nearness to Him. Living habits and day-to-day matters, however, did not originate with the Law-Giver; they were originated and acted upon by human beings themselves. Thus the Law-Giver intervenes only to rectify, to moderate, or to refine them, and occasionally to identify some practices which are harmful or which may lead to strife.

The great Islamic scholar Ibn Taymiyyah states,

> Peoples' sayings and actions are of two kinds: acts of worship by which their religion is established, and customary practices which are required for day-to-day living. From the principles of the *Shari'ah,* we know that acts of worship are those acts which have been prescribed by Allah or approved by Him; nothing is to be affirmed here except through the *Shari'ah.* However, as far as the wordly activities of people are concerned, they are necessary for everyday life. Here the principle is freedom of action; nothing may be restricted in this regard except what Allah Subhanahu wa Ta'ala has restricted. This is the case because commanding and prohibiting are both in Allah's hands. As far as worship is concerned, there has to be a command from Him concerning it. Thus, when it requires a command

---

[1]This *hadith* is classified as *muttafaq 'alayh* ("agreed upon" by the two great scholars al-Bukhari and Muslim).

(from Allah) to establish something, how can we say that something is restricted without His command?

This is why Ahmad (bin Hanbal) and other jurists, who base their judgements on *ahadith*,[1] say: In relation to acts of worship, the principle is limitation (*tawqeef*); that is to say, nothing can be legislated in this regard except what Allah Himself has legislated. To do otherwise is to incur the risk of being included in the meaning of the *ayah*: 'Do they have partners (with Allah) who have prescribed for them in religion that concerning which Allah has given no permission?' (42:21) But as far as living habits are concerned, the principle is freedom because nothing can be restricted in this regard except what Allah Himself has prohibited. Here, to do otherwise, is to be included in the meaning of His saying: 'Say: Do you see what Allah has sent down to you for sustenance? Yet you have made some part of it *halal* and some part *haram*.' (10:59)

This is a great and beneficent principle, on the basis of which we can say that buying, selling, leasing, giving gifts, and other such matters are necessary activities for people, as are eating, drinking, and the wearing of clothes. If the *Shari'ah* says something concerning these mundane matters, it is in order to teach good behavior. Accordingly, it has prohibited whatever leads to strife, has made obligatory that which is essential, has disapproved that which is frivolous, and has approved that which is beneficial. All this has been done with due consideration for the kinds of activities involved, their magnitudes, and properties.

Since this is the stand of the *Shari'ah*, people are free to buy, sell, and lease as they wish, just as they are free to eat and to drink what they like as long as it is not *haram*. Although some of these things may be disapproved, they are free in this regard, since the *Shari'ah* does not go to the extent of prohibiting them,

---

[1] Plural of *hadith*. (Trans.)

and thus the original principle (of permissibility) remains.[1]

This principle is also supported by what is reported in a sound *hadith* by the Prophet's Companion, Jabir bin 'Abdullah. He said, "We used to practice *'azl (coitus interruptus,* or withdrwal before ejaculation during intercourse) during the period when the Qur'an was being revealed. If the practice were to have been prohibited, the Qur'an would have prohibited it." He therefore concluded that if the divine revelation was silent about something, it was permissible and people were free to practice it. Assuredly the Prophet's Companions (may Allah be pleased with them) had a perfect understanding of the *Shari'ah.* Accordingly, this great principle — that no worship can be legislated except by the command of Allah, and no practice can be prohibited except by His prohibition — is firmly established.

2. To Make Lawful and to Prohibit Is the Right of Allah Alone

The second principle is that Islam has restricted the authority to legislate the *haram* and the *halal,* taking it out of the hands of human beings, regardless of their religious or worldly position, and reserving it for the Lord of human beings alone. Neither rabbis nor priests, kings or sultans, have the right to prohibit something permanently to Allah's servants; if someone does this, he has certainly exceeded his limits, usurping the sovereignty which, with respect to legislating for the people, belongs to Allah Subhanahu wa Ta'ala alone. Others who acquiese with this transgression of such usurpers and act upon what they have legislated thereby elevate them to the rank of partners or associates with Allah:

> Do they have partners (with Allah) who have prescribed for them in religion that concerning which Allah has given no permission? (42:21)

---

[1]*Al-Qawa'id al-Nuraniyah al-Fiqhiyah* by Ibn Taymiyyah, pp. 112-113. In accordance with this principle, Ibn Taymiyyah, his pupil, Ibn al-Qayyim, and the Hanbali jurists in general hold that contracts and the conditions laid down in them are essentially permissible, as any contract not involving any matter which is textually established as *haram* is valid.

18

They have taken their rabbis and priests as lords besides Allah, and the Messiah, son of Mary, although they were commanded to worship no one except the One Allah. There is no Deity but He, glory be to Him above what they associate with Him! (9:31)

The Qur'an took to task the People of the Book, that is, Christians and Jews, for putting the power to make lawful and to prohibit things and actions into the hands of their rabbis and priests.

'Adi bin Hatim, who had been a Christian before accepting Islam, once came to the Prophet (peace be on him). When he heard him reciting the above *ayah* he said, "O Messenger of Allah, but they do not worship them." The Prophet (peace be on him) replied,

Yes, but they prohibit to the people what is *halal* and permit them what is *haram,* and the people obey them. This is indeed their worship of them.[1]

Christians still claim that Jesus (peace be on him), before ascending to heaven, vested in His apostles the authority to delcare things permissible or prohibited as they saw fit, as reported in Matthew 18:18:

I tell you this: whatever you forbid on earth shall be forbidden in heaven, and whatever you allow on earth shall be allowed in heaven.

The Qur'an also took the polytheists to task for legislating and prohibiting things without any authority from Allah:

Do you see what Allah has sent down to you for sustenance and yet you have made some part of it *halal* and some part *haram*? (10:59)

And do not say, concerning the falsehood which your tongues utter, 'This is *halal* and that is *haram*,' in order to fabricate a lie against Allah; assuredly those who fabricate a lie against Allah will not prosper. (16:116)

From these explicit verses of the Qur'an and from clear *ahadith* of the Prophet (peace be on him), the jurists of Islam grasped with certainty that it is Allah Subhanahu wa Ta'ala alone Who has the right to make lawful or to prohibit a matter, either through His Book

---

[1]Reported and classified as *hasan* by al-Tirmidhi and others.

19

or through the tongue of His Messenger (peace be on him). The jurists' task does not go beyond explaining what Allah has decreed to be *halal* or *haram* "when He has explained to you in detail what He has made *haram* for you." (6:119) It is definitely not their task to decide what is to be allowed and what is to be prohibited to human beings. Thus the great jurists, in spite of their scholarship and ability of *ijtihad* (deduction from analogy), shied away from pronouncing judgements concerning matters of *halal* and *haram*, passing the problem from one to the other out of fear of committing the error of declaring *halal* what is actually *haram* and vice-versa.

In his book *Al-Umm*, Imam Shafi'i narrated that Abu Yusuf, a companion of Abu Hanifah and a chief judge (*qadi*), said:

> I know that our knowledgeable teachers avoided saying,'This is *halal* and that is *haram*,' apart from what they found clearly stated without requiring an interpretation in the Book of Allah. We have been told by Ibn al-Saib that al-Rabi' bin Khaytham, one of the greatest of the second generation Muslims, said, 'Beware that none of you says, "Allah has made this lawful or approves of it," and that Allah may then say that He did not make it lawful nor approve it, or that you say, "Allah has prohibited this," and that Allah may then say, "You lie! I did not prohibit it nor disapprove of it." Some companions of Ibrahim al-Nakh'i, a great jurist of Kufah among the second generation Muslims, have told us of his mentioning his colleagues as saying, when they gave a judgement concerning something, 'It is disapproved' or 'There is no harm in it,' rather than, 'It is *haram*' or 'It is *halal*,' as *haram* and *halal* are terms of much greater import.[1]

This is what Abu Yusuf has reported concerning our righteous forebearers and what al-Shafi'i has quoted from him, in agreement with his position. Similarly, Ibn Muflih reported the great scholar Ibn Taymiyyah, as saying that the jurists of the early days of Islam

---

[1] *Al-Umm*, vol. 7, p. 317.

did not term anything *haram* unless it was definitely known to be so.[1] In the same spirit, the great *imam* Ahmad ibn Hanbal, when asked about some matter, would say, "I disapprove of it" or "It does not appeal to me," or "I do not like it" or "I do not prefer it." Similar reports are narrated concerning Malik, Abu Hanifah, and all the other *imams* (may Allah be pleased with them).[2]

3. Prohibiting the *Halal* and Permitting the *Haram* Is Similar to Committing *Shirk*[3]

While Islam reprimands all those who, on their own authority, declare what is lawful and what is prohibited, it is more strict with respect to those who voice prohibitions; for the tendency to set up prohibitions results in hardship for human beings, unjustifiably narrowing what Allah has made spacious for His creatures. Moreover, this tendency is prevalent among some of those who go to extremes in matters of religion and must be checked. The Prophet (peace be on him) fought against this pseudo-pietism and zealotry by every means, warning those who indulged in it with the words, "The zealots will perish," repeated three times.[4]

The Prophet (peace be on him) characterized his Message by saying,

"I have been sent with what is straight and easy".[5]

The straightness of his Message consists of belief in *tawheed* (the unity of Allah) and its ease in practice and legislation, in contrast to *shirk* and to the prohibiting of good things of this life. The Prophet

---

[1] This is further supported by the fact that the Companions did not give up the drinking of alcohol after the revelation of the Qur'anic verse, "They ask thee concerning wine and gambling. Say: In them is great sin and some benefit," (2:219) since this verse did not definitely prohibit drinking prior to the revelation of the verses in *Surah al-Maida.* (5:93-94 (90-91))

[2] This is a lesson to the followers of such *imams* who freely use the word *"haram"* without having a proof, or even a semblance of proof.

[3] See footnote (2) p. 11.

[4] Reported by Muslim, Ahmad, and Abu Daoud.

[5] Reported by Ahmad.

21

(peace be on him) has mentioned all this in a *hadith qudsi*[1], reporting the saying of Allah Ta'ala:

They prohibited to people what I had made lawful for
I created people upright *(hunafah)*. Then the evil ones
came to them and led them astray from their religion.
them and commanded them to associate with Me that
for which I had not sent down any authority.[2]

Prohibiting something which is *halal* is similar to committing *shirk*, and this is why the Qur'an censures the idolaters of Arabia for their polytheism, their idols, and for prohibiting to themselves, without any authority from Allah, the eating and the use of certain kinds of produce and cattle. Among these prohibited animals were those which were called *bahirah, saibah, wasilah,* and *ham* during the pre-Islamic period of *jahiliyyah.*[3] *Bahirah* (the slit-eared) denoted a female camel which had given birth to five calves, the last of which was a male. The ear of such a camel was slit and she was loosed to roam freely; she was not to be ridden, milked, or slaughtered, and was free to eat and drink from any place she liked without hindrance. *Saibah* referred to a male or female camel which was released to roam freely because of a vow, usually made following a safe return from a journey, the cure of an illness, or for some other reason. As for *wasilah*, if the firstborn of a female goat were a male, the polytheists would sacrifice him to their gods, while if it were a female they would keep her for themselves. In the case of twin offspring, one female and the other male, they would say, "He is her brother," and instead of sacrificing the male they would release him to roam free; he was known as *wasilah*. And if a male camel's second generation offspring was capable of carrying a rider, they would let the older camel go free, saying, "He saved his back," and calling him *al-ham*.

While there are other interpretations of these four terms, they are

---

[1]A *hadith* in which the Prophet (peace be on him) refers a saying to Allah, the Prophet himself being merely the narrator. Unlike the Qur'an, one cannot say of a *hadith qudsi* that "Allah said it." In the case of a *hadith qudsi*, the meaning is from Allah but the words are the Prophet's, transmitted to him either through a vision or revelation. (Trans.)

[2]Reported by Muslim.

[3]The state of mind and conditions of life prior to the advent of Islam, characterized by deviation from the guidance of Allah and the adoption of ungodly systems and ways of life. (Trans.)

all of a similar nature. The Qur'an rejected these prohibitions and left no excuse for those who practiced them to follow the errors of their forefathers:

Allah did not institute *bahirah* or *saibah* or *wasilah* or *ham*; but those who disbelieve forge a lie against Allah, and most of them do not use their reason. When it is said to them, 'Come to what Allah has revealed and to the Messenger,' they say, 'What we found our fathers doing is enough for us.' What! And even though their fathers did not know anything and were not rightly guided? (5:106-107 (103-104))

In *Surah al-An'am*, there is a detailed discussion of what such people claimed to be *haram* of camels, oxen, sheep, and goats. In this context the Qur'an uses an ironic style of rhetorical questioning to convince them of their error:

Eight pairs (of cattle), two of sheep and two of goats. Say: Has He forbidden the two males or the two females or that which the wombs of the two females hold? Inform me with knowledge if you are truthful. And two (pairs) of camels and two of oxen. Say: Has He forbidden the two males or the two females? (6:143-144)

In another discussion contained in *Surah al-A'raf*, Allah Subhanahu wa Ta'ala rejects the claims of all prohibitors, laying down the final criteria governing prohibitions:

Say: Who has forbidden the adornment of Allah which He has brought forth for His servants, and the good things of His providing?...Say: What my Lord has indeed prohibited are shameful deeds, whether open or secret, and sin and rebellion without just cause, and that you associate with Allah that for which He has sent down no authority, and that you say concerning Allah that about which you do not know. (7:32-33)

A significant aspect of these discussions is that they were revealed in Makkah. The Makkan revelations invariably dealt with matters of faith, the oneness of Allah Ta'ala, and the Hereafter. We may therefore deduce that, in the sight of Allah, this matter of declaring things to be prohibited without any authority from Him

23

was not a minor matter but one which pertained to the fundamentals and general principles of the faith.

In Madinah certain Muslims showed a tendency toward asceticism, denying themselves some permissible pleasures. Then, in order to keep them within the limits set by Himself and bring them back to the straight path of Islam, Allah revealed the following strongly-worded verses:

> You who believe! Do not make *haram* the good things which Allah has made *halal* for you, and do not transgress; indeed, Allah does not like the transgressors. And eat of what Allah has provided for you, lawful and good, and fear Allah, in Whom you are believers. (5:90-91 (87-88))

4. The Prohibition of Things Is Due to Their Impurity and Harmfulness

It is the right of Allah, the One Who created human beings and bestowed innumerable gifts on them, to legalize or prohibit as He deems proper, and to place obligations and responsibilities upon them as He sees fit. As His creatures, they have neither the right to question nor to disobey Him. But Allah Subhanahu wa Ta'ala is not arbitrary in what He commands. Because He is merciful to His servants, He makes things *halal* and *haram* for a reason, with peoples' well-being in view. Accordingly, He has neither permitted anything except what is pure nor has He prohibited anything except what is impure.

It is true that Allah Ta'ala had prohibited certain good things to the Jews, but this was only as a punishment for their rebelliousness and transgression of the limits set by Allah. Thus He says:

> And to the Jews We forbade every animal with claws, and of cattle and sheep We have forbidden them their fat, except what is carried on their backs or entrails, or what is connnected to the bone; thus did We recompense them for their rebelliousness, and indeed, We speak the truth. (6:146)

Elsewhere in the Qur'an Allah has described other manifestations of this rebellious attitude:

24

Because of the wrongdoing of the Jews, We prohibited to them some of the good things which had been permitted to them, and because of their hindering many from the path of Allah, and their taking usury although they had been forbidden to do it, and their wrongfully devouring peoples' wealth...(4:160-161)

When Allah sent His final Messenger (peace be on him) with the eternal complete religion to humanity after it had developed to a state of maturity, He demonstrated His mercy by removing these prohibitions, which had been a temporary penalty for a rebellious, stiff-necked people.[1] And the coming of the Prophet (peace be on him) who would relieve them of this burden was foretold to the Jews and Christians, who, as the Qur'an states:

...they find described in their own scriptures, in the *Taurat* and the *Injeel*.[2] He commands them what is right and forbids them what is evil; He makes lawful to them what is good and makes unlawful what is foul; He releases them from their burdens and from the yokes which were upon them...(7:157)

In Islam, ways other than prohibiting the good things were prescribed by Allah Ta'ala for the eradication of sins: sincere repentance, which cleanses sins as water cleanses dirt; good deeds, which compensate for evil ones; spending in charity, which extinguishes fire; and trials and sufferings, which disperse sins as the winter wind disperses dry leaves. Accordingly, we know that in Islam things are prohibited only because they are impure or harmful. If something is entirely harmful it is *haram*, and if it is entirely beneficial it is *halal*; if the harm of it outweighs its benefit it is *haram*, while if its benefit outweights its harm it is *halal*. This principle is explained in the Qur'an in relation to wine and gambling:

They ask thee concerning wine and gambling. Say (O Prophet): In them is great sin and some benefit for

---

[1] See, for example, Exodus 32:9. (Trans.)
[2] *Taurat* refers to the original scripture revealed to the Prophet Moses by God, and *Injeel* to what He revealed to the Prophet Jesus. These are not to be confused either with the existing Torah or Old Testament, or the four Gospels of the New Testament. (Trans.)

25

human beings, but the sin is greater than the benefit....(2:219)

By the same logic, if it is asked, what is *halal* in Islam, the answer is, the good things. Good things are those which moderate people acknowledge to be wholesome and which are approved by human beings in general without relation to the habits of a particular group. Allah Ta'ala says:

They ask thee what is lawful to them (as food). Say: Whatever is good is lawful to you....(5:5 (5:4))
He also says:
Today whatever is good is made lawful to you....(5:6 (5:5)

The Muslim is not required to know exactly what is unclean or harmful in what Allah has prohibited; it may be hidden from him but be apparent to someone else, or its harm may not have been discovered during his lifetime but may be understood at a later period. What is required of a Muslim is simply to say, "We have heard and we shall obey." Do we not observe that Allah prohibited the eating of pork without the Muslims being aware of the reason for its prohibition apart from the fact that the pig is a filthy animal? Centuries passed, and then scientific research discovered the presence of parasites and deadly bacteria in its flesh. Yet even if scientific research had discovered nothing in pork, or if it had discovered much more than this, the Muslim would still continue to believe it to be unclean.

Another example of this is in the Prophet's saying:

Avoid three abominable acts (that is, the one who does them is cursed by Allah and by the people): defecating in streams, defecating on roadways, and defecating in shaded places."[1]

People of earlier times merely knew that these were filthy acts, abhorrent to civilized taste and public manners. With the advancement of science, we now know that these "three abominable acts" are hazards to public health, as they are the root cause of the

---

[1]Reported by Abu Daoud, Ibn Majah and al-Hakim, and classified as *sahih* by Baihaqi.

spread of such dangerous diseases as hookworm (ankylostoma) and bilharzia (schistosomiasis).

Thus, as the light of knowledge penetrates more deeply and new discoveries are made, the beneficial aspects of the Islamic legislation relating to the lawful and the prohibited—in fact, the benefits of all its legal injunctions—become apparant to us. How could it be otherwise when they come from the Wise, All-Knowing, and Merciful God?

> ...and Allah knows the mischief-monger from the one who puts things aright. And if Allah had willed, He could have put you into difficulties; indeed, Allah is Mighty, Wise. (2:220)

5. What is *Halal* Is Sufficient, While What is Is *Haram* Is Superfluous

One of the beauties of Islam is that it has prohibited only such things as are unnecessary and dispensible, while providing alternatives which are better and which give greater ease and comfort to human beings. This point has been explained by Ibn al-Qayyim:

> Allah has prohibited seeking omens by drawing lots but has provided the alternative of *istikhara*[1] which is a supplication for seeking Allah's guidance.
>
> He has prohibited usury but has encouraged profitable trade. He has prohibited gambling but has permitted betting on forms of competition which are useful for their (the Muslims) religious striving, such as horse or camel racing and competing in marksmanship.
>
> He has prohibited (to men) the wearing of silk but has given them the choice of other materials such as wool, linen, and cotton.

---

[1] Islam teaches that if the Muslim faces a problem he should consult with others and seek guidance from Allah. The meaning of *istikhara* is to ask guidance from Allah in making a choice between two conflicting decisions. For this there is a *salat* and a *du'a* (supplication).

He has prohibited adultery, fornication, and homosexuality but has encouraged lawful marriage.

He has prohibited intoxicating drinks in order that they may enjoy other delicious drinks which are wholesome for the body and mind.

And He has prohibited unclean food but provides alternative wholesome food.[1]

Thus, when we survey the Islamic injunctions in their totality, we find that if Allah limits the choice of His servants in relation to some things, He provides them with a still wider range of more wholesome alternatives in. relation to other things of a simliar kind. For assuredly Allah has no desire to make peoples' lives difficult, narrow, and circumscribed; on the contrary; He desires ease, goodness, guidance, and mercy for them, according to His saying:

Allah desires to make clear to you and to guide you to the ways of the (righteous) people before you and to turn to you in mercy; and Allah is Knowing, Wise. And Allah desires to lighten your burden, for man was created weak.   (4:26-28)

6. Whatever Is Conducive to the *Haram* Is Itself *Haram*

Another Islamic principle is that if something is prohibited, anything which leads to it is likewise prohibited. By this means Islam intends to block all avenues leading to what is *haram*. For example, as Islam has prohibited sex outside marriage, it has also prohibited anything which leads to it or makes it attractive, such as seductive clothing, private meetings and casual mixing between men and women, the depiction of nudity, pornographic literature, obscene songs, and so on.

Accordingly, Muslim jurists have established the criterion that whatever is conducive to or leads toward the *haram* is itself *haram*. A similar principle is that the sin of the *haram* is not limited only to the person who engages in it but extends to others who have

---

[1]*Rawdah al-Muhibbeen, p. 10, and A'alam al-Muwaqq'in,* vol. 2, p.111.

supported him in this, materially or morally; each is held accountable according to his share. For example, in the case of intoxicating drinks, the Prophet (peace be on him) cursed not only the one who drinks them but also the one who produces them, the one who serves them, the one to whom they are served, the one to whom the price of them is paid, etc. This point will be discussed again later. Again, in the matter of usury, the Prophet (peace be on him) cursed the one who pays it, the one to whom it is paid, the one who writes the contract, and the one who acts as a witness thereto. Accordingly, we derive the rule that anything which assists in the doing of what is *haram* is itself *haram*, and anyone who helps another person to do it shares in the sin of it.

7. Falsely Representing the *Haram* as *Halal* Is Prohibited

Just as Islam has prohibited whatever leads toward the *haram*, it has also prohibited resorting to technical legalities in order to do what is *haram* by devious means and excuses inspired by Satan. It has reprimanded the Jews for resorting to such practices. The Prophet (peace be on him) said:

"Do not do what the Jews did in order to (technically) legalize Allah's prohibitions by flimsy excuses."[1]

This is a reference to the fact that Allah had prohibited the Jews to hunt on the Sabbath (Saturday). To get around this prohibition, they would dig ditches on Friday so that the fish would fall into them on Saturday, to be caught on Sunday. Those who resort to rationalizations and excuses to justify their actions consider such practices to be permissible, but the jurists of Islam consider them *haram*, since Allah's purpose was to prevent them from hunting on the Sabbath, whether by direct or indirect means.

Calling a *haram* thing by a name other than its own or changing its form while retaining its essence is a devious tactic, since obviously a change of name or of form is of no consequence as long

---

[1]This *hadith* is in *Ighathat al-Lahfan* by Ibn al-Qayyim, vol. 1, p. 308. The author says: "This was reported by 'Abdullah bin Battah on good authority, and al-Tirmidhi classifies a similar *hadith* as *sahih*."

as the thing and its essence remain unchanged. Thus, when some people invent new terms in order to deal in usury or to consume alcohol, the sin of dealing in usury and drinking remains. As we read in the collections of *ahadith*,

> A group of people will make peoples' intoxication *halal*
> by giving it other names.[1]

> A time will come when people will devour usury, calling
> it "trade."[2]

And among the strange phenomena of our time is that people term obscene dance "art," liquor "spirits," and usury "interest."

8. Good Intenions Do Not Make the *Haram* Acceptable

In all its legislations and moral injunctions, Islam lays great stress on nobility of feelings, loftiness of aims, and purity of intentions. The Prophet (peace be on him) said,

> "Actions will be judged by intentions, and everyone
> will be recompensed according to what he intended."[3]

Indeed, in Islam the routine matters of life and its mundane affairs are transformed into acts of worship and devotion to Allah by good intentions. Accordingly, if one eats food with the intention of sustaining life and strengthening his body in order that he may be able to carry out his obligations to his Creator and to other human beings, his eating and drinking are considered worship and devotion to Allah Ta'ala. Again, if one enjoys sexual intimacy with his wife, desiring a child and seeking to keep himself and his wife chaste, it is considered an act of worship on his part, deserving of reward in the Hereafter. Concerning this the Prophet (peace be on him) said:

> When you satisfy your desire with your wife, it is
> counted for you as an act deserving of reward. Those
> who were listening to him said: Messenger of Allah,

---

[1]Reported by Ahmad.
[2]Reported by al-Bukhari and Muslim.
[3]Reported by al-Bukhari.

how can it be that one of us satisfies his desire and will then be rewarded for it? The Prophet (peace be on him) replied: Would he not be sinful if he had satisfied it in a prohibited manner? Consequently, if he satisfies it in a permissible manner, there is a reward for him.[1]

He also said:

> Anyone who desires what is permissible from the world, keeping himself away from sins, working for the sake of his family, and taking care of his neighbor, will meet his Lord with a face shining like the full moon.[2]

In this manner, whenever any permissible action of the believer is accompanied by a good intention, his action becomes an act of worship. But the case of the *haram* is entirely different; it remains *haram* no matter how good the intention, how honorable the purpose, or how lofty the aim may be. Islam can never consent to employing a *haram* means to achieve a praiseworthy end. Indeed, it insists that not only the aim be honorable but also that the means chosen to attain it be pure. "The end justifies the means" is not the maxim of the *Shari'ah*, nor is "Secure your right even through wrong-doing." This can never be, for the *Shari'ah* demands that the right should be secured through just means only.

If someone accumulates wealth through usury, forgery, gambling, prohibited games, or in any other *haram* manner in order to build a mosque, establish a charitable foundation, or to do any other good work, the guilt of having done what is *haram* will not be lifted from him because of the goodness of his objective; in Islam good aims and intentions have no effect in lessening the sinfulness of what is *haram*. This is what the Prophet (peace be on him) taught us when he said:

> Allah is good and does not accept anything but good, and Allah has commanded the Believers, as He commanded His messengers, saying 'O you mesengers! Eat of whatever is good and work righteousness. Indeed, I am aware of what you do.'[3] He also said, 'O

---

[1] Reported by al-Bukhari and Muslim.
[2] The text of the *hadith* was narrated by al-Tabarani.
[3] The Qur'an 35:31.

31

you who believe! Eat of the good things which We provide for you.'¹ The Prophet (peace be on him) then said, A man travels far, unkempt and dust-stained (for *hajj*, *umrah*, or the like), raising his hands to the sky (and saying), 'O Lord! O Lord!' while eating what was *haram*, drinking what was *haram*, wearing what was *haram*, and nourishing himself through *haram* means. How then could his prayers be accepted?²

He also said:

If anyone amasses wealth through *haram* means and then gives charity from it, there is no regard for him and the burden of sin remains.³

Again he said:

If a person earns property through *haram* means and then gives charity, it will not be accepted (by Allah); if he spends it there will be no blessing on it; and if he leaves it behind (at his death) it will be his provision in the Fire. Indeed, Allah Ta'ala does not obliterate one bad deed by another bad deed, but He cancels out a bad deed by a good deed. An unclean thing does not wipe away another unclean thing.⁴

9. Doubtful Things Are To Be Avoided

It is Allah's mercy to human beings that He did not leave them in ignorance concerning what is lawful and what is prohibited. Indeed, He has made explicit what is *halal* and explained what is *haram*, as He says:

...He has explained to you what He has made *haram* for you....(6:119)

Accordingly, one may do what is lawful and must avoid what is

---

¹2:172.
²Reported by Muslim and al-Tirmidhi on the authority of Abu Hurairah.
³Reported by Ibn Khazimah, Ibn Hibban, and al-Hakim on the authority of Abu Hurairah.
⁴Reported by Ahmad and others on the authority of Ibn Mas'ood.

prohibited insofar as he has the choice. However, there is a gray area between the clearly *halal* and the clearly *haram*. This is the area of what is doubtful. Some people may not be able to decide whether a particular matter is permissible or forbidden; such confusion may be due either to doubtful evidence or because of doubt concerning the applicability of the text to the particular circumstance or matter in question.

In relation to such matters, Islam considers it an act of piety for the Muslim to avoid doing what is doubtful in order to stay clear of doing something *haram*. This is similar to what was discussed earlier concerning the blocking of the avenues which lead to what is *haram*. Such a cautious approach, moreover, trains the Muslim to be farsighted in planning and increases his knowledge of affairs and people. The root of this principle is the saying of the Prophet (peace be on him):

> The *halal* is clear and the *haram* is clear. Between the two there are doubtful matters concerning which people do not know whether they are *halal* or *haram*. One who avoids them in order to safeguard his religion and his honor is safe, while if someone engages in a part of them he may be doing something *haram*, like one who grazes his animals near the *hima* (the grounds reserved for animals belonging to the King which are out of bounds for others' animals); it is thus quite likely that some of his animals will stray into it. Truly, every king has a *hima*, and the *hima* of Allah is what He has prohibited.[1]

10. The *Haram* Is Prohibited to Everyone Alike

In the *Shari'ah* of Islam the *haram* has universal applicability; here there is no such thing as that which is prohibited to a non-Arab but permitted to an Arab, nor anything which is restricted to a Black but allowed to a White. For in Islam there are no privileged classes or individuals who, in the name of religion, can do whatever they

---

[1]Reported by al-Bukhari, Muslim, and others; the narration is taken from al-Tirmidhi.

please according to their whims. Muslims do not have any privilege of making something *haram* for others while it is lawful for themselves; this cannot be, for truly Allah is the Lord of all, and the *Shari'ah* of Islam is the guide for all. Whatever Allah has legislated through His *Shari'ah* is lawful for all human beings and whatever He has prohibited is prohibited to all human beings until the Day of Resurrection.

As an example, stealing is equally *haram* for the Muslim and the non-Muslim; the punishment for it is the same, regardless of the family or the origin of the thief. The Prophet (peace be on him) firmly enforced this rule, proclaiming,

> "By Allah, if Fatimah, the daughter of Muhammad, were to steal, I would have her hand cut off."[1]

A case of theft was brought before the Prophet (peace be on him) involving two suspects, the one a Jew and the other a Muslim. Some relatives of the Muslim advanced circumstantial evidence to cast doubt on the Jew in order to save their man while he was, in fact, guilty. The Prophet (peace be on him) was almost persuaded to believe that the Muslim was innocent. Then a revelation was sent down exposing the conspiracy, clearing the Jew of the crime and directing the Prophet (peace be on him) to establish justice without any bias:

> Indeed, We have sent down to thee the Book with the truth, so that thou mightest judge between the people as shown by Allah; then do not be an advocate for the treacherous, and seek forgiveness of Allah; indeed, Allah is Forgiving, Merciful. And do not plead on behalf of those who deceive themselves; indeed, Allah does not like the one who is treacherous and sinful. They may hide from men, but they cannot hide from Allah, for He is with them even when they hold, by night, discourse not pleasing to Him, and Allah encompasses what they do. Ah! You are the ones who pleaded for them in the life of this world, but who will plead for them with Allah on the Day of Ressurection, or who will be their guardian? (4:105-109)

---

[1]Reported by al-Bukhari.

In the distorted scripture of the Jews, it is alleged that while usury or interest is prohibited to the Jew when lending money to a brother Jew, there is no harm in charging it to a gentile, as stated in Deuteronomy 23:19-20:

> You must not lend on interest (usury) to your brother, whether the loan be of money or food or anything else that may earn interest. You may demand interest on a loan of a foreigner, but you must not demand interest from your brother, so that Yahweh your God may bless you in all your giving in the land you are to enter and make your own.

The Qur'an also speaks about another similar tendency among the Jews, that of cheating others who are not of their race or faith without feeling anything wrong in it. The Qur'an says:

> And among the People of the Book is he who, if entrusted with a single gold coin, would not return it to thee unless thou constantly stood over him. This is because they say: We have no duty toward the gentiles,[1] but they utter a falsehood concerning Allah, and they know it. (3:75)

They have unquestionably uttered falsehood in what they have ascribed to Allah, for the law of Allah does not discriminate between one people and another, and insofar as cheating is concerned, Allah has condemned it through the tongue of all His messengers and prophets.

With due apologies, we may say that this tendency to use a double standard, one for one's "brother" and another for a "foreigner" or outsider, is a characteristic of primitive ethics. It can never be ascribed to a divinely revealed religion, for high morality — that is, true morality — is distinguishable by its universality and comprehensiveness and by its lack of a double standard. The distinction between us and primitive peoples is not in the existence or absence of a moral code but in the enlargement of the area of its application. As an example, such people also consider honesty as a praiseworthy quality, but they restrict its practice to the people of

---

[1] "Gentiles" here refers to the Arabs, who before Islam possessed neither religion nor a divinely revealed sripture.

35

their own tribe. When dealing with people from outside their tribe or clan, they see nothing wrong with cheating them, or in fact recommending or even requiring it.

The author of *The Story of Civilization* writes,

> Almost all groups agree in holding other groups to be inferior to themselves. The Amerian Indians looked upon themselves as the chosen people, specially created by the Great Spirit as an uplifting example for mankind. One Indian tribe called itself 'The Only Men;' another called itself 'Men of Men;' the Caribs said, 'We alone are people.' The Eskimos believed that the Europeans had come to Greenland to learn manners and virtues. Consequently, it seldom occured to primitive man to extend to other tribes the moral restraints which he acknowledged in dealing with his own; he frankly conceived it to be the function of morals to give strength and coherence to his group against other groups. Commandments and taboos applied only to the people of his tribe; with others, except when they were his guests, he might go as far as he dared[1].

11. Necessity Dictates Exceptions

While Islam has narrowed the range of what is prohibited, it is, at the same time, very strict in seeing that its prohibitions are observed. Accordingly, it has blocked the ways, apparent or hidden, leading to what is prohibited. Thus, what is conducive to the *haram* is itself *haram*, what assists in commiting the *haram* is *haram*, any rationalization for engaging in the *haram* is *haram*, and so on, to the last of the principles which we have elucidated. At the same time, Islam is not oblivious to the exigencies of life, to their magnitude, nor to human weakness and capacity to face them. It permits the Muslim, under the compulsion of necessity to eat a

---

[1]Will Durant, *The Story of Civilization*, Simon and Schuster, New York, 1935, vol. 1, pp. 54-55.

prohibited food in quantities sufficient to remove the necessity and save himself from death.

In this context, after listing the prohibited foods in the form of dead animals, blood, and pork, Allah Ta'ala says:

> ...But if one is compelled by necessity, neither craving
> (it) nor transgressing, there is no sin on him; indeed,
> Allah is Forgiving, Merciful.   (2:173)

And this is repeated at four places in the Qur'an after each mention of the prohibited foods.

On the basis of these and similar veres of the Qur'an, Islamic jurists formulated an important principle, namely, that "necessity removes restrictions." However, it is to be noted that the individual experiencing the necessity is permitted to eat the *haram* food with the stipulation that he is "neither craving it nor transgressing." This is interpreted to mean that he should not desire to relish it nor transgress by eating more than the bare amount needed to satisfy his hunger. From this stipulation, jurists have derived another principle, that "The quantity permitted is determined by the (magnitude) of the necessity." Here the underlying idea is that, even though compelled by necessity, a person need not surrender to it or embrace it with eagerness; rather he must live with what is essentially *halal* and seek a way to return to it so that he may not become accustomed to the *haram* or begin enjoying it under the pretext of necessity.

In permitting the use of the *haram* under necessity, Islam is true to its spirit and general principles. This spirit, which we find permeating its laws, is to make life easy and less oppressive for human beings, and to lift the burdens and yokes imposed by earlier systems and religions. True is the saying of Allah, the Almighty:

> ...Allah desires ease for you, and He does not desire
> hardship for you....   (2:185)

> ...It is not Allah's desire to place a burden upon you, but
> He desires to purify you and to perfect His favor on you
> in order that you may be thankful.   (5:7 (5:6))

> Allah desires to lighten your burden, for man was
> created weak. (4:28)

CHAPTER TWO
THE *HALAL* AND THE *HARAM* IN THE PRIVATE LIFE OF THE MUSLIM

1. **Food and Drink**
   The Islamic Manner of Slaughtering
   Hunting
   Intoxicants

2. **Clothing and Adornments**
   Gold and Silk
   The Dress of the Muslim
   Artificial Change of Features

3. **The Home**
   The Use of Gold and Silver
   Statues
   Photographs

4. **Work**
   Music and Dance
   Making Statues and Crosses
   Intoxicants
   Prohibited Trade

1. Food and Drink

Since ancient times, peoples have differed in their eating and drinking habits and in relation to what is to be allowed and avoided, especially with regard to food of animal origin.

Concerning food and drink of vegetable origin, the peoples of the earth have been close to a consensus. Islam does not prohibit vegetable foods, with the exception of what is fermented, whether it be grapes, dates, barley, or any other substance, as long as it remains in the unfermented state; similarly, Islam prohibits anything which intoxicates, affects the functioning of the brain, or harms the body, as we shall see later. However, with regard to foods derived from animal sources peoples and nations have held widely varying attitudes.

The Attitude of the Brahmins Toward Slaughtering Animals and Eating Meat

The Brahmins and a group of philosophers, subsisting on vegetarian food, only prohibit to themselves the killing and eating of animals. They claim that the slaughtering of animals is a cruelty inflicted by men on these creatures, who are living beings like themselves and that they must not deprive the animals of their right to live.

However, when we ponder the creation, we realize that these animals have not been created for their own sake, because they have not been endowed with intellect or freedom of choice; we also see that their natural position is such that they have been subjected to the service of man. It is therefore not to be doubted that man should benefit from their flesh after slaughter just as he benefits from their service while they are alive.

Again, we realize that it is the law of Allah in His creation that the lower order of species be sacrificed for the benefit of the higher. Thus green plants are cut and fed to an animal, the animal is slaughtered to be food for man, and a man must also fight and risk his life for the sake of the group. Moreover, even if

39

a man refrains from slaughtering an animal, it will not thereby be saved from death and destruction; it will either become prey to some other animal or will die in some other way, possibly in a much more painful manner than by a quick stroke of a sharp knife.

Animals Prohibited to the Jews and Christians

Among the people possessing a religion based on a divinely revealed scripture,[1] Allah prohibited to the Jews the eating of many land and marine animals; for a description of these one may refer to the Old Testment book of Leviticus, chapter eleven. The Qur'an mentions some of the things which Allah prohibited to them, as we mentioned previously, to punish them for their transgressions and sins:

> And to the Jews We forbade every animal with claws, and of oxen and sheep We have forbidden them their fat, except what is carried on their backs or entrails or what is connected to the bone; thus did We recompense them for their rebelliousness, and indeed We speak the truth. (6:146)

These prohibitions applied to the Jews, and it may be assumed that the Christians were also supposed to observe them since the *Injeel* declares that Jesus (peace be on him) did not come to abolish the Law of Moses but to fulfill it. However, the Christians made permissible things which had been prohibited in the *Torah*, although not abrogated in the *Injeel*, or scripture revealed to Jesus (peace be on him). The Christians followed the teachings of Paul, who declared all foods and drinks permissible with the sole exception of the flesh of animals sacrificed to idols, [2] since "to the pure everything is pure."[3] Accordingly, Christians permitted to themselves the eating of pork, despite the fact that the text of the *Torah* prohibits it to this day.

---

[1]See footnote [1], page 5.
[2]1 Cor. 8:4-10, 10:19-29; Col. 2:13-14, 16; 1 Tim. 4:4-5. (Trans.)
[3]Rom. 14:14-17; Tit. 1:15. (Trans.)

The Attitude of the Pre-Islamic Arabs

The pre-Islamic Arabs prohibited certain animals as being unclean, together with some other animals which were considered sacred and dedicated to their gods; we have already mentioned *bahirah, saibah, wasilah,* and *ham,* which fall into the latter category. In contrast to this, they permitted many kinds of impure foods, such as the flesh of dead animals and flowing blood.

Islam Permits What Is Wholesome

This was the state of the world in relation to the eating of food at the advent of Islam. At one extreme every kind of meat was permitted and at the other all meat was prohibited. Then Allah addressed all human beings saying,

> O mankind! Eat of what is permissible and good on
> earth, and do not follow the footsteps of Satan; truly he
> is an open adversary to you. (2:168)

Thus He speaks to all the people on this globe, calling on them to eat of the good things which He has provided for them on this vast, outspread table, the Earth, and not to follow the ways of Satan, who has made it alluring to some people to prohibit for themselves various wholesome things which Allah has made *halal,* thus leading them toward the pitfalls of self-destruction. Then Allah addressed the Believers in particular saying,

> O you who believe! Eat of the good things that We have
> provided for you, and be thankful to Allah if it is He
> alone whom you worship. Indeed, what He has
> forbidden to you is the flesh of dead animals and blood
> and the flesh of swine, and that which has been
> sacrificed to anyone other than Allah. But if one is
> compelled by necessity, neither craving (it) nor
> transgressing, there is no sin on him; indeed, Allah is
> Forgiving, Merciful. (2:172-173)

In this particular message to the Believers, Allah Subhanahu wa Ta'ala tells them to eat of the good things of His providing and to

41

give thanks to Him for His favors. He then explains that no food is *haram* to them except the four kinds mentioned in the *ayah*. The same four kinds, with some further details, are mentioned at other places in the Qur'an:

> Say: I do not find in what is revealed to me anything prohibited to an eater in his food unless it be (the flesh of) that which is dead, or flowing blood,or the flesh of swine, for that is indeed foul, or the abomination which has been dedicated to anyone other than Allah. But if one is compelled by necessity, neither craving (it) nor transgressing, then, indeed, thy Lord is Forgiving, Merciful.   (6:145)

And in even greater detail:

> Forbidden to you are the flesh of dead animals and blood and the flesh of swine, and that which has been dedicated to any other than Allah, and that which has been killed by strangling or by beating or by falling or by being gored, and that which has been (partly) eaten by a wild beast except that which you make lawful by slaughtering (before its death), and that which has been sacrificed to idols....   (5:4 (5:3))

There is no contradiction between this verse, which lists ten prohibited categories, and the previous verse which lists four, since animals which are killed by strangulation, by a blow, by a fall, by being gored, or which are partly eaten by wild animls all belong in the category of dead animals. Similarly, what is sacrificed to idols falls into the category of that which is dedicated to anyone other than Allah. Accordingly, the foods which are prohibited fall into four broad categories which may be reclassified into ten detailed categories, as follows:

The Prohibition of Eating What Is Dead and Its Wisdom

1. The first thing mentioned in these verses concerning prohibited foods is the flesh of "dead animals," that is, the beast or fowl which dies of natural causes, without being slaughtered or hunted by men. There are obvious reasons for this prohibition:

42

(a) Eating the flesh of a dead animal is repugnant to civilized taste and is considered by thinking people in all societies to be contrary to human dignity. We also observe that all peoples possessing a divinely revealed scripture have prohibited it and that they do not eat the flesh of an animal unless it is slaughtered. However, the methods of slaughter may vary.

(b) In whatever he does, the Muslim acts with a set purpose and intention; he does not use a thing nor reap its benefit without directing his intention, aim, and effort toward it. The significance of slaughtering, which is a purposeful act, the intention of which is to take the life of the animal in order to use it as food, is to remove the slaughtered animal from the category of "dead animals." Allah Subhanahu wa Ta'ala does not desire that man should eat of what he did not intend or think of eating, as is the case with the dead animal; conversely, slaughtering an animal or hunting it as game both require an intention followed by effort and subsequent action.

(c) If the animal died a natural death, it is quite likely that it died of some acute or chronic disease, through eating a poisonous plant, or other similar causes; hence eating its flesh would probably be harmful. The same is the case when the cause of death is old age or starvation.

(d) By prohibiting the flesh of a dead animal to human beings, Allah in His Mercy provides source of food to animals and birds, who, in the words of the Qur'an, constitute an *ummah* (nation) like themselves. The truth of this is demonstrated by the fact that the carcasses of animals lying out in the open are devoured by birds and animals.

(e) This prohibition encourages the owner of an animal to guard it from disease and malnutrition lest it die and be wasted. Accordingly, in the case of disease, he will be quick to seek a cure for it or will hasten to slaughter the animal.

43

The Prohibition of Flowing Blood

2. The second prohibition relates to flowing or liquid blood.[1] Ibn Abbas was asked about the spleen and he replied, "You can eat it." The questioners said, "But it is blood."[2] He answered, "Only flowing blood is prohibited to you." The reason for this prohibition is both that the drinking of blood is repugnant to human decency and that it may likewise be injurious to health.

    During the period of *jahiliyyah*,[3] a person who felt hungry might jab a bone or sharp object into the flesh of his animal, and collect and drink the flowing blood. It was concerning this that the poet al'Ashi said:

    Never approach animals that are dead, Nor take a sharp bone to pierce the live one.

Thus, since piercing the flesh of a living animal injures and weakens it, Allah Ta'ala prohibited such a practice.

Pork

3. The third prohibited food is pork, that is, the flesh of swine. Since the pig relishes filth and offal, its meat is repugnant to persons of decent taste; moreover, recent medical research has shown that eating swine-flesh is injurious to health in all climates, especially hot ones. Scientific research has also shown that pork carries a deadly parasite (trichina), among others, and no one can say what science may discover in the future which will shed more light on the wisdom of this prohibition. Allah the Almighty spoke the truth in describing His Messenger, Muhammad (peace be on him), as the one who "makes unlawful what is foul." (7:157)

    In addition to this, there are also some scholars who say that eating pork frequently diminishes the human being's sense of shame in relation to what is indecent.

----

[1] It is not prohibited to eat the blood which remains in the flesh of the slaughtered animal after one has done his best to remove it. (Trans.)
[2] In early times the spleen was believed to be congealed blood. (Trans.)
[3] See footnote (3), page 22.

44

That Which Is Dedicated to Anyone Other Than Allah

4. The fourth prohibited category refers to an animal which is dedicated to anyone other than Allah, that is to say, one which is slaughtered with the invocation of a name other than the name of Allah — for example, the name of an idol. When slaughtering an animal, the Arab polytheists would invoke the names of their idols, such as al-Lat or al-Uzza. Such a practice is a devotional act addressed to someone other than Allah and is a form of worship in which His glorious name is not mentioned. In this case the reason for the prohibition is entirely related to faith: to safeguard the belief in the Oneness of Allah, to purify worship, and to fight *shirk* and polytheism in whatever form they may be expressed.

Indeed, it is Allah who created man and gave him control over everything on the earth, subjecting the animal to his power and permitting him to take its life for food on the condition that His name be pronounced at the time of slaughter. Pronouncing the name of Allah while slaughtering the animal is a declaration that one is taking the life of this creature by the permission of its Creator, while if one invokes any other name, he has forfitted this permission and must be denied the use of its flesh.

Types of Dead Animals

The preceding are the four principal categories of prohibited animal foods. As revealed in the verse of *Surh al-Maidah* (5:4 (3)), to these four are added five more categories which pertain to further classifications of the "dead animal," as follows:

5. *The strangled:* an animal which has been strangled, for example, by a rope around its neck, or suffocated, as for instance by putting its head into something which produces suffocation.
6. *The beaten:* an animal which has been beaten to death by a club or similar object.
7. *The fallen:* an animal which dies as a result of a fall from a high place, or by falling into a gully or ravine.

8. *The gored*: an animal which dies as a result of being gored by the horns of another animal.

9. *That which has been (partly) eaten by wild beasts*: an animal which has been partially devoured by wild animals and dies as a result.

After naming these five categories, Allah makes an exception of "that which you make lawful by slaughtering," meaning that if one comes upon such an animal while it is still alive, slaughtering renders it *halal* as food. The correct understanding of "still alive" is that some sign of life remains in it. 'Ali ibn Abu Talib said, "If you can slaughter the beaten, the fallen or the gored animal while it (still) moves its hoof or leg, you may eat it." Commented al-Dahak, "The people of the time of *jahiliyyah* used to eat them (dead animals); then Allah prohibited them in Islam, excepting what is slaughtered. If it is slaughtered while it (still) moves a leg, its tail, or an eye, it is *halal*[1]

Reasons for the Prohibition of the Foregoing Categories

We need not repeat the reasons stated in the preceding discussion concerning dead animals, with the possible exception of the danger to health, which is not clear in such cases. However, we wish to emphasize again the significance of prohibitions 5 through 9 above. The All-Wise Law-Giver wants to teach people to be kind to the animal and to protect it from harm. One should not neglect it so that it can be strangled, fall from a high place, or be gored in a fight with other animals, nor torture it by severe beating, possibly resulting in its death, as vicious herdsmen, particularly hired ones, sometimes do, even goading animals such as two bulls or sheep to fight each other until one wounds or gores the other to death.

It is solely for this reason that Islamic jurists have prohibited the eating of the flesh of an animal which has been gored to death, even if it was wounded by the horns of the other and its blood has flowed; this prohibition holds even if the blood flowed from a wound in the

---

[1]Some jurists have said that there must be life in it, the signs of which are the flow of blood and reflex movements.

46

usual site of slaughter, the throat. According to my understanding, the purpose behind this is to penalize the owner of such animals who has left them unattended to gore each other to death; he is not to be rewarded for this negligence by being permitted to make use of their flesh for food.

The reason for prohibiting the eating of animals partially devoured by wild beasts is to preserve human dignity; a Muslim is not to degrade himself by eating the leavings of animals. The people of the period of *jahiliyyah* were in the habit of eating what had been left by wild animals, whether of sheep, camel or cow, but subsequently Allah prohibited this to the Believers.

Animal Sacrifices

10. The tenth category of prohibited animal food is that which has been sacrificed to idols. During the period of *jahiliyyah*, stone altars stood in front of the idols around the *Ka'aba*, and the polytheists would slaughter animals on or close to these altars in order to seek nearness to the deities to which the altars were assigned.

    Such immolation is similar to "that which has been dedicated to anyone other than Allah," as both involve the glorification of false deities. The difference is that in case of "that which has been dedicated to anyone other than Allah," the slaughtering did not take place in the vicinity of the idol and only its name was mentioned over the object of sacrifice, while in the latter case the immolation was done in front of the idol or on the altar assigned to it, and it was therefore unnecessary to mention its name.

    Since these altars were in the vicinity of the *Ka'aba*, it was possible to imagine that these sacrifices were meant to render homage to the Sacred House. The Qur'an, through an explicit declaration, removed this possibility from the minds of people, classifying this practice in the same category as that which is dedicated to anyone other than Allah.

47

The Exemption of Sea Food and Locusts

The Islamic *Shari'ah* has exempted fish, whales, and other sea creatures from the category of "dead animals." When the Prophet (peace be on him) was asked about the sea, he replied,

Its water is pure and its dead are *halal*.[1]

Says Allah Ta'ala:

The game of the sea is permitted to you and so is its food.... (5:99 (96))

and 'Umar explained, "Its game is what is caught from it and its food is what is thrown out from it," while Ibn 'Abbas said, "Its food is its dead (animals)."

In the two *Sahihs* of al-Bukhari and Muslim, it is reported on the authority of Jabir that the Prophet (peace be on him) once sent some of his Companions on an expedition. They found a dead whale by the sea and subsisted on it for more than twenty days. On their return to Madinah, they told the Prophet (peace be on him) about this and he said,

Eat the food which Allah has brought forth for you, and feed us from it if you have any left.

They then brought him some whale meat and he ate it.[2]

By the same token, locusts are exempted from the category of "dead animals." The Prophet (peace be on him) gave permission to eat dead locusts, as the question of slaughtering them does not arise. Said Ibn Abu Awfa, "We went with the Prophet (peace be on him) on seven expeditions, and we ate locusts with him."[3]

Making Use of the Skin, Bones, and Hair of the Animal

The prohibition concerning the dead animal is limited to the eating of its flesh. One can — in fact, one should — make use of its skin, horns, bones and hair, for throwing them away is a waste, and waste is not permitted. Concerning this, Ibn 'Abbas narrated:

---

[1] Reported by Ahmad and other compilers of the *Sunnah*.
[2] Reported by al-Bukhari.
[3] Reported by all the authentic collections of *ahadith* excepting that of Ibn Majah.

The freed maid-servant of the Prophet's wife, Maymunah, was given a sheep, and it died. The Prophet (peace be on him) passed by its carcass and said, 'Why did you not take its skin to be tanned and use it?' They replied, 'But it is dead.' The Prophet (peace be on him) said, 'What is prohibited is eating it."[1]

The Prophet (peace be on him) made it clear that the way to purify the skin of a dead animal is to tan it. He is reported to have said,

"The tanning of the skin is its slaughtering,"[2]

meaning that just as slaughtering makes the eating of the flesh of a sheep or cow *halal*, likewise tanning makes the use of the skin *halal*. He also said,

"Tanning removes its impurity,"[3]

and

"If the skin is tanned, it is purified."[4]

The application of these latter *ahadith* is quite general, including the skin of the dog or the pig. This was the opinion of the jurists of the Zahiri school, of Abu Yusuf, the pupil of Abu Hanifah, and of al-Shawkani. Sawdah, the wife of the Prophet (peace be on him), said "One of our sheep died, so we tanned its skin and used it as a waterskin, putting dates in it to sweeten the water. We used it until it wore out."[5]

Necessity Dictates Exceptions

All the above-mentioned prohibitions apply in situations in which one has a choice. However, in case of a necessity a different rule applies, as was discussed earlier. Allah Ta'ala says:

...He has explained to you what He has made *haram* for you, except that to which you are compelled... (6:119)

And after mentioning the prohibitions concerning the flesh of dead animals, blood, and so, He says:

---

[1]Reported in all the authentic collections of *ahadith* excepting that of Ibn Majah
[2]Reported by Abu Daoud and al-Nisai.
[3]Reported by al-Hakim.
[4]Reported by Muslim and others.
[5]Reported by al-Bukhari and others.

...but if one is compelled by necessity, neither craving
(it) nor transgressing, there is no sin on him; indeed,
Allah is Forgiving, Merciful. (2:172-173)

The consensus of the jurists is that necessity in this case signifies
the need for food to alleviate hunger when no food other than the
prohibited food is available, some jurists holding the opinion that at
least one day and one night should pass without food. In such a
situation a person may eat as much will satisfy his hunger and thus
save himself from death. Said Imam Malik, "The amount of it is
what will alleviate his hunger, and he should not eat more than
what will keep him alive." This, perhaps, is the meaning of Allah's
words, "neither craving (it) nor transgressing," — that is, neither
desiring it nor eating more than necessary. That hunger can be a
compelling need is expressly mentioned in the Qur'anic *ayah*:

...but if one is compelled by hunger, without any
inclination to sin, then indeed Allah is Forgiving,
Merciful. (5:4 (3))

Medical Necessity

Concerning the question of whether some of the prohibited food
substances can be used as medicine, there is a difference of opinion
among jurists. Some do not consider medicine to belong in the
category of a compelling necessity like food, and in support of their
position they cite the *hadith:*

"Assuredly Allah did not provide a cure for you in what
He has prohibited to you."[1]

Others consider the need for medicine equal to that of food, as both
are necessary for preserving life. In support of their position that
prohibited food substances may be used as medicine, they argue
that the Prophet (peace be on him) allowed 'Abd al-Rahman bin
'Awf and al-Zubair bin al-'Awwam to wear silk because they were
suffering from scabies.[2]

---

[1] Reported by al-Bukhari on the authority of Ibn Mas'ood.
[2] The text of this *hadith* is quoted in the subsection of this book entitled "Clothing and
Ornaments."

Perhaps this latter view is closer to the spirit of Islam which, in all its legislations and teachings, is concerned with the preservation of human life. However, taking medicine containing some of the *haram* substances is permissible only under the following conditions:

1. The patient's life is endangered if he does not take this medicine.
2. No alternative or substitute medication made from entirely *halal* sources is available.
3. The medication is prescribed by a Muslim physician who is knowledgeable as well as God-fearing.

We may, however, add that on the basis of our own observations and the opinions of expert physicians, we have arrived at the conclusion that there hardly exists any medical necessity which requires ingesting what is *haram*, as for example, taking medicine. Nevertheless, we have stated this principle in case a Muslim happens to be in a place where he cannot find medications other than those which contain *haram* substances.

Necessity Does Not Exist if the Society Possesses Excess Food

Consider a situation in which an individual does not have enough to eat but other people, Muslims or *dhimmis*,[1] in his community have excess food. In such a case he does not fulfill the stipulation of being in a state of necessity and consequently *haram* foods do not become permissible to him, for an Islamic community is like a single body supporting its members or like a fortified wall in which each brick strengthens the other.

The concept of social solidarity is expressed very forcefully by the great jurist Imam Ibn Hazm, who said,

> The Muslim is not in a state of necessity such that it becomes permissible for him to eat the flesh of dead

---

[1]*Dhimmis*: non-Muslims living under the protection of an Islamic government. (trans.)

51

animals or swine as long as someone else, whether a Muslim or a *dhimmi*, has excess food. It is obligatory on the person having food to feed the one who is hungry, and that being the case, the hungry person is not compelled to resort to the flesh of dead animals or swine. If the person having excess food denies it to him, he has a right to fight for it. If he (the hungry person) is killed, the killer is guilty of murder and consequently subject to *qisas* (retaliation), while if he kills the denier of food he has dispatched him to the curse of Allah, as he denied him his right and was one of the rebellious. Allah Ta'ala says: 'And if one of them transgresses against the other, fight against the one who transgresses until he complies with the command of Allah.' (49:9)

One who denies the rights of his brother is a rebel against Allah. That is why Abu Bakr al-Siddiq fought against those who refused to pay *zakat* (while professing to be Muslims).[1]

The Islamic Manner of Slaughtering

All Marine Animals Are Halal

Depending on their habitats, animals are of two kinds: either marine or terrestrial. Marine animals, that is, those which live in water and cannot survive outside it, are all *halal*. It does not matter in what way they are obtained: whether they are taken out of the water dead or alive, whole or in pieces, whether they are fish or marine animals, whether they are called sea dogs or sea hogs, or whether they are caught by a Muslim or a non-Muslim. The Most Generous Lord has opened wide His bounty upon His servants by permitting them to eat all marine animals, without the requirement of bleeding; man has been left free to catch them in whatever

---

[1]*Al-Muhalla* by Ibn Hazm, vol. 6, p. 159.

manner he is able, avoiding any unnecessary cruelty as far as possible. Reminding us of His favors, Allah Ta'ala says,

And it is He Who has subjected the sea (to you) in order that you may eat fresh meat from it.... (16:14)

The game of the sea is permitted to you and so is its food, a provision for you and for travelers by sea.... (5:99 (96))

Praise be to Him for not having excluded anything, for

Thy Lord is not forgetful. (19:64)

Prohibited Terrestrial Animals

As far as terrestrial or land animals are concerned, Allah has prohibited only the eating of pork, the flesh of any animal which dies of itself or is sacrificed to anyone other than Allah, and the drinking of blood. These prohibitions are explicitly mentioned in the text of the Qur'an, comprising, as we have seen, four major and ten minor categories.

At the same time, the Qur'an says concerning the Messenger of Allah (peace be on him):

He...makes lawful to them what is good and makes unlawful what is foul....(7:157)

Foul things are those which, although some individuals may like them, people generally find detestable. As an instance of this, on the day of the confrontation of Khaibar, the Prophet (peace be on him) forbade the eating of the flesh of domesticated donkeys.[1]

Another example of the same thing is provided by a *hadith* narrated by both al-Bukhari and Muslim, which states that the Prophet (peace be on him) "forbade the eating of any wild animals with a canine tooth and of any bird with talons." "Wild animals" denotes those which prey on others and devour them by tearing them apart, e.g., the lion, leopard, wolf, and the like; birds with talons such as the hawk, eagle, falcon, etc., do the same.

---

[1]Reported by al-Bukhari. Concerning this *hadith*, it is said that the prohibition of eating donkeys was temporary and was due to an emergency, as donkeys were needed for riding. This is similar to a situation in which, due to a shortage of meat, a government may prohibit the slaughtering of young animals so they may grow bigger or the hunting of deer in a particular season, etc.

According to Ibn 'Abbas, nothing is *haram* other than the four categories mentioned in the Qur'an, while what the Prophet (peace be on him) forbade, such as beasts of prey, are to be regarded as *makruh* (detestable) rather than reaching the degree of *haram*. Said Ibn 'Abbas:

> The people of the time of *jahiliyyah* ate certain foods and avoided others, according to their whim. Then Allah sent His Prophet (peace be on him) and revealed His Book, and He legislated what is permissible and what is prohibited. Accordingly, what He permitted is *halal*, what He prohibited is *haram*, and that concerning which He is silent is allowed.

Ibn 'Abbas then recited,

> Say: I do not find in what is revealed to me anything prohibited to an eater in his food. (6:145)[1]

On the basis of this *ayah*, Ibn 'Abbas argued that the flesh of domesticated donkeys is permissible. Imam Malik agrees with him on this matter, considering beasts of prey *makruh* rather than *haram*.

The jurists agree that cutting the throat of a prohibited animal does not render it *halal*. However, it then becomes permissible to use its skin without tanning it.

The Requirement of Slaughtering in the Islamic Manner

Land animals which are permissible as food are of two kinds. The first consists of those animals which are tame or domesticated, such as camels, cows, goats, poultry, and other fowl which are raised on a farm or in the house, while untamed and wild animals are of the second type. In order to render their flesh *halal*, Islam requires that animals of the first category be slaughtered in the manner prescribed by Islam.

The Conditions of Islamic Slaughtering

According to the *Shari'ah*, the legal purification of the flesh of animals requires that the following conditions be met:

---

[1]Reported by Abu Daoud as the saying of Ibn 'Abbas.

1. The animal should be slaughtered by a sharp object which is capable of making it bleed by severing blood vessels, even if the sharp object is a stone or a piece of wood. 'Adi bin Hatim narrated that he said to the Prophet (peace be on him), "O Mesenger of Allah, we go hunting and sometimes we do not have a knife with us. We may find a sharp rock or a piece of wood or a reed." The Prophet (peace be on him) said:

> "The object is to make it bleed with whatever you have and mention the name of Allah over it."[1]

2. The slaughtering is to be done by cutting the throat of the animal or by piercing the hollow of the throat, causing its death. The best way is to cut the windpipe, the gullet, and the two jugular veins.[2]

However, if it becomes impossible to slaughter the animal in the specified manner, this second condition is cancelled; for example, the animal may have fallen headlong into a well so that its throat is inaccessible, or it may become wild and start kicking and running. Such cases are treated in the manner of game animals and it is sufficient to wound the animal at any place to make it bleed. On the authority of Raf'i ibn Khadij, both al-Bukhari and Muslim report the former as narrating:

> We were on a journey with the Prophet (peace be on him) when one of the camels bolted away. As the people did not have a horse, a man shot an arrow which struck the camel and wounded it. The Prophet (peace be on him) said, 'Some of these animals are like wild beasts. If any of them behaves like this, treat it in this fashion.'[3]

---

[1] Reported by Ahmad, Abu Daoud, Nisai, Ibn Majah, al-Hakim, and Ibn Hibban.

[2] Some jurists have cited further conditions, but we have omitted them as we did not find explicit texts mentioning them. The slaughtering of animals is known instinctively to all people, and to go into depth and detail concerning it does not accord with Islam, which keeps matters easy and simple. The more details these jurists have attempted to list, the more confusion they have caused; for example, is it necessary to cut all four parts - the windpipe, the gullet and the two jugular veins - or only some of them? Should the knife point downward or upward? Can the hand be raised before the slaughtering is completed or not? and so on, without end, with each alternative answer to these questions finding support among some jurists.

[3] Reported by al-Bukhari and Muslim.

3. No name other than Allah's should be mentioned over the animal at the time of slaughter; concerning this condition there is a consensus among all the jurists. The people of the time of *jahiliyyah* sought to propitiate their deities and idols by sacrificing animals to them, either by invoking their names while slaughtering or by immolating them on altars specified for them. As mentioned previously, the Qur'an prohibited all this in the words,

> Forbidden to you are...that which has been dedicated to anyone other than Allah...and that which has been sacrificed to idols. (5:4 (3))

4. The name of Allah should be mentioned while slaughtering the animal.[1] This is clear from Qur'anic texts and *ahadith*. Allah Ta'ala says:

> Then eat of that over which the name of Allah has been mentioned, if you believe in His signs. (6:118)

> And do not eat of that over which the name of Allah has not been mentioned, for truly that is impiety.... (6:121)

And the Messenger of Allah (peace be on him) said:

> If the blood is drained (from the animal) and the name of Allah has been mentioned over it, you may eat of it.[2]

This condition is further supported by other sound *ahadith* which state that Allah's name must be pronounced while hunting just before an arrow is shot or a hunting dog is sent for the chase. This point will be discussed later in the section on hunting.

Some scholars are of the opinion that although the name of Allah must be mentioned, it is not necessary to mention it at the time of slaughtering the animal; one can mention it at the time of eating, since in that case it cannot be held that it was eaten without mentioning the name of Allah over it. In the *Sahih* of al-Bukhari we find a *hadith* narrated by 'Aisha, who said,

> Some people who had recently become Muslims said to

---

[1] The correct manner of mentioning the name of Allah at slaughtering is, *"Bismillah, Allahu akbar"* (in the name of God, God is the most great). On this occasion the words *al-Rahman al-Raheem* (the Compassionate, the Merciful) do not follow *Bismillah* as they ordinarily do, since slaughtering is not an act of mercy. (Trans.)
[2] Reported by al-Bukhari and others.

the Prophet (peace be on him), 'People bring us meat and we do not know whether they have mentioned the name of Allah over it or not. Shall we eat of it or not?' The Prophet (peace be on him) replied, 'Mention the name of Allah (over it) and eat.'[1]

The Wisdom of the Islamic Manner of Slaughtering

The wisdom of the Islamic rules of slaughtering is to take the animal's life in the quickest and least painful way; the requirements of using a sharp instrument and of cutting the throat relate to this end. It is forbidden to rend the throat by using teeth or nails since this will cause pain to the animal and is likely to strangle it. The Prophet (peace be on him) recommended sharpening the knife and putting the animal at ease, saying,

> Allah has ordained kindness (or excellence) in everything. If killing is to be done, do it in the best manner, and when you slaughter, do it in the best manner by first sharpening the knife and putting the animal at ease.[2]

In another *hadith* narrated by Ibn 'Umar, the Prophet (peace be on him) said,

> "When one of you slaughters, let him complete it,"[3]

meaning that one should sharpen his knife well and feed, water, and soothe the animal before killing it.

Ibn 'Abbas reported that once the Prophet (peace be on him) saw a man who was sharpening his knife after laying down a sheep to be slaughtered. The Prophet (peace be on him) rebuked him saying,

> "Do you intend to make it die two deaths? Why did you not sharpen your knife before laying it down?"[4]

---

[1]The correct invocation when one begins to eat or drink is *Bismillah ar-Rahman ar-Raheem*, "In the name of God, the Compassionate, the Merciful," coupled with a supplication such as, *Allahumma, barik lana fi ma razaqtana wa qina adhab an-nar*, "Our Lord, bless us in what You have provided for us and save us from the punishment of the Fire." (Trans.)

[2]Reported by Muslim on the authority of Shaddad bin Aus.

[3]Reported by Ibn Majah.

[4]Reported by al-Hakim, who classified it as "sound" according to the standard of al-Bukhari.

Once 'Umar saw a man dragging a sheep by its leg to be slaughtered. He said, "Woe to you! Lead it to its death in a decent manner."[1]

Thus the main intent here is to be kind to the unfortunate animal and spare it unnecessary suffering insofar as this is possible. The people of *jahiliyyah* were fond of cutting off the humps of live camels and the fat tails of live sheep in order to eat them. In order to put a stop to this barbaric practice, the Prophet (peace be on him) forbade the eating of any part obtained in this fashion, saying,

"Any part cut off a living animal is dead flesh,"[2]

The Significance of Mentioning Allah's Name

Mentioning the name of Allah to purify the act of slaughtering has a subtle significance which we would do well to ponder. First, this practice is in opposition to the practice of the idolaters and the people of *jahiliyyah*, who mentioned the names of their non-existent deities while slaughtering animals. Since the polytheist mentions the name of a false deity, how can the Believer fail to mention the name of the true God?

Second, these animals, like human beings, are creatures of Allah, and like them they have life. How then can a man take control of them and deprive them of life unless he first obtains permission from his, and their, common Creator, to Whom everything belongs? Mentioning the name of Allah while slaughtering the animal is a declaration of this divine permission, as if the one who is killing the animal were saying, "This act of mine is not an act of aggression against the universe nor of oppression of this creature, but in the name of Allah I slaughter, in the name of Allah I hunt, and in the name of Allah I eat."

---

[1]Reported by 'Abd ur-Razzaq.
[2]Reported by Ahmad, Abu Daoud, al-Tirmidhi, and al-Hakim.

58

Animals Slaughtered by the People of the Book

We have seen that Islam emphasizes that the animal must be slaughtered in a prescribed manner. The polytheists of Arabia and other nations had made animal sacrifice an act of worship, or rather an integral part of their belief system and a pillar of their religion, seeking to propitiate their deities by sacrificing animals either at their special altars or by mentioning their names over them. Islam abolished these pagan rites and ordained that no name except that of Allah be mentioned while slaughtering, and it prohibited what was sacrificed at an altar or dedicated to anyone other than Allah Subhanahu wa Ta'ala.

Now although the People of the Book — the Jews and Christians — are essentially believers in one God, some Muslims nevertheless supposed that in matters related to food the People of the Book were to be treated in the same manner as idolators. Thereupon Allah Ta'ala granted special permission to Muslims in the matter of eating with the People of the Book and in the matter of marriage to their women. In *Surah al-Maidah*, the last *surah* of the Qur'an to be revealed, Allah says,

> Today whatever is good is made lawful to you. And the food of those who were given the Scripture (before you) is permitted to you and your food is permitted to them....(5:6 (5))

The meaning of these verses is, in brief, that from this day forward all good, pure, and wholesome things are permitted to you Muslims; consequently, there can be no more *bahirah, saibah, wasilah,* or *ham*. Since Allah did not prohibit it, the food of the Jews and the Christians is permitted to you on the basis of the original permissibility of things, and likewise you can share your food with them. Accordingly, you can eat the flesh of the animals they have slaughtered or hunted, and they can eat what you have slaughtered or hunted.

While Islam takes an uncompromising attitude toward polytheists, it is lenient toward the People of the Book, for they are closer to Muslims in their belief in divine revelation, prophethood, and other fundamentals of religion. Islam permits us to eat with them, to marry their women, and , in general, to have social relations with them. It may be that, by interacting with Muslims in

59

an Islamic environment and observing the beliefs, practices, and characters of Muslims, they may come to realize that Islam is in truth their own religion but with a higher level of spirituality, a more perfect *Shari'ah*, and books of greater authenticity,[1] while also free of the influence of paganism, man-made concepts, and falsehood.

The application of the phrase, "the food of those who were given the Scripture," is general and includes their meats, produce, and other foods. All of these are *halal* for us excepting what is *haram* in itself, e.g., the flesh of a dead animal, pork, and flowing blood, as these are *haram* regardless of whether they are obtained from a Christian, a Jew or a Muslim.

We now turn to various questions which are of sufficient importance to Muslims to require an answer here.

Animals Slaughtered for Churches and Christian Festivals

If one does not hear from a Christian or a Jew that a name other than Allah's such as that of Jesus or a saint, was mentioned at the time of slaughter, the meat he offers is *halal*. If, however, he says that a name other than Allah's has been mentioned, it is *haram*, according to the opinion of some jurists who argue that it falls under the heading of what has been dedicated to other than Allah. Some others hold the opinion that the food of the People of the Book has been permitted to us by Allah, Who is aware of what they say when slaughtering an animal.

Someone asked Abu al-Darda whether he could eat the flesh of a lamb, slaughtered for the Church of St. George, which had been given to him. Abu al-Darda answered, "O Allah, may You pardon us! Are they not the People of the Book, whose food is *halal* for us and ours for them? He then told the person to eat it.[2]

Imam Malik was once asked about eating the flesh of animals slaughtered for Christian festivals and churches. He replied,

> I classify it as *makruh* but not *haram: makruh* because
> I am afraid it may have been dedicated to someone

---

[1]That is, the Holy Qur'an, the books of *Ahadith*, and the *Sirah* (biography) of the Prophet. (Trans.)
[2]Reported by al-Tabari.

other than Allah but not *haram* because perhaps, with respect to the People of the Book, the meaning of the phrase, 'that which has been dedicatd to any other than Allah,' applies only to those animals which they slaughter for the purpose of seeking the pleasure of their deities[1] and not to eat. As for what they slaughter to eat, it is their food, and Allah says, 'The food of those who were given the Scripture is permitted to you.'[2] (5:6 (7))

Animals Slaughtered By Electric Shock and Other Methods

The second question is this: Is it necessary that the method of slaughter of an animal employed by the People of the Book so that it is *halal* in their religion be the same as ours, which is to cut the throat? A majority of jurists stipulate this as a condition, while a number of Maliki jurists have ruled that it is not a condition.

Qadi Ibn al-Arabi, in explaining the verse of *Surah al-Maidah,* "The food of those who were given the Scripture is permitted to you," (5:6 (7)) says:

This is a decisive proof that the game and food of the People of the Book are among the good things which Allah has allowed for us. He, the Most High, has repeated it twice in order to allay doubts and to seal the mouths of those mischevious objectors, who would raise questions and prolong the discussion. I was asked: 'If a Christian kills a chicken by cutting off its head and then cooks it, is it permissible to eat with him or to partake of his food?' I said: 'Eat it, as this is his food and the food of his priests and monks. Although this is not our way of slaughtering the animal, yet Allah has permitted their food to us unconditionally,

---

[1]This may refer to Jesus, Mary, or to other saints. (Trans.)
[2]This ruling by Imam Malik demonstrates his humility, piety, and caution in religion. He did not rush to the conclusion that it was *haram*, as some jurists do today, but confined himself to stating that it was *makruh*. As we can see, faced with the problem of reconciling two conflicting general categories, that which is dedicated to anyone other than Allah and the permissibility of the food of the People of the Book, he exercised caution and deliberation.

and also other things in their religion excepting those which Allah says they have falsified.' Our scholars have said: They give us their women in marriage and it is permissible to engage in sexual intercourse with them. In matters concerning *halal* and *haram*, sexual intercourse is of graver import than eating; how then does it make sense to say that their food is not *halal*?

This is the opinion of Ibn al-Arabi. On another occasion he says: "What they eat without intending to make it lawful for eating, as for example by strangling the animal or smashing its head, is *haram*." There is no contradiction between these two statements of his. What is meant here is that what they consider as religiously lawful to eat is *halal* for us, even though the method of killing the animal in their religion may be different from ours, and what is not religiously lawful to them is *haram* for us. What is meant by killing the animal in their religion is killing it with the intention of making it lawful as food according to their religion. This is the opinion of a group of Maliki jurists.

In the light of this ruling, we know that imported meats, such as chicken and canned beef, originating with the People of the Book are *halal* for us, even though the animal may have been killed by means of electric shock or the like. As long as they consider it lawful in their religion, it is *halal* for us. This is the application of the above verse from *Surah al-Maidah*.

The Meat of Zoroastrians and Others Like Them

A difference of opinion exists among jurists concerning the meat of animals slaughtered by the Zoroastrians or Parsees (*Majus*). The majority forbids the eating of it because they are polytheists, while others say that it is *halal* because the Prophet (peace be on him) said,

"Treat them as you treat the People of the Book."[1]

The Prophet (peace be on him) acccepted *jizyah* from the Zoroastrians of Hajar.[2] In the chapter on slaughtering in Ibn

---

[1] Reported by Malik and al-Shafi'i. What comes at the end of this *hadith*, "Do not marry their women nor eat their meat," is not considered authentic by the compilers of *Ahadith*.
[2] Reported by al-Bukhari and others.

Hazm's book, *Al-Muhalla,*[1] the author says, "They are also a People of the Book; hence all the rules related to the People of the Book apply to them."[2] Likewise the Sabeans are classified by Abu Hanifah as belonging to the category of People of the Book.[3]

A Rule: What We Do Not See Should Not Be Probed Into

It is not required of the Muslim to inquire about what he has not witnessed, i.e., How was the animal killed? Did the manner of slaughter meet the Islamic conditions? Was the name of Allah mentioned while slaughtering or not? If the animal was slaughtered by a Muslim, even if he is ignorant or sinful, or by someone from among the People of the Book, eating it is *halal* for us.

We have already narrated a *hadith* in which it was said to the Prophet (peace be on him): "People bring us meat and we do not know whether they have mentioned the name of Allah over it or not. Shall we eat it or not?" and the Prophet (peace be on him) replied,

"Mention the name of Allah (over it) and eat."

Concerning the application of this *hadith*, scholars say: This is proof that the actions and practices of people are ordinarily considered to be correct and appropriate, while deviation or error must be proved.

Hunting

Many Arabs and peoples of other nations formerly lived by hunting; hence the Qur'an and *Sunnah* have addressed themselves to this matter. Muslim jurists have always treated the subject of

---

[1] Vol. 7, p. 456.
[2] Ibn Hazm's opinion undoubtedly carries great weight. He was very meticulous in applying the texts of the Qur'an and *Ahadith,* as well as being knowledgeable concerning the history of nations and their customs. Al-Baghdadi, in his book *Al-Farq Bayn al-Firaq,* states: "The Magians (Zoroastrians) claim that Zoraster was a prophet." Some modern Islamic scholars who have conducted researches into ancient cultures, such as Abul Kalam Azad, support this view.
[3] Some researchers of our time have attempted to extend the circle of People of the Book to include idolators such as Hindus and Buddhists, but they are stretching the matter too far. See, for example, *Tafsir al-Manar,* vol. 6, in the interpretation of the *ayah,* "The food of those who were given the Scripture is permitted to you," in the chapter dealing with the food of idolators and marriage to their women.

hunting under a separate heading, explaining what is lawful and what is prohibited, what is obligatory and what is commendable in this regard, since many animals and birds whose flesh is wholesome are neither tamed nor under man's control.

In order to render eating them *halal*, Islam does not require that the throats of such creatures be cut or that the hollow of their throat be pierced, as is required for the slaughter of tame and domesticated animals. It is sufficient to do something of this sort but to a lesser degree, as the circumstances of the hunt permit. People have always followed their instincts while hunting, and Islam does not oppose what is natural and instinctive, but merely adds a few conditions in order to bring hunting, as it brings all the other affairs of Muslims, in accord with its general belief system. Some of these conditions apply to the hunter, others to the game, and still others to the instrument of hunting.

These conditions apply, naturally, only to land game. As for sea game, Allah has permitted all of it without restriction, as was mentioned earlier:

> The game of the sea is permitted to you and so is its food, a provision for you and for travellers by sea.... (5:99 (96))

Conditions Pertaining to the Hunter

The conditions pertaining to the hunter are the same as those which pertain to the butcher: that he should be either a Muslim, a Jew, a Christian, a Zoroastrian, or a Sabean.

Islam teaches the hunter that he should not hunt merely for sport, taking the life of animals without intending to eat them or otherwise benefit from them. The Prophet (peace be on him) said:

> If someone kills a sparrow for sport, the sparrow will cry out on the Day of Judgement, 'O Lord! That person killed me in vain! He did not kill me for any useful purpose.'[1]

Again, he said:

> Whoever kills a sparrow or anything bigger than that

---

[1]Reported by al-Nisai and by Ibn Hibban in his *Sahih*.

without a just cause, Allah will hold him accountable on the Day of Judgement. The listeners asked, O Messenger of Allah, what is a just cause? He replied, That he kill it to eat, not to simply chop off its head and then throw it away.[1]

Another condition is that the Muslim should not be in the state of *ihram*[2] for *hajj* or *'umrah*, for at that time he is in a state of total peace and serenity, the sphere of which extends to the animals and birds around him. Even if some game should appear right in front of him so that he could catch or kill it with a spear, it is not permissible for him to do so. This is to test and train the Believer in order to make him strong and patient. As Allah Ta'ala says:

O you who believe! Do not kill game while you are in the state of *ihram*.... (5:98 (95))

...And hunting is *haram* for you while you are in the state of *ihram*....(5:2(1))

Conditions Pertaining to the Game

One of the conditions pertaining to game is that it should be an animal which man is not able to bring under control in order to slaughter it properly, for, according to principle, if it is possible to slaughter it, this must be done, and no other choice remains.

Similarly, if one shoots an arrow at the animal or if his hunting dog has brought it down, as long as he reaches the animal while there is still abundant life remaining in it, its throat must be cut. However, although cutting the throat is preferable, if it is barely alive and the hunter leaves it to die without cutting the throat there is no harm in it. According to the two *Sahih's* of al-Bukhari and Muslim, the Prophet (peace be on him) said:

When you set your dog (for the chase), mention the name of Allah. If he catches the game, and you reach it while it is still alive, cut its throat.

---

[1]Reported by al-Nisai and al-Hakim, who said that its transmission is sound.
[2]*Ihram* refers to the state of consecration, physical and spiritual, of the Muslim who is performing *hajj*, the obligatory pilgrimage, or *'umrah*, the lesser and voluntary pilgrimage. (Trans.)

Conditions Pertaining to the Instrument

Instruments of hunting are two kinds:

(a) Weapons, such as swords, arrows, and spears, as mentioned in the *ayah*:

> ...in the game which you take with your hands and your spears.... (5:97 (94))

(b) Hunting animals which can be trained, such as the dog and the leopard among beasts, and the falcon and hawk among birds. Allah Ta'ala says:

> Say: Whatever is good is lawful for you. And eat of what is caught for you by those you have trained among hunting animals, teaching them as Allah has taught you....(5:5 (4))

Hunting with Weapons

Two conditions must be met if the game is killed by a weapon. First, the weapon should pierce the body of the animal, making a wound; death by mere impact does not render it *halal*. 'Adi bin Hatim narrated, "I asked the Messenger of Allah (peace be him) about game killed with a weapon (*m'irad*). He said,

> "If you hurl the weapon and it pierces the game, eat it, but if it is killed by the blow of its side, do not eat it."[1]

This *hadith* is proof that what makes the game *halal* is that the body of the animal be pierced, even if the weapon is blunt. Accordingly, game killed by a rifle or pistol or the like is *halal* as the bullet will penetrate its body even more deeply than an arrow, spear, or sword.

With reference to the *hadith* reported by Ahmad,

> "Do not eat what is killed by a *banduqah* unless you slaughter it,"

and the one reported by al-Bukhari on the authority of Ibn 'Umar, which states that the animal killed by a *banduqah* is like an animal killed by a blow, it should be noted that *banduqah* here refers to a ball of clay and not to the modern bullet. The Prophet (peace be on him) likewise forbade throwing stones at the hunted animal, saying,

---

[1]Reported by al-Bukhari and Muslim.

66

"Throwing stones will not hunt the game or kill an
enemy, but it may break a tooth or gouge out an eye."[1]

The second condition to be met when hunting with a weapon is
that the name of Allah must be mentioned when hurling or striking
with the weapon, as the Prophet (peace be on him) instructed 'Adi
bin Hatim, whose reports of a *hadith* are the source material for this
topic.[2]

Hunting with Dogs and the Like

If hunting is done with a dog or falcon or the like, the following is
required: first, it should be a trained animal; second, it should catch
the game for its owner and not for itself, as the Qur'an specifies; and
third, the name of Allah must be mentioned while sending it for the
chase. The source of these conditions is the following *ayah:*

They ask thee (O Muhammad) what is lawful to them
(as food). Say: Whatever is good is lawful for you. And
eat of what is caught for you by those you have trained
among hunting animals, teaching them as Allah has
taught you, and mention the name of Allah over it....(5:5
(4))

1. The definition of "training" is well known. It means that the
animal so trained is under the control of its owner so that when he
calls it, it responds; when he sends it toward the game, it hunts it;
and when he restrains it, it halts. The jurists have laid down various
criteria for this; however, common sense is a better guide in deciding
whether a hunting animal is trained or not.

2. The definition of "catching the game for its owner" is that it
does not itself eat the game. The Prophet (peace be on him) said:

"If you send your dog after the game, and it eats part of
it, you should not eat of it, for the dog has hunted the
game for itself and not for you; but if you send the dog
and it kills the game without eating it, you can eat it, as
it has caught it for its master."[3]

Some jurists make a distinction between hunting animals such as

---

[1] Reported by al-Bukhari and Muslim.
[2] The above instructions likewise apply to hunting with a gun. (Trans.)
[3] Narrated by Ahmad; also reported by al-Bukhari and Muslim.

dogs and hunting birds such as falcons. Their opinion is that eating game which has been partly eaten by a bird is permissible, while if a dog has eaten from it, it is not allowed.

The reason for laying down these two conditions is, first, to emphasize that the hunting dog should be well-trained, always being under the control of its master, and second, to preserve human dignity by not allowing man to eat the leavings of animals. Finally, we note that a well-trained dog which catches the game for its master is very similar to an inanimate weapon in his hands such as an arrow.

3. Mentioning the name of Allah while sending the dog for the chase is like mentioning His name while shooting the arrow, hurling the spear, or striking with the sword. The Qur'anic injunction, "mention the name of Allah over it," has also been emphasized in *ahadith*, such as that of 'Adi bin Hatim.

The mandatory nature of this condition has also been demonstrated by the fact that if a dog other than that of the hunter is found at the game, eating of it is not lawful. 'Adi said to the Prophet (peace be on him), "Suppose I send my dog but I find another dog at the game, and I do not know which dog caught it?" The Prophet (peace be on him) replied,

> "Do not eat it, for while you mentioned the name of Allah over your dog, you did not mention it over the other dog."

However, if one forgets to mention Allah's name while dispatching his weapon or the hunting animal, he can make up for it by mentioning it at the time of eating, for Allah has forgiven the Muslim *ummah* for the errors it commits due to forgetfulness or error. As was mentioned earlier, this also applies in the case of forgetting to pronounce the name of Allah at the time of slaughtering.

The significance of mentioning the name of Allah over the animal need not be repeated here, as it was explained earlier in connection with slaughtering.

When the Game is Found Dead

It may happen that although the game is struck by the arrow it may nevertheless escape; the hunter may find it some time —

perhaps even days — later, dead. In such a case, the game is lawful as food under the following conditions:

(1) That it is not found in water. The Prophet (peace be on him) said:

> "If you shoot an arrow and it kills the animal, you can eat it. But if it is found in water, you do not know whether its death was caused by drowning or by your arrow."[1]

(2) That it has no wounds other than the wound inflicted by the arrow. 'Adi bin Hatim asked the Prophet (peace be on him), "What if I shoot an arrow and find the game the next morning with my arrow in it?" The Prophet (peace be on him) replied:

> "If you know that your arrow killed it, and you do not find any wound inflicited by wild beasts, you may eat it."[2]

(3) That the game has not reached the stage of decay. People of sound taste are naturaly revolted and nauseated by rotten meat, and eating it is also likely to be injurious. It is narrated in the *Sahih* of Muslim that the Prophet (peace be on him) told Abu Th'alabah al-Khashini,

> "You shoot an arrow but the game disappears for three days. If you then come upon it, you may eat what is not decayed of it."

INTOXICANTS

The Arabic word *khamr* signifies any alcoholic drink which causes intoxication. We would be stating the obvious if we were to discuss the harmful effects of drinking on the individual's mind, his health, his religion, and his work; or if we discussed the disasters which he brings upon his family by neglecting their needs and by not fulfilling his obligations, as the head of the family, toward his wife and children; or if we elaborated on the spiritual, material, and moral evils which proliferate in societies and nations due to the widespread consumption of alcohol.

---

[1] Reported by al-Bukhari and Muslim.
[2] Reported by al-Tirmidhi, who classifies it as *sahih*.

69

A researcher in this area has rightly stated that:

> Mankind has not suffered any greater calamity than that brought about by the use of alcohol. If statistics were collected worldwide of all the patients in hospitals who, due to alcohol, are suffering from mental disorders, *delerium tremens*, nervous breakdowns, and ailments of the digestive tract, to which are added the statistics of suicides, homicides, bankruptcies, sales of properties, and broken homes related to the consumption of alcohol, the number of such cases would be so staggering that, in comparison to it, all exhortation and preaching against drinking would seem too little.

The Arabs during the period of *jahiliyyah* were very fond of wine and drinking parties. This love of wine is reflected in their language, which has nearly one hundred names for it, and in their poetry, which celebrates the praises of wine, goblets, drinking parties, and so on.

To eradicate this pervasive evil from society, Allah Subhanahu wa Ta'ala adopted a wise course of education and training, prohibiting it in measured stages. First, He made it clear to them that the harm of drinking wine is greater than its benefit; next, He told them not to come to *salat* while intoxicated; and finally, He revealed the verse in *Surah al-Maidah* which prohibited it totally and decisively:

> O you who believe! Truly, intoxicants and gambling and divination by arrows are an abomination of Satan's doing: avoid it in order that you may be successful. Assuredly Satan desires to sow enmity and hatred among you with intoxicants and gambling, and to hinder you from the remembrance of Allah and from *salat*. Will you not then desist? (5:93-94 (90-91))

In these two verses, Allah strictly prohibited wine and gambling, linking them to idols and seeking omens by means of divining arrows, and declared them to be *rijs* (abominable or filthy), a term which the Qur'an reserves for extremely indecent and evil things. He ascribes them to the work of Satan, which indeed consists only of obscenity and evil, and commands the Believers to abstain from

70

them as the only way to attain success. Allah Ta'ala then mentions the harmful effects of wine and gambling on society, namely, the breaking of relationships and ensuing enmity and hatred, in addition to the harm they do to man's soul by causing him to neglect the religious obligations of remembering Allah and of performing *salat*. The verses end with a very stern admonition to abstain: "Will you not then desist?" And when the Prophet (peace be on him) had finished reciting these verses for the first time, the listeners answered with the fervent cry, "We have desisted, O Lord! We have desisted!"

The response of the Muslims to these verses was remarkable indeed. At the time some people were drinking, with partly-filled cups in their hands. As soon as they heard someone announcing, "Wine has indeed been prohibited," they poured the remaining drinks upon the ground and broke the big clay pots in which other drinks were being fermented.

Many present-day governments throughout the world are convinced of the harmful effects of alcohol on individuals, families, and society. Some governments, such as that of the United States, have even tried to abolish alcohol by passing, and attempting to enforce, laws prohibiting the drinking of alcohol. It is only Islam which has succeeded in combatting and eradicating it.

The churchmen hold differing opinions concerning the position of alcohol in Christianity. Some argue that the Biblical text permits drinking in small quantities, since it is good for the digestion.[1] But if this should be true, even though a little wine may be beneficial to the digestion, this little must be prohibited, as a small amount leads to large amounts and one glass to other glasses, until one becomes' addicted to it. For this reason Islam's stand in prohibiting alcohol and in blocking all avenues which lead to drinking is very clear and unequivocal.

All That Intoxicates Is Haram

The first declaration made by the Prophet (peace be on him) concerning this matter was that not only is wine prohibited but that the definition of *khamr* extends to any substance which intoxicates,

---

[1]See, for example, I Tim. 5:23.

in whatever form or under whatever name it may appear. Thus, for example, beer and similar drinks are *haram.*

The Prophet (peace be on him) was once asked about certain drinks made from honey, corn, or barley by the process of fermenting them until they became alcoholic. The Messenger of Allah (peace be on him), blessed as he was with the best of speech, replied succinctly,

> "Every intoxicant is *khamr,* and every *khamr* is *haram.*"[1]

And 'Umar declared from the pulpit of the Prophet, "*Khamr* is that which befogs the mind."[2]

Whatever Intoxicates in Large Amounts is Haram in Any Amount

Islam takes an uncompromising stand in prohibiting intoxicants, regardless of whether the amount is little or much. If an individual is permitted to take but a single step along this road, other steps follow; he starts walking and then running, and does not stop at any stage. This is why the Prophet (peace be on him) said,

> "Of that which intoxicates in a large amount, a small amount is *haram.*"[3]

And again,

> "If a bucketful intoxicates, a sip of it is *haram.*"[4]

Trading in Alcohol

The Prophet (peace be on him) did not stop at prohibiting the drinking of alcohol, whether much or little, but he also forbade any trading in it, even with non-Muslims. It is not permissible for a Muslim to import or export alcoholic beverages, or to own or work in a place which sells them. In connection with alcohol, the Prophet (peace be on him) cursed ten categories of people saying:

> Truly, Allah has cursed *khamr* and has cursed the one who produces it, the one for whom it is produced, the one who drinks it, the one who serves it, the one who carries

---

[1]Reported by Muslim.
[2]Reported by al-Bukhari and Muslim.
[3]Reported by Ahmad, Abu Daoud, and al-Tirmidhi.
[4]Reported by Ahmad, Abu Daoud, and al-Tirmidhi.

72

it, the one for whom it is carried, the one who sells it, the one who earns from the sale of it, the one who buys it, and the one for whom it is bought.[1]

When the above verse of *Surah al-Maidah* was revealed, the Prophet (peace be on him) announced:

Truly, Allah has prohibited *khamr*. Therefore, whoever hears this verse and possesses some of this substance should neither drink it nor sell it.

The narrator of this *hadith* says, "The people brought forth whatever they possessed of it and poured it out in the streets of Madinah."[2]

Since the Islamic method is to block all avenues which lead to the *haram*, it is also *haram* for a Muslim to sell grapes to a person whom he knows will make *khamr* from them. A *hadith* states:

If someone stockpiles grapes during harvest time and holds them in order to sell them to a Jew or Christian or anyone else (even if he be a Muslim) who produces *khamr*, he will be leaping into the Fire with his eyes open.[3]

Alcohol Cannot Be Given as a Gift

Just as the sale of alcohol or receiving the price of it is *haram* for the Muslim, likewise giving it as a gift to anyone, such as a Christian or Jewish friend, is *haram*. Alcoholic beverages cannot be received or given by a Muslim as gifts because a Muslim is pure and neither gives nor receives anything except what is pure.

It is reported that a man brought a cask of wine to the Prophet (peace be on him) as a gift. The Prophet (peace be on him) informed him that Allah had prohibited it.

'Shall I not sell it?' asked the man. 'The One Who Prohibited drinking it has also prohibited selling it,' replied the Prophet (peace be on him). 'Shall I not give it to a Jew as a gift?' asked the man. 'The One Who has

---

[1] Reported by al-Tirmidhi and Ibn Majah, on reliable authority.
[2] Reported by Muslim.
[3] Reported by al-Tabarani in *Al-Awsat*, and classified as *sahih* by al-Hafiz in *Bulugh al-Maram*.

73

prohibited it has also prohibited that it be given as a gift to the Jew,' said the Prophet. 'Then what shall I do with it?' asked the man. 'Pour it on the ground,' the Prophet replied.[1]

Avoiding Drinking Parties

In the same spirit, the Muslim is ordered to stay away from drinking parties or gatherings at which drinks are served. 'Umar narrated that he heard the Messenger of Allah (peace be on him) saying,

"Whoever believes in Allah and the Last Day must not sit at table at which *khamr* is consumed."[2]

While it is the duty of a Muslim to eradicate the evil he sees, if he is unable to do so, he must stay away from it, leaving the place where people are engaged in such things.

It is reported that the rightly-guided Caliph 'Umar ibn 'Abdul-'Aziz used to flog not only those who drank but those who sat with them as well, even if they were not themselves drinking. When once he was told of a group of people who were at a drinking party, he ordered that all of them be flogged. He was told that a person who was fasting was among them. "Begin with him," he said. "Have you not heard Allah's saying, 'And He has revealed to you in the Book that when you hear the revelation of Allah rejected and mocked, you are not to sit with them until they turn to some other theme; for if you do so, you will be like them....' " (4:140)

Alcohol, Itself a Disease, Cannot Be a Medicine

From all the explicit texts of the Qur'an and *ahadith* quoted above, we see that Islam is very firm in combating alcohol, as well as in keeping the Muslim away from it by erecting barriers between him and it so that no opening, either wide or narrow, is left for him either to consume alcohol or to touch it. The Muslim is not allowed to drink it in large or small amounts; he is not permitted to handle it through selling or buying, manufacturing, or giving it as a gift; he is not allowed to bring it to his home or shop; he is not allowed to serve

---

[1]Reported by al-Hameedi in his *Musnad.*
[2]Reported by Ahmad; al-Tirmidhi also reports something similar to it.

74

it at gatherings, for a joyous occasion or otherwise, or to serve it to a non-Muslim guest; and he is not allowed to mix it with any food or beverage.

A question raised by some people which still remains to be answered concerns the use of alcohol as a medicine. This question was answered by the Prophet (peace be on him) when a man told him that he used wine as a medicine. The Prophet (peace be on him) said,

"It is not a medicine but a disease,"[1]

He also said,

Allah has sent down the disease and the cure, and for every disease there is a cure. So take medicine but do not use anything *haram* as medicine.[2]

With regard to intoxicants Ibn Mas'ud said, "Allah has not made a cure for you in what He has prohibited to you."[3] It is therefore not surprising that Islam forbids the use of alcohol and other prohibited substances as medicines. As explained by Ibn Qayyim, the prohibition of a thing implies avoiding and staying way from it by every means, while taking it as a medicine renders it desirable and reuires keeping it on hand, and this is against the Law-Giver's purpose. Ibn Qayyim, said, "If alcohol were permitted as medicine when people are already inclined toward it, it would provide them with an excuse to drink it for pleasure and enjoyment, especially since people have the impression that it is beneficial for their health, alleviates their complaints, and cures their diseases."[4]

One may also mention that the attitude of the patient toward the medicine he takes has a considerable effect in hastening or delaying the cure. Ibn Qayyim, who had considerable insight into human psychology, elaborates on this point in the following manner:

One condition for the efficacy of the medicine is that the patient believes in its efficacy and that Allah has placed the blessing of cure in it. Now the Muslim patient's belief that a particular substance, such as

---

[1]Reported by Muslim, Ahmad, Abu Daoud, and al-Tirmidhi.
[2]Reported by Abu-Daoud.
[3]Reported by al-Bukhari as a comment on the preceding hadith.
[4]*Zad al-Ma'ad,* vol. 3, pp. 115-116.

alcohol, is *haram* prevents him from believing that it can at the same time be beneficial or blessed. Thus he will not have any trust in it nor will he take it approvingly. On the contrary! The stronger the Muslim's faith, the greater will be his aversion to it and the greater his mistrust of it. If he then grudgingly takes what he hates and loathes, it will not be a cure for him but a disease.[1]

Having said this, we must again mention the exempted case of necessity; the Islamic *Shari'ah* has a different ruling for such a case. Supposing a man's life were in danger and no substitute for a medication containing alcohol were available; a Muslim physician, who was at once an expert in his field and at the same time zealous in safeguarding the commands of religion, would then find no alternative except to prescribe a medication containing alcohol. As its aim is always the welfare of human beings, the *Shari'ah* permits the taking of such a medicine in such a case. However, one must be aware that this concession is strictly limited to that quality which is deemed essential:

> ...But if one is compelled by necessity, neither craving (it) nor transgressing, then, indeed, thy Lord is Forgiving, Merciful. (6:145)

DRUGS

"*Khamr* is what befogs the mind." These are the words spoken by 'Umar ibn al-Khattab from the pulpit of the Prophet (peace be on him), providing us with a decisive criterion for defining what falls under the prohibited category of *khamr*. There remains then no room for doubts and questions: any substance which has the effect of befogging or clouding the mind, impairing its faculties of thought, perception, and discernment is prohibited by Allah and His Messenger (peace be on him) until the Day of Resurrection.

Drugs such as marijuana, cocaine, opium, and the like are

---

[1]Adapted from his discussion in *Zad al-Ma'ad*, vol. 3.

definitely included in the prohibited category of *khamr*. It is well known that the use of such drugs affects the sensory perceptions, making what is near seem distant and what is distant seem near; that their use produces illusions and hallucinations, so that the real seems to disappear and what is imaginary appears to be real; and that drug usage in general impairs the faculty of reasoning and decision-making. Such drugs are taken as a means of escape from the inner reality of one's feelings and the outer realities of life and religion into the realm of fantasy and imagination. Added to this psychological fact are the physical effects: bodily lassitude, dullness of the nerves, and decline in overall health. The moral consequences, moral insensitivity, weakening of the will-power, and neglect of responsibilities are also well known. Eventually, addiction to drugs renders a person a diseased member of society. Furthermore, drug addiction may result in the destruction of the family or even in a life of crime. Since obtaining drugs involves a great outlay of money, a drug addict may well deprive his family of necessities in order to buy drugs and may resort to illegal means to pay for them.

When we recall the principle that impure and harmful things have been made *haram*, there can be no doubt in our minds concerning the prohibition of such detestable substances such as drugs, which cause so much physical, psychological, moral, social and economic harm.

The Muslim jurists were unanimous in prohibiting those drugs which were found during their respective times and places. Foremost among them was Sheikh al-Islam Ibn Taymiyyah, who said,

> This solid grass (hashish) is *haram*, whether or not it produces intoxication. Sinful people smoke it because they find it produces rapture and delight, an effect similar to drunkenness. While wine makes the one who drinks it active and quarrelsome, hashish produces dullness and lethargy; furthermore, smoking it disturbs the mind and temperament, excites sexual desire, and leads to shameless promiscuity, and these are greater evils than those caused by drinking. The use of it has spread among the people after the coming of

77

the Tartars. The *hadd* punishment[1] for smoking hashish, whether a small or large amount of it, is the same as that for drinking wine, that is, eighty or forty lashes.

He explained the imposition of *hadd* for smoking hashish in the following manner:

> It is the rule of the Islamic *Shari'ah* that any prohibited thing which is desired by people, such as wine and illicit sexual relations, is to be punished by imposing *hadd*, while the violation of a prohibited thing which is not desired, such as (eating) the flesh of a dead animal, calls for *ta'zir*.[2] Now hashish is something which is desired, and it is hard for the addict to renounce it. Accordingly, the application of the texts of the Qur'an and *Sunnah* to hashish is similar to that of wine.[3]

The Consumption of Harmful Things is Haram

A general rule of the Islamic *Shari'ah* is that it is *haram* for the Muslim to eat or drink anything which may cause his death, either quickly or gradually, such as poisons, or substances which are injurious to health or harmful to his body. It is also *haram* to eat or drink large quantities of a substance if large quantities of it cause illness. For the Muslim is not entirely his own master; he is also an asset to his religion and his *ummah* (the Muslim nation), and his life, health, wealth, and all that Allah has bestowed upon him are a trust with him which he is not permitted to diminish. Says Allah Subhanahu wa Ta'ala:

> And do not kill yourselves; indeed, Allah is ever Merciful to you. (4:29)

---

[1]The Qur'an specifies the punishments for certain crimes, such as lashing for drinking wine and equal retaliation or compensation in the case of murder or injuries. These punishments are called *hadd* (plural, *hudud*), meaning "the limit set by Allah." (Trans.)

[2]For crimes concerning which no specified punishment is mentioned in the Qur'an or Ahadith, the Muslim government may introduce its own punishments, such as fines or imprisonment. Such a punishment is called *ta'zir*. (Trans.)

[3]*Fatawa Ibn Taymiyyah*, vol. 4, p. 262 f. Also see his book, *Al-Siyasah al-Shar'iyyah*.

He also says:

> And do not be cast into ruin by your own
> hands....(2:195)

And His Messenger (peace be on him) said:

> "Do not harm yourself or others."[1]

As an application of this principle, we may say that if it is proved that the use of tobacco is injurious to health, it is *haram*, especially for a person whose physician has advised him to stop smoking. Even if it is not injurious to health, it is still a waste of money, spent neither for religious nor for secular benefit, and the Prophet (peace be on him) forbade wasting of property.[2] This becomes the more serious when the money is otherwise needed for the sustenance of oneself or one's family.

2. Clothing and Adornment

Islam permits, and in fact requires, that the Muslim be careful about his appearance, dress decently, maintain his dignity, and enjoy what Allah has created for the purpose of clothing and adornment.

From the Islamic point of view, clothing has two purposes: to cover the body and to beautify the appearance. Allah Subhanahu wa Ta'ala counts His bestowal of clothing and adornment upon human beings as one of His favors to mankind:

> O children of Adam! Verily, We have bestowed upon
> you clothing to cover your shame as well as to be an
> adornment to you....(7:26)

Whoever neglects either of these two aspects, covering or adornment, has deviated from the way of Islam toward the path of Satan. Accordingly, Allah warns people concerning both nakedness and neglect of good appearance, as these are snares of Satan, in the following verses:

> O children of Adam! Do not let Satan seduce in the same

---

[1]Reported by Ahmad and Ibn Majah.
[2]Reported by al-Bukhari.

79

manner as he expelled your parents (Adam and Eve) from the Garden, stripping them of their raiment in order to expose their shame....(7:27)

O children of Adam! Wear your beautiful apparel at every place of worship, and eat and drink, but do not be wasteful....(7:31)

Islam has made it obligatory on Muslims to cover their private parts, which everyone naturally feels a sense of shame at exposing, in order that they may be distinguished from the naked animals; in fact, it instructs them to avoid uncovering these parts of their bodies even when they are alone so that they may attain perfection in morals and religion.

Bahaz ibn Hakim, on the authority of his grandfather, reported the latter as saying:

I asked, 'O Messenger of Allah! What should we conceal and what can we show of our private parts?' He replied, 'Let no one see them except your wife or your bondwoman.' I then asked, 'What if some people live together (e.g., during travel, or camping)?' He replied, 'If you can manage it, try not to let anyone see them.' I then said, 'And what if no one is present (meaning if one is alone)?' He said, 'Allah Tabarak wa Ta'ala is most deserving of your modesty.'[1]

Cleanliness and Beautification Are Characteristics of Islam

Before directing its attention to the questions of adornment and good appearance, Islam addressed itself in considerble depth to the question of cleanliness, for cleanliness is the essence of good appearance and the beauty of every adornment.

It is reported that the Prophet (peace be on him) said:

"Cleanse yourself, for Islam is cleanliness."[2]

---

[1]Reported by Ahmad, Abu Daoud, al-Tirmidhi, and Ibn Majah.
[2]Reported by Ibn Hayyan.

"Cleanliness invites toward faith, and faith leads its
possessor to the Garden.[1]"

The Prophet (peace be on him) placed a great emphasis on keeping
the body, clothing, houses, and streets clean, and he laid special
stress on cleaning the teeth, hands, and hair. This emphasis on
cleanliness is not to be wondered at in a religion which makes
cleanliness the key to its principle form of worship, *salat,* for the
Muslim's *salat* is not acceptable unless his body, clothing, and the
place where he performs his *salat* are all clean. In addition to this
requirement, there are the obligatory types of cleansing, either of the
entire body in the form of *ghusl* (total washing), or of those parts of
the body which are exposed to dirt, in the form of *wudu* (ablution for
salat).

The desert environment of Arabia and the nomadic life of its
people were not very conducive to cleanliness and refinement, and
most of them neglected these aspects. The Prophet (peace be on him),
with his lively instruction and to-the-point admonition, gradually
led them out of their uncouth habits and taught them refinement
and civil manners. Once a man approached the Prophet (peace be
on him) with his hair and beard dishevelled. The Prophet (peace be
on him) made some gestures as if asking the man to comb his hair.
He did so, and when he returned the Prophet (peace be on him) said
to him,

"Is not this better than that one should come with
dishevelled hair, looking like a devil?"[2]

On another occasion the Prophet (peace be on him) saw a man with
unkept hair and remarked,

"Does he have nothing with which to comb his hair?"[3]

Upon seeing another man with dirty clothes he remarked,

"Cannot he find anything with which to wash his
clothes?"[4]

A man came to the Prophet (peace be on him) wearing cheap-
looking garments. "Do you have property?" the Prophet (peace be on

---

[1] Reported by al-Tabarani.
[2] Reported by Malik in *Al-Muwatta.*
[3] Reported by Abu Daoud.
[4] Reported by Abu Daoud.

81

him) asked him. "Yes," the man replied. "What kind of property?" asked the Prophet (peace be on him). "Allah has given me all kinds of wealth," he said. The Prophet (peace be on him) then said to him,

> "Since Allah has given you wealth, let Him see the effects of His favor and bounty upon you."[1]

The Prophet insisted that people come to general gatherings, such as the Friday and the 'Eid prayers, nicely dressed and well-groomed. He said,

> If you can afford it, it is befitting that you wear garments other than your working clothes to Friday prayer.[2]

Gold and Pure Silk are Haram for Men

Beautification and elegance are not merely permitted but are required by Islam, and in general it repudiates any attempts to prohibit them.

> Say: Who has forbidden the adornment of Allah which He has brought forth for His servants, and the good things of His providing? (7:32)

Islam has, however, prohibited two kinds of adornment for men, while permitting them to women. These are, first, gold ornaments and, second, clothing made of pure silk. 'Ali reported that the Prophet (peace be on him) took some silk in his right hand and some gold in his left, declaring,

> "These two are *haram* for the males among my followers."[3]

'Umar reported that he heard the Prophet (peace be on him) say,

> "Do not wear silk, for those who wear it in this life shall not wear it in the Hereafter."[4]

On another occasion, referring to a silken garment, he said,

> "This is the dress of a man who has no character."[5]

---

[1]Reported by al-Nisai.
[2]Reported by Abu Daoud.
[3]Reported by Ahmad, Abu Daoud, al-Nisai, Ibn Hayyan, and Ibn Majah, who reports the additional phrase, "but *halal* for the females."
[4]Reported by al-Bukhari and Muslim. A similar *hadith* is reported by them on the authority of Anas.
[5]Reported by al-Bukhari and Muslim.

The Prophet (peace be on him) once saw a gold ring on a man's hand. He immediately took it from him and threw it down saying,

'Does a person pick up a piece of burning coal and hold it in his hand?' After the Prophet (peace be on him) had left the place, someone asked the man, 'Why do you not pick it up and benefit from it?' He replied, 'No, by Allah! I shall not pick it up after the Messenger of Allah (peace be on him) has thrown it away.'[1]

The same prohibition which applies to the gold ring likewise applies to what we observe among conspicuous spenders, i.e., the gold pen, gold watch, gold cigarette case and lighter, gold teeth, etc.

The Prophet (peace be on him), however, permitted men to wear silver rings. On the authority of Ibn 'Umar, al-Bukhari reported the former saying, "The Messenger of Allah (peace be on him) wore a silver ring. After him, Abu Bakr and then 'Umar and 'Uthman wore it, until it fell off his finger into the well of Arees."[2] As for other metals such as iron, there are no sound texts prohibiting them. On the contrary, in the *Sahih* of al-Bukhari we find that the Messenger of Allah (peace be on him) advised a man who wanted to marry a woman to,

"Present her with a gift, even if it be ring made of iron."

On the basis of this *hadith* al-Bukhari inferred the permissibility of iron rings.

The Prophet (peace be on him) made concessions in the wearing of silken garments for medical reasons, as he gave 'Abd al-Rahman bin 'Auf and al-Zubayr bin al-'Awwam, both of whom suffered from scabies, permission to wear silk.[3]

The Wisdom of These Two Prohibitions Concerning Men

By means of these two prohibitions which concern men, Islam's aim is to achieve certain noble educational and moral objectives.

---

[1] Reported by Muslim.
[2] Reported by al-Bukhari in the chapter on "Clothing" (*Al-Libas*).
[3] Reported by al-Bukhari.

Since it is the religion of *jihad* (striving) and strength, Islam must safeguard the manly qualities of men from any show of weakness, passivity, and lethargy. Allah has made the physique of the man different from that of the woman, and it does not befit a man to wear clothes made of fine material or to adorn his body with costly ornaments.

There is, however, a social aim underlying these prohibitions. The prohibition of gold and silk to males is part of a broader Islamic program of combating luxuriousness in living. From the Qur'anic point of view, luxurious living leads to weakness among nations and to their eventual downfall; the existence of luxury is also an expression of social injustice, as only a few can afford luxurious items at the expense of the deprived masses of people.

In addition to this, luxurious living is an enemy of every call towards truth, justice, and social reform. The Qur'an says:

> And when We intend that We should destroy a township, we permit its luxury-loving people to commit wickedness therein.
> Then the word is proved true against it, and We then destroy it utterly.   (17:16)

and again,

> And We did not send a warner to any township without its luxury-loving people saying, 'Assuredly we are disbelievers in that with which you have been sent.' (34:34)

In keeping with the spirit of the Qur'an, the Prophet (peace be on him) forbade Muslims any indulgence in conspicuous consumption. He not only forbade the use of gold and silk to men but also forbade men and women alike the use of gold and silver utensils.

Finally, economic considerations also carry some weight here. Since gold is a universal medium of exchange, using it to make household utensils or ornaments for men does not make sense in economic terms.

Why Gold and Silk are Permitted to Women

Woman has been exempted from this prohibition out of consideration for her feminine nature, as the love of jewelry and ornaments is quite natural and becoming for a woman. However, she is not to use her adornments to attract men and arouse their sexual desires. According to a *hadith*,

> When a woman puts on perfume and goes among people so that its scent reaches them, she is an adulteress, and any eye which is attracted to her is that of an adulterer.[1]

And Allah Ta'ala warns women

> ...that they should not stamp their feet in order to make apparent what is hidden of their adornment....(24:31)

The Dress of the Muslim Woman

Islam makes it *haram* for women to wear clothes which fail to cover the body and which are transparent, revealing what is underneath. It is likewise *haram* to wear tightly fitting clothes which delienate the parts of the body, especially those parts which are sexualy attractive. Abu Hurairah narrated that the Messenger of Allah (peace be on him) said,

> I will not be a witness for two types of people who are destined for the Fire: people with whips, like the tails of cows, who beat the people (i.e., tyrannical rulers who are the enemies of their own people), and women who, although clothed, are yet naked, seducing and being seduced, their hair styled like the tilted humps of camels. These will not enter the Garden nor will its fragrance even reach them, although its fragrance reaches a very great distance.[2]

The Prophet (peace be on him) described such women as being clothed, yet naked, since their clothing, being transparent and fine, does not do the job of conceling the body but is rather intended to reveal it; such is the dress of the women of our time. The Prophet (peace be on him) likened their hair-style to the hump of a special breed of camel (*bakht*) which has very large humps, because they put up their hair in a beehive shape from the middle of their heads. It is as if the Prophet (peace be on him) were looking beyond the centuries to the present age, when dressing the hair of women and

---

[1]Reported by al-Nisai, and also by Ibn Khazimah and Ibn Hayyan in their respective *Sahih's*.
[2]Reported by Muslim.

85

styling it in variety of shapes has become a profession dominated by men who charge top prices for their work. And this is not all. Many women, not satisfied with what Allah gave them in the way of natural hair, buy wigs made of artificial hair to add to their own in order to increase its body, beauty, and luster, imagining that this renders them better looking and more sexually attractive.

The astonishing thing about this *hadith* is the connection of political opression with moral laxity. This connection is borne out by facts, since it is the way of rulers to keep people preoccupied with their personal desires and lusts so that they have no time to think about public affairs.

Concerning Woman's Imitating Man and Vice Versa

The Prophet (peace be on him) declared that a woman should not wear a man's clothing nor a man a woman's. He cursed men who imitate women and women who imitate men.[1] Aspects of such imitation include the manner of speaking, walking, dressing, moving and so on.

The evil of such conduct, which affects both the life of the individual and of society, is that it constitutes a rebellion against the natural ordering of things. According to this natural order, there are men and there are women, and each of the two sexes has its own distinctive charcteristics. However, if men become effeminate and women masculinized, this natural order will be reversed and will disintegrate.

Among those who are cursed by Allah and His angels, both in this world and in the Hereafter, the Prophet (peace be on him) has mentioned the man whom Allah has made a male but who becomes effeminate by imitating women, and a woman whom Allah has made a female but who becomes masculinized by imitating men.[2]

For this reason the Prophet (peace be on him) forbade men to wear fabric decorated with large, loud, or bold designs. In his *Sahih*, Muslim reported 'Ali as saying,

---

[1] Reported by al-Bukhari and others.
[2] Reported by al-Tabarani.

86

The Messenger of Allah (peace be on him) forbade me the wearing of a gold ring, a silken garment, and clothing with bold designs.

Muslim also reports a *hadith* from Ibn 'Umar, who said, "The Messenger of Allah (peace be on him) saw me wearing two garments having bold designs, and he said,

"This is what unbelievers wear. Do not wear such things."

Dressing for the Sake of Ostentation and Pride

The general rule for the enjoyment of the good things of life, such as food, drink, and clothing, is that their use should be without extravagance or pride.

Extravagance consists of exceeding the limits of what is beneficial in the use of the *halal*, while pride is something related to the intention and the heart rather than to what is apparent. Pride is the intention to look superior and above others, and

Allah does not love any proud boaster. (57:23)

The Prophet (peace be on him) said:

"On the Day of Resurrection, Allah will not look at the person who trails his robe behind him out of pride."[1]

In order to avoid even the suspicion of pride, the Prophet (peace be on him) forbade Muslims to wear garments of "fame" that is, clothes which are worn in order to impress others and which generate competition in vain and idle pursuits. According to a *hadith*,

On the Day of Resurrection, Allah will clothe the one who wears garments of fame with the garments of humiliation.[2]

A man asked Ibn 'Umar, "What kind of clothes shall I wear?" Ibn 'Umar replied, "Such as would neither invite the scorn of the weak-minded (because of their being cheap and ugly) nor the blame of the wise (because of their being immoderately expensive)."[3]

---

[1]Agreed upon by Bukhari and Muslim.
[2]Reported by Ahmad, Abu Daoud, al-Nisai, and Ibn Majah.
[3]Reported by al-Tabarani.

Going to Extremes in Beautification by Changing What Allah Created

Islam denounces such excesses in beautifying oneself as require altering one's physical features as Allah created them. The Qur'an considers such alerations as inspired by Satan, who

> ...will command them (his devotees) to change what Allah has created...(4:119)

The Prohibition of Tattooing, Cutting the Teeth, and Undergoing Surgery for Beautification

Among such excesses are tattooing and shortening the teeth.[1]
> The Messenger of Allah (peace be on him) cursed the tattooer and the one who is tattooed, the shortener of teeth and the one whose teeth are shortened.[2]

As far as tattooing is concerned, it permanently disfigures the face and other parts of the body with blue pigment and repulsive designs. Some Arabs, especially women, were in the habit of tattooing large portions of their bodies, while people of certain religious sects tattooed pictures of their deities or religious rituals on their hands and chests. To all these abominations is added the pain and agony which the person being tattooed must undergo from the pricking of the needles. Because all of this, both the tattooer and the one who is tattooed have been cursed.

As for cutting or shortening the teeth, the Prophet (peace be on him) cursed both the men and the women who do it and the women who request it. If a man does it, he merits an even greater curse. Similarly, the Prophet (peace be on him) prohibited widening the spaces between the teeth, and he cursed

> ...Women who widen the gaps between their own or others' teeth for the sake of beauty, changing what Allah has created.

---

[1]A beautification practice of the pre-Islamic Arabs. (Trans.)
[2]Reported by Muslim.

Now, Allah obviously created some women with gaps between their teeth and others without. Some women who have no such gaps desire to create them artifically, either by filing or by cutting away parts of the adjoining teeth. Islam considers this a form of deception and excessive involvement with personal beauty, both of which it discourages.

From these *ahadith* of the Prophet (peace be on him), we also know the ruling of the Islamic *Shari'ah* concerning plastic surgery. Surgeries for beautification are in vogue today as the result of the materialistic outlook of Western civilization, a civilization stressing the body and its desires. Men and women spend hundreds and thousands of dollars to reshape their noses or breasts, or whatever they consider misshapen. This behavior most certainly belongs in the category of excessive beautification, unnecessarily changing what Allah has created, and it merits the curse of Allah and His Prophet (peace be on him). It likewise involves torture, pain, and waste of money merely for the sake of one's appearance; it is, moreover, an expression of an individual's preoccupation with form rather than substance, with body rather than with spirit.

> It may happen that a person has an unusual physical defect which attracts the attention of others to the point of inflicting physical and psychological pain every time he meets people. In this case, he may treat the defect and thus alleviate the embarassment which made his life miserable. Allah the Most Merciful has imposed no hardship on us in religion....[1]

This statement is perhaps supported by the *hadith* concerning widening the gap between the teeth for the sake of beautification, for what is disapproved here is doing this merely for the sake of achieving good looks and artificial beauty. However, if it is needed to eliminte pain or distress, there is nothing wrong with it; but Allah knows best.

---

[1] Al-Bahee al-Khooly, *Al-Mar'ah Bain al-Bait wal-Mujtama'*, 2nd edition, p. 105.

Plucking the Eyebrows

Among the extremes of beautification prohibited by Islam is *al-nams*, which denotes removing the hair of the eyebrows by plucking in order to thin or shape them. The Prophet (peace be on him) cursed both the women who do the plucking and those who seek to have it done.[1] This practice is particularly frowned upon because it is customarily done by prostitutes.

According to some Hanbali scholars, if the husband approves it, the removal of facial hair (other than that of the eyebrows) and the use of powder, creams, and other beauty aids are permitted to women, as this is part of feminine adornment. Al-Nawawi is somewhat more strict, considering the removal of facial hair to be *al-nams* and hence forbidden. In contrast to his opinion, we may, however, mention Abu Daud's statement in his *Sunan* that *"al-nams* is plucking the eyebrows in order to thin them," from which we may conclude that *al-nams* does not include the removal of facial hair.

Al-Tabari reports a narrative concerning the wife of Abu Ishaq, who loved to beautify herself. Once she visited 'Aisha and asked, "What if a woman removes the hair from her forehead to please her husband?" 'Aisha replied, "Remove what is harmful from yourselves whenever possible."[2]

Wigs and Hairpieces

In the category of female adornments, the addition of any other hair, real or artificial, to one's own hair — that is, the wearing of wigs and hairpieces — is also prohibited.

It is reported by al-Bukhari on the authority of 'Aisha, her sister Asma, Ibn Mas'ood, Ibn 'Umar, and Abu Hurairah that

"The Messenger of Allah (peace be on him) cursed *al-wasilah* and *al-mustawsilah*,"

---

[1] Narrated by Abu Daoud on good authority.
[2] *Fath al-Bari*, under the explanation of the *hadith* by Ibn Mas'ood in the chapter entitled "Pluckers of Eyebrows," in the book *Clothing*.

wasilah denoting a woman whose profession is making wigs and hairpieces, and *mustawsilah* a woman who uses them.

Men are prohibited such things to an even greater degree, whether they are a *wasil* (coiffeur or hairdresser) or a *mustawsil*, like today's effeminate, long-haired young men of the "hippie" mould.

The Prophet (peace be on him) was very strict in combating such deceptions, so much so that if a woman lost her hair due to some illness, he did not permit her to add other hair to that on her head, even if she were soon to be married. Al-Bukhari reports 'Aisha's narrative concerning a girl of the Ansar who was married and subsequently fell ill, losing her hair. Some people wanted to add other hair to her own, but when they asked the Prophet (peace be on him) about this he replied,

Allah has cursed the *wasilah* and the *mustawsilah*[1]

Al-Bukhari also reports Asma's narrative concerning a woman who said to the Prophet (peace be on him), "O Messenger of Allah, since my daughter has had measles, her hair has fallen out, and I am about to give her in marriage. Shall I add some strands of hair to her hair?" and the Prophet (peace be on him) replied,

"Allah has cursed the *wasilah* and the *mustawsilah*.[2]"

Sa'id ibn al-Musayab narrated that Mu'awiyah delivered a public address during his last visit to Madinah. In the course of it he took out a strand of hair, saying, "I have not seen anyone using this besides the Jews. Indeed, the Prophet (peace be on him), referring to the adding of hair to one's own hair, called it forgery." According to another report, he said to the people of Madinah, "Where are your scholars? I heard the Prophet (peace be on him) prohibiting the use of this and saying, 'The Children of Israel were destroyed when their women started using this.' "

The Prophet's terming the use of false hair "a forgery" indicates the reason for its prohibition. It is, in fact, fraud, falsification, and deception, and Islam condemns deception and dissociates itself from those who practice it either by material or psychological means, for

---

[1]Reported by al-Bukhari, in his book *Clothing*, in the chapter entitled "Adding to the Hair."
[2]Reported by al-Bukhari.

"The one who decieves us is not of us."[1]

Khattabi said,

> Harsh punishments are promised (in the Hereafter for such practices because they involve deception and fraud. If any of these is allowed, the door will be open for other types of forgeries. Moreover, this involves the alteration of God-given features, as mentioned in the *hadith* of Ibn Mas'ood concerning 'The alterers of Allah's creation.[2]

What is prohibited in these *ahadith* is the addition of other hair, whether natural or artificial, to one's own, as this is a form of deceit and fraud. What is not included in this prohibition is the use of material other than hair, such as thread or cloth, which can be interwover with natural hair. On the authority of Sa'id ibn Jubair, we have the saying of the Prophet (peace be on him):

> There is nothing wrong with *tawamil*,[3]

meaning the use of wool or silk to make braids. Imam Ahmad bin Hanbal has also commented on its permissibility.[4]

Dyeing the Hair

Another aspect of beautification relates to dyeing the gray hair of the head or the beard. It was reported that the Jews and Christians refrained from dyeing the hair, regarding such beautification and adornment as contrary to piety and devotion, and not befitting rabbis, priests, and ascetics. The Prophet (peace be on him) forbade Muslims to imitate these people or follow their ways, in order that Muslims might develop their own distinctive and independent characteristics in appearance and behavior.

Al-Bukhari, on the authority of Abu Hurairah, reported the Messenger of Allah (peace be on him) as saying,

---

[1]Reported by a number of *sahabah* (Companions of the Prophet).
[2]*Fath al-Bari*, in the chapter entitled "Adding to the Hair."
[3]Mentioned in *Fath al-Bari* on the authority of Abu Daoud.
[4]*Fath al-Bari*.

92

"The Jews and Christians do not dye their hair, so be different from them."[1]

This is, however, not a command but only a recommendation, as is evident from the actions of the *sahabah,* such as Abu Bakr and 'Umar, who used to dye their hair, while others, such as 'Ali, Ubay ibn Ka'b, and Anas did not.

The question now remains as to what type of dye is to be used. Should its color be black or can there be other colors? Or should black be avoided? If a man is of a very advanced age, with white hair and beard, it would hardly be appropriate for him to use black dye. On the day of the conquest of Makkah, Abu Bakr brought his aged father, Abu Qahafah, carrying him until he had seated him in front of the Prophet (peace be on him). On seeing Abu Qahafah's snow-white hair, the Prophet (peace be on him) said,

"Change this, but avoid black."[2]

However, if a man is not of such advanced age or feebleness as Abu Qahafah then was, there is no harm in his using black dye. In this regard al-Zuhri said, "We dyed our hair black when the face looked young, but discarded it when the face became wrinkled and the teeth decayed."[3]

Some of the early Muslims, including some *sahabah* such as Sa'd ibn Abi Waqqas, 'Uqbah ibn 'Amr, al-Hassan, al-Hussain, Jarir, and others permitted the use of black dye. Some scholars, on the other hand, do not consider the use of black hair dye as permissible except during time of war, when the enemy might be impressed by the fact that all the soldiers of the Muslim army look young.

Abu Dharr narrated the *hadith,*

The best thing with which to dye gray hair is henna and *katm.*[4]

Henna makes the hair red, while *katm,* a plant from Yemen, colors it black tinged with red. Said Anas, "Abu Bakr dyed his hair with henna and *katm,* and 'Umar dyed it with henna only."

---

[1]Reported in al-Bukhari's chapter on "Dyeing the Hair" in his book *Clothing.*
[2]*Fath al-Bari,* in explaining the above mentioned *hadith* (in the chapter on "Dyeing the Hair").
[3]Reported by Ibn Abu 'Asim in the book on "Dyeing the Hair."
[4]Mentioned in *Fath al-Bari.*

Letting the Beard Grow

The growing of beards is also related to our topic. Al-Bukhari, on the authority of Ibn 'Umar, reported the Prophet (peace be on him) as saying,

> "Be different from the polytheists (*mushrikeen*): let the beard grow and trim the moustache."

The purpose here, as the hadith states, is to be different from the polytheists, who, in the particular instance cited, were Zoroastrians, the worshippers of fire, whose practice was either to clip or shave their beards. The Prophet's command to be different from them was intended to train the Muslims in developing an independent personality, distinct in its inner reality as well as in outward appearance, in substance as well as in form. At the same time, shaving the beard is an affront to the masculine nature, as it is an attempt to resemble women, while the beard is an integral part of masculinity and a distinctive feature of the male sex.

However, letting the beard grow does not mean letting it grow wild or so long that it becomes a nuisance. One should certainly trim it in both length and breadth. This has been recommended in a *hadith* reported by al-Tirmidhi; moreover, the Muslims of the first generations did so. Said 'Ayyad,[1] "It is *makruh* to shave the beard or to drastically cut or shorten it, but it is *mustahab* (commendable) to remove something from its length and breadth if it grows big."

Abu Shamah voiced the complaint that "Some people have started shaving their beards, and that is a step further than the Zoroastrians, who used only to trim them."[2] In my view it is regrettable that at the present time the majority of Muslims shave their beards in imitation of the foreign elements who have occupied their lands. It is an unfortunate fact that the conquered always imitate their conquerors. Today's Muslims have ignored the Prophet's command that they be different from non-believers and avoid imitating them. Indeed, anyone who "imitates a people is one of them."[3]

---

[1]The twelfth century author of a well known book about the characteristics of the Prophet. (Trans.)
[2]*Fath al-Bari*, in the chapter entitled "Growing Beards."
[3]A *hadith* reported by Abu Daoud on the authority of Ibn 'Umar.

A large number of jurists consider shaving the beard to be *haram* on the basis of the Prophet's command. This command to let the beard grow renders it an obligation, especially because it is for the purpose of being different from non-Muslims, since maintenance of this distinction from those who do not believe is obligatory for Muslims.

It has never been reported that any of the Muslims of the earliest generations neglected this obligation. However, some modern scholars permit the shaving of the beard under the impact of events in response to public opinion, arguing that the growing of the beard was a personal preference of the Prophet (peace be on him) which was not related to religious practice, and hence it need not be followed. But the truth of this matter is that growing the beard is required not merely because the Prophet (peace be on him) had one but because he explicitly commanded it in order to maintain the distinction from non-believers. Ibn Taymiyyah has convincingly argued that to make the Muslims different from non-believers was the aim of the Law-Giver, for resemblance in appearance produces love, friendship, and affinity in feeling, just as love in the heart produces resemblance in outward appearance. This psychological fact is borne out by experience and observation. Says Ibn Taymiyyah:

> The Qur'an, the *Sunnah*, and the consensus of Muslim scholars all teach Muslims to be distinct from non-believers and in general to avoid resembling them. Anything which is likely to cause corruption in a hidden and diffuse manner is related to this matter and is likewise prohibited. The imitation of the appearance of the non-believers will lead to imitation of their immoral behavior and evil qualities — indeed, even of their beliefs. Such influences can neither be brought under control nor easily detected, and consequently it becomes difficult or even impossible to eradicate them. Accordingly, whatever is a cause of corruption has been prohibited by the Law-Giver.[1]

Thus, we note that there are three opinions with regard to the shaving of the beard: one, that it is *haram*, which is the opinion of

---

[1]Refer to *Kitab Iqtida al-Sirat al-Mustaqeem.*

Ibn Taymiyyah and others; two, that it is *makruh*, the opinion of 'Ayyad as mentioned in *Al-Fatah al-Bari* but of no one else; and three, that it is permitted, which is the opinion of some modern scholars. Perhaps the second opinion, that it is *makruh*, is nearer to the truth and more moderate. As the stated reason for growing the beard is to be different from the non-believers, it is similar to the matter of dyeing gray hair in order to be distinct from the Jews and Christians; it is known that some of the *sahabah* did not dye their gray hair, signifying that it was commendable rather than obligatory. Similarly, growing the beard may be regarded as commendable but not obligatory, and, accordingly, shaving it would be classified as *makruh* rather than *haram*. It is true that none of the *sahabah* was known to have shaved his beard. Perhaps there was no need to shave, and perhaps growing the beard was a custom among them.

3. In the Home

The home is the place in which an individual protects himself from the elements and in which he finds freedom from the restrictions and pressures of society. It is a place of rest for the body and relaxation for the mind. That is why Allah Ta'ala, in mentioning His favors to His servants, says:

And Allah has made for you in your houses, places of rest.... (16:80)

The Prophet (peace be on him) loved spaciousness in the home and considered it as an element conducive to happiness in this life, saying,

Happiness has four elements: a good wife, a spacious house, a good neighbor, and a comfortable riding beast.[1]

He often used to pray fervently, "Our Lord, forgive me my sin, make my house spacious, and bless me in my sustenance." He was asked, "O Messenger of Allah, why do you supplicate so often in these words?" He replied, "Is anything left out?"[2]

---

[1] Reported by Ibn Habban in his *Sahih*.
[2] Reported by al-Nisai and Ibn al-Sunni with a sound chain of transmitters.

The Prophet (peace be on him) urged people to keep their houses clean as a vital expression of Islam, which is a religion of cleanliness. Cleanliness is a distinctive characteristic of a Muslim. The Messenger of Allah (peace be on him) said,

> Assuredly, Allah Ta'ala is good and loves goodness, is clean and loves cleanliness, is generous and loves generosity, is hospitable and loves hospitality. So keep your rooms and courtyards clean, and do not be like the Jews.[1]

Items Related to Luxurious Living and Paganism

The Muslim may adorn his house with various kinds of flowers, decorated fabrics, and other permitted ornamental objects:

> Say: Who has forbidden the adornment of Allah which He has brought forth for His servants? (7:32)

The Muslim is certainly free to desire beauty in his home and elegance in his clothing, shoes, and other items related to personal appearance. Once the Prophet (peace be on him) said,

> 'Anyone who has an atom of pride in his heart will not enter the Garden'. A man then asked, 'What about the one who likes to wear a handsome robe and good shoes?' The Prophet (peace be on him) replied, 'Surely Allah is beautiful and loves beauty.'[2]

In another version of this *hadith*, a handsome man came to the Prophet (peace be on him), saying, "I love beauty and have been given some of it, as you can see, to the extent that I dislike anyone's having a better pair of sandals than I. Is this pride, O Messenger of Allah?" The Prophet (peace be on him) replied,

> "No. Pride is to reject the truth and to view other people with contempt."[3]

---

[1] Reported by al-Tirmidhi.
[2] Reported by Muslim.
[3] Reported by Abu Daoud.

However, Islam disapproves of excess, and the Prophet (peace be on him) disliked the Muslim's filling his house with items of luxury and extravagance, traits condemned by the Qur'an, or with items related to paganism, the very thing against which the religion of the Oneness of God has fought with every weapon.

Gold and Silver Utensils

In accordance with what has been stated above, Islam has prohibited the use of gold and silver utensils, and of pure silk spreads in the Muslim house. The Prophet (peace be on him) warned that anyone who deviates from this path may incur severe punishment in the Hereafter. On the authority of Umm Salmah, Muslim reported in his *Sahih* the Prophet's saying,

> "Whoever eats or drinks from gold or silver untensils is indeed filing his stomach with the fire of hell."[1]

Al-Bukhari reported on the authority of al-Hudhaifah that "The Mesesenger of Allah (peace be on him) forbade us to drink or eat from gold or silver dishes or to wear silken garments or to sit on silken cloth. He said,

> 'They are for them (the unbelievers) in this world and for us in the Hereafter.'[2]

Moreover, what is prohibited for practical use is also forbidden to be given as a gift or used as an ornament.

These prohibitions concerning utensils, spreads, and similar articles apply to men and women alike, for the purpose of this legislation is to rid the house of excessively luxurious items. Ibn Qudamah expresses this idea in clear terms as follows:

> Men and women are equal in this regard because of the generality of the *hadith*, and because the reason for this prohibition is the show of extravagance and pride on the one hand and the injury to the feelings of the poor on the other. The wearing of gold and silk has been

---

[1]Reported by Muslim.
[2]Reported by al-Bukhari.

permitted to women so that they may beautify themselves for their husbands; this is an exemption which does not extend to other uses. If it is said, 'If the reason you have stated is correct, then utensils made of rubies and other precious materials would also have been prohibited because they are more expensive (than gold and silver)' to this we reply, 'The poor are not familiar with such things, and their feelings will not be injured even if they see the rich using them.' Moreover, the rarity of such things in itself makes their use prohibitive, and hence the need for prohibiting them on the basis of extravagance becomes superfluous.[1]

Earlier we mentioned the economic reasons for prohibiting the use of gold ornaments for men. In the present case this reason is even weightier and more obvious. Gold and silver are universal monetary standards which facilitate the establishing of prices and the carrying out of transactions between nations, thus promoting trade and commerce. It is Allah's favor that He guided people to use them as a means of exchange. The proper economic usage of gold and silver, then, is their free circulation; they are not to be hoarded in houses as coins or, worse yet, to be tied up in household articles and ornamental objects.

Imam al-Ghazzali has beautifully enunciated this point in the chapter entitled *"Al-Shukr"* (Thankfulness) in his book, *Ihya al-'Ulum al-Din*, in the following manner:

Anyone who melts down gold and silver coins to make vases and containers is ungrateful for Allah's bounty and is worse than the one who hoards them. It is like using the mayor of a city for sweeping its streets or for sewing garments, or to do jobs which are normally carried out by the lowliest of people. To imprison him would be less insulting. Now, materials such as porcelain, iron, lead, and copper can replace gold and silver for making vases and containers, but they cannot replace them as money or as standards of exchange. If a person cannot grasp this point (through his own

---

[1] *Al-Mughni*, vol. 8, p. 323.

reasoning and knowledge), we would tell him that the spokesman of Allah has explained it: 'Whoever eats or drinks from gold or silver utensils is indeed filling his stomach with the fire of hell.'[1]

Let no one suppose that this prohibition constitutes a severe restriction on the Muslim in his own home, for among wholesome and permissible things there is a great variety from which to choose. What beautiful vases, containers, and pots have been made of glass, porcelain, copper, and many other materials! Likewise, bedspreads, cushions, and tablecloths of great beauty are fabricated from cotton, linen, and various other materials.

Islam Prohibits Statues

Islam has prohibited the keeping of statues in the Muslim home. By statues is meant complete, solid figures which have not been disfigured or otherwise defaced. Their presence in a house is considered sufficient to drive away the angels, who represent Allah's mercy and His pleasure. As the Messenger of Allah (peace be on him) said,

> "Assuredly the angels do not enter a house in which there are statues (or figures)."[2]

According to the commentary of scholars, a person who keeps statues in his house is similar to unbelievers, whose practice it is to keep and venerate idols in their homes. The angels are repelled by this; they do not enter such a house and abandon it.

It is also forbidden to the Muslim to engage in manufacturing statues, even if he makes them for non-Muslims. The Prophet (peace be on him) said:

> "Among the people receiving the harshest punishment on the Day of Resurrection will be the makers of figures,"

---

[1]*Ihya al-'Ulum al-Din.* See vol. 4, *Thanksgiving and Praise.*
[2]Reported by al-Bukhari and Muslim; the wording is from Muslim.

or, in another version,

"the imitators of Allah's creation."[1]

He also said,

On the Day of Resurrection, the maker of a figure will be asked to breathe a spirit into it, and he will never be able to do so,[2]

meaning that he will be asked to bring it to life in order to reproach and humiliate him.

The Wisdom of Prohibiting Statues

(a) One of the reasons for this prohibition, although not the only one, as some people may suppose, is to safeguard the belief in the Oneness of God and to be far-removed from the practices of idolaters, who fashion statues and idols with their own hands and then sanctify them, standing before them in adoration.

Islam's sensitivity in safeguarding the belief in the Unity of God is very acute, and assuredly this caution and concern is quite justified. In the final analysis, the worship of idols originated when people began making statues of their dead or pious ancestors in order to remember them. Gradually they began to venerate them, adding to this veneration little by little until they had made the statues into gods, worshipping them besides God, asking them for help, fearing their anger, and imploring them for blessings. This is what happened, among earlier communities such as the people of Wadd, Suwwa' Yaghuth, Ya'uq, and Nasra.[3]

It is not surprising that a religion which seeks to halt all corruption should block every passage through which *shirk* (polytheism), either open or hidden, may slip into the minds and hearts of the people. Among such passageways is the imitation of idolaters or of the followers of other religions who have exaggerated

---

[1]Reported by al-Bukhari and Muslim.
[2]Reported by al-Bukhari and others.
[3]Names of pagan deities of antiquity who are mentioned in the Qur'an (71:23). For an explanation, see for example, the commentary in Yusuf 'Ali's translation of the Holy Qur'an, Appendix XIII, following *Surah Nuh* (71). (Trans.)

respect for their saints. Moreover, Islam's legislation is not merely intended for one or two generations but is for all mankind for as long as it shall exist on this planet. What may seem unlikely in one environment may become acceptable in another, and what appears impossible at one time may materialize into reality at another.

(b) Another reason for this prohibition concerns the maker of statues, the sculptor, himself. Sculptors tend to feel pride in their work, as if they had created something out of nothing or had given life to clay or stone. A sculptor once completed a figure after a great deal of labor; it was so perfect and so beautiful that he stood before it, lost in admiration of its fine lines and features until, overwhelmed with pride and exhilaration, he said to it, "Speak! Speak!" This is why the Noble Messenger (peace be on him) said,

> Those who make figures will be chastised on the Day of Ressurection. They will be told, 'Put life into what you have created.'[1]

And in a *hadith qudsi*, Allah Ta'ala says:

> Who does greater wrong than he who desires to create the like of what I create? Let them create an atom! Let them create a grain of barley![2]

(c) Those who engage in this art stop at nothing, producing statues of nude or erotic figures and the deities and saints of other religions. A Muslim is not permitted to acquiese in regards to such practices.

(d) Finally, statues have been, and still are, symbols of aristocratic and luxurious living. People in high places fill their palaces, halls, and chambers with statues fabricated of many materials. It is not surprising that a religion which declares war on luxury in all its manifestations, should prohibit the Muslim from having statues in his home.

The Islamic Manner of Commemorating the Great

Now someone may ask, "Is it not an expression of a people's loyalty to the memory of its heroes, whose great deeds are recorded

---

[1] Reported by al-Bukhari and Muslim.
[2] Reported by al-Bukhari and Muslim.

102

in the annals of history, to erect statues in their honor as a reminder to future generations of their achievements and greatness? Peoples' memories are short, and the passage of time will make them forget the past."

The answer is that Islam abhors excessive glorification of people, no matter how "great" they may be, whether they are living or dead. The Prophet (peace be on him) said,

> Do not glorify me in the same manner as the Christians glorify Jesus, son of Mary, but say, 'He is a slave of Allah and His Messenger.'[1]

When his Companions wanted to stand up to greet him out of respect, he forbade them, saying,

> "Do not stand up as the Persians do, some people honoring the others."[2]

And he warned his followers against praising him excessively after his death, saying,

> "Do not make of my grave a site for festivals,"[3]

and he prayed to his Lord,

> "O my Lord, do not let my grave be made into an idol to be worshipped."[4]

Once some people came to the Prophet (peace be on him) and addressed him in the following words: "O Messenger of Allah, the best of us and the son of the best of us, our leader and the son of our leader." He said,

> O people, say what you said previously or a part of it, and do not let Satan mislead you. I am Muhammad, a slave of Allah and His Messenger. I do not like your raising my status above the status which Allah, the Mighty and Glorious, has given me.[5]

A religion whose teachings concerning even the Messenger of Allah (peace be on him) is one of such moderation can never tolerate

---

[1]Reported by al-Bukhari and others.
[2]Reported by Abu Daoud and Ibn Majah.
[3]Reported by Abu Daoud.
[4]Reported by Malik in *Al-Muwatta*.
[5]Reported by al-Nisai on good authority.

the erecting of idol-like statues for some individuals, involving expenditures running into thousands of dollars so that people may point to them with admiration and esteem. Many pretenders to greatness and self-proclaimed makers of history have slipped into the hall of fame through this open door, since anyone who is able to do so erects statues or monuments to himself, or lets his admirers do it for him, so that people are misled from appreciating those who are truly great.

The Believers aspire only to that true immortality which can be bestowed by Allah alone, Who knows the secret and the hidden, Who neither misleads nor forgets. In His register of immortality there is the name of many a person whose greatness has remained unrecognized by the people. Indeed, the Most High loves those God-fearing and religious souls who remember Him in the secrecy of their hearts, who do great service without fanfare, whose presence is not felt in a gathering of people and whose absence is not missed.

When the greatness of some of these noble souls is recognized by the people, its perpetuation for coming generations is not to be achieved by erecting statues of them. The correct Islamic method of commemoration is to keep their memory alive in the hearts and minds by speaking about their good deeds, ideas, and achievements.

The Messenger of Allah (peace be on him), the caliphs, the leaders, and the *imams* of Islam were never immortalized in figures or statues. In this faith the fathers tell their children, and they in turn pass on to their own children, the stories of such peoples' achivments and ideas. At meetings and gatherings these stories are like breaths of fresh air, filling the hearts and minds of Muslims without any need for pictures or statues.

I quote here part of a lecture entitled "Toward a New Understanding of Islam," by Professor Muhammad al-Mubarak, Dean of the College of the Shari‘ah, University of Damascus, delivered at al-Azhar University. The section quoted here contains an incisive analysis of the whole question of how to perpetuate the memory of the great.

> We are faced with the situation that many new modes, systems, and habits which are inconsistent with our correct beliefs and established moral principles have found their way into our social life. Among these is the

104

manner in which Europeans and Americans commemorate their heroes by erecting statues of them. If we examine this matter with an open mind, free of subservience to whatever comes from the West, and reflect on ways of commemorating the lofty achievements of the great, we find the Arabs, in particular, memorialized nothing of their great personages except their noble deeds and good qualities such as fidelity, generosity, and courage. Their manner of perpetuating their memories was to recount tales of their heroes, passing them down form one generation to another, and to compose and recite eulogies in the form of poetry. In this manner the generosity of Hatim and the bravery of 'Antarah became proverbial in the days before Islam.

When Islam came, it emphasized the meaning underlying this method. It declared that the best of Allah's creation and the last of His Messengers (peace be on him) was but a mortal man: 'Say: Indeed, I am a mortal like you; my Lord inspires me.' (18:111) It emphasized that the worth of human beings lies in their deeds and not in their physical form; it made the Messenger (peace be on him) an example for all mankind to follow; and it forbade such sanctification and exaggerated respect for men which resembles adoration and which, by implication, signifies the denigration of the rest of mankind.

When the Messenger of Allah (peace be on him) passed away to meet his Lord, the first caliph drew peoples' attention to this fact, saying, 'If anyone worshipped Muhammad, then (know that) Muhammad is dead, but if anyone worshipped Allah, then Allah is living and does not die.' He then recited the words of Allah Ta'ala: 'Muhammad is but a messenger, messengers (the like of whom) have passed away before him. If, then, he dies or is killed, will you turn back on your heels?' (3:144)

Islam immortalizes the memories of people because of their good and beneficent deeds; the remembrance of

105

them remains in the hearts of Muslims. Thus, the literate and illiterate, the young and the old, know about the justice of 'Umar, the firmness and wisdom of Abu Bakr, and the piety and courage of 'Ali. No statue made of stone was needed to commemorate any of them because their deeds and qualities are inscribed in peoples' hearts.

Commeration by means of erecting statues is in reality a regression to the remote past, a descent from a higher plane; it was the method of the Greeks and Romans which was adopted by Europeans....

In respect to the concept of the nature of man and his true worth, they are far inferior to the Muslims, even to the pre-Islamic Arabs, since because of their inability to grasp the true stature of man and his potentialities, they are able only to conceive of great men as gods, and of their gods as men incarnate.

What we are pointing out is that it does not befit us to imitate this alien practice which is inferior to our own, and we must not deviate from the ruling of the *Shari'ah* that making statues is *haram* and is harmful to human psychology and morals.

The Exemption of Children's Toys

If there are some kinds of three-dimensional figures which are not intended to be accorded respect or to be displayed as an expression of high living, then the above cautionary statements do not apply. Islam does not close its mind to them, nor does it see any harm in their use.

Children's playthings such as dolls, in the form of humans, animals, and the like fall into this category. Said the Prophet's wife 'Aisha (may Allah be pleased with her):

I used to play with dolls in the house of the Messenger of Allah (peace be on him) and my friends would come over to play with me. They would hide when they saw the Messenger of Allah (peace be on him) approaching,

106

but he was in fact very happy to see them with me, and so we played together.[1]

'Aisha also reported,

> One day the Messenger of Allah (peace be on him) asked me, 'What are these?' 'My dolls,' I replied. 'What is this in the middle?' he asked. 'A horse,' I replied. 'And what are these things on it?' he asked. 'Wings,' I said. 'A horse with wings?' he asked. 'Have not you heard that Solomon, the son of David, had horses with wings?' I said. Thereupon the Messenger of Allah (peace be on him) laughed so heartily that I could see his molars.[2]

The dolls mentioned in the above *hadith* are the dolls with which children play, as 'Aisha was quite young when she married the Prophet (peace be on him). Al-Shawkani says that these *ahadith* are sufficient proof of the permissibility of children's playing with statue-like three dimensional figures (i.e., dolls of human or animal shape). It is reported that once Imam Malik saw a man buying dolls for his daughter and he disliked it, but Qadi 'Ayyad says that it is permissible for girls to play with dolls.[3]

This permission also applies to figures made of sweets for festive occasions since they are used only as food.

Incomplete or Defaced Statues

It is reported in the books of *Hadith* that the angel Gabriel (Jibril) once refused to enter the house of Allah's Messenger (peace be on him) because there was a statue by its door. He did not enter it again the following day but said to the Prophet (peace be on him), "Order that the head of the statue be broken off so that it resembles the trunk of a tree."[4]

---

[1]Reported by al-Bukhari and Muslim.
[2]Reported by Abu Daoud.
[3]Because girls are more likely to play with dolls than boys, only girls have been mentioned here. However, this does not imply any prohibition for boys to do so. (trans.)
[4]Reported by Abu Daoud, al-Nisai, al-Tirmidhi, and Ibn Hibban.

On the basis of this *hadith* some scholars have argued that what is *haram* are complete figures, but if some part of them is missing without which a human being cannot survive, they are allowed. However, the true and correct interpretation of Jibril's asking that the head be broken off in order to make it look like a tree trunk is not that without the head life is impossible, but that the statue was then defaced and consequently viewing it would not generate feelings of respect toward it.

If we ponder over the matter objectively, we will undoubtedly conclude that it is more *haram* to set up busts in public places in order to perpetuate the memory of kings and great men than to have full figured statues in the home for the purpose of decoration.

Paintings and One-Dimensional Ornaments

We have explained the Islamic position concerning the solid figures we term "statues," but what about figures and art work executed on plane surfaces such as paper, cloth, curtains, walls, coins, paper currency, and the like?

Concerning this issue, we say that no general ruling is possible here and that each case is to be judged individually. What does the picture depict? Where is it placed? What is its use? What was the artist's purpose in making the picture? It is these questions which must be looked into.

If the pictures become objects of worship, as for example the cow does for Hindus, whoever makes them with this purpose is in reality nothing but an unbeliever propagating *shirk* and error. Again, the Prophet (peace be on him) threatened such people with dire punishment in the Hereafter saying,

> "On the Day of Resurrection the most severe chastisement will be for the makers of figures."[1]

Al-Tabari, explaining the meaning of this *hadith*, says, "What is meant here by makers of figures are those who make figures in order that they may be worshipped besides Allah, and this is unbelief (*kufr*). As for those who do not make them for this purpose, they will

---

[1] Reported by Muslim.

be guilty only of making a representation (*suar*)." Similarly, if someone hangs such pictures on the wall in order to venerate them, his act is not that of a Muslim, for Islam has departed from his heart.

We next examine the case of the person who makes pictures not so that they should be worshiped but so that they may be likened to Allah's creation; he feels a sense of pride that he has created as Allah, the Exalted and Mighty, has created. Such an individual has rebelled against belief in *tawheed*, and concerning him the Prophet (peace be on him) said,

> The most severly punished among people (on the Day of Resurrection) will be those who try to create something similar to what Allah has created.

This pertains directly to the intention of the artist. Perhaps the *hadith qudsi* cited earlier,

> Who does greater wrong than he who desires to create the like of what I create? Let them create an atom! Let them create a grain of barley!

bears this out as well. Again, what is referred to here is the intention of those artists who want to imitate Allah's attributes of Creator and Originator. Allah's challenge to them to create an atom or a grain of barley points to the fact that their artistic work implies an intention to create something similar to what He has created. To shame them for this on the Day of Resurrection, they will be told publicly, "Bring to life what you created," which of course they can never do. It is prohibited to make or to acquire portraits of individuals who are either revered in a religion or respected for their wordly status. Examples of the first category are representations of prophets such as Abraham, Isaac, David, and Jesus; of angels such as Jibril and Mika'eel (Michael); and of saints and righteous individuals such as Maryam (Mary) and the like. This is a Jewish or Christian custom. Unfortunately, some Muslims, making innovations in religion and imitating the People of the Book, have begun to make and to acquire portraits of 'Ali, Fatimah, and others.

The second category includes portraits of kings, leaders, and artists in our time. Although there is less evil in this case, nevertheless we must emphasize its evil, especially if those portrayed are non-believers, tyrants, or wrong-doers, such as rulers who do not judge according to what Allah has revealed, leaders who call people to a message other than the message of Allah Subhanahu wa Ta'ala, and artists who glorify falsehood and propagate lewdness and immorality among people.

It appears that many of the portraits made during the time of the Prophet (peace be on him) and thereafter were of the kind which glorify personages; most probably they were painted by Greeks or Persians, and consequently were never free of the imprint of their beliefs and the sanctification of their saints and rulers. Muslim reported that AbuDuha said,

> I was with Masrooq in a house which had statues. Masrooq asked me, 'Are these statues of Khosrau?'[1] I said, 'No these are statues of Mary.' Masrooq assumed them to be the handiwork of a Magian, because the Magians used to portray the figures of their kings even on jars, but when it became clear that they were the work of a Christian, he said, 'Abdullah ibn Mas'ud said that he heard the Messenger of Allah (peace be on him) say, "Among the people receiving the harshest punishment on the Day of Resurrection will be the makers of figures." '

Drawing, painting, and acquiring pictures of plants, trees, and inanimate objects such as lakes, oceans, ships, mountains, the sun, moon, stars, and the like from scenes of nature is permitted. There is no difference of opinion in this regard. Moreover, if someone wants to make a picture of an animate being with no intention of competing with Allah as creator or for its glorification or respect, there is no prohibition of doing so; there are numerous sound *ahadith* in this regard.

Muslim reported in his *Sahih*, on the authority of Basr ibn Sa'id, who heard it from Zayd ibn Khalid, who heard it from Ibn Talha, a Companion of the Prophet (peace be on him), that the Messenger of Allah (peace be on him) said,

> "The angels do not enter a house in which there are figures."[2]

Basr said, "Thereafter Zayd became ill and we went to visit him.

---

[1]The ruler of Persia. (Trans.)
[2]Reported by Muslim.

There was a picture on the curtain of his door. I said to my companion, 'Ubayd Allah al-Khulani, who was the servant of the Prophet's wife Maymunah, 'Was it not Zayd who told us about pictures the other day?' 'Ubayd Allah replied, 'Did you not hear him when he said, "Except if it is made of cloth?" ' "

Al-Tirmidhi reported on the authority of 'Utbah that once the latter went to visit Abu Talhah al-Ansari, who was ill, and he found Sahl ibn Hanif (another Companion) there. Abu Talhah called someone to come and tear up the sheet which was under him. "Why tear it up?" Sahl asked. "There are pictures on it, and you know what the Prophet (peace be on him) said concerning that," Abu Talhah replied. "Did he not also say, 'Except if it is made on cloth?' " Sahl asked. "Yes, but it makes me feel better," Abu Talhah replied. al-Tirmidhi classifies this *hadith* as good and sound (*hasan wa sahih*).

Do not these two *ahadith* prove that the figures which are prohibited are those which are solid, that is to say "statues?" As for figures drawn or printed on wood, paper, cloth, rugs and carpets, walls, and the like, there is no sound, explicit, and straightforward text to prove that they are forbidden. True, there are sound *ahadith* which merely indicate the Prophet's dislike for such types of pictures because they are reminiscent of those who live in luxury and love things of inferior value.

Muslim reported from Zayd ibn Khalid al-Juhani, who quoted Abu Talhah al-Ansari as saying,

> I heard the Messenger of Allah's statement, 'The angels do not enter a house in which there is a dog or statues.' I then went to see 'Aisha and asked her, 'Are you aware that the Messenger of Allah (peace be on him) said, "The angels do not enter a house in which there is a dog or statues?" Did you hear the Messenger of Allah (peace be on him) mention this?' She replied, 'No, but I will tell you what he did. Once when he had gone on an expedition I draped the door with a curtain having pictures on it. When he returned and saw it, I could discern from his face that he disliked it. He pulled it down and tore it apart, saying, "Allah has not commanded us to clothe stone and clay." ' She said, 'We

111

cut it and made two pillows out of the cloth, stuffing them with palm fibres. He did not criticize me for that.'

Nothing can be inferred from this *hadith* except that to decorate walls and such things with curtains on which there are pictures is mildly disapproved. Al-Nawawi said, "There is nothing in the *hadith* implying prohibition. In fact, the crucial words are, 'Allah has not commanded us to do that.' This implies that such a thing is not obligatory or meritorious; in no way does it imply prohibition."

Muslim has also reported from 'Aisha that she said, "We had a curtain with the figure of a bird on it. When the Messenger of Allah (peace be on him) entered the house, he saw it right in front of him and he said, 'Remove it from here. When I enter and see it, I am reminded of this world.' "

The Prophet (peace be on him) did not tell 'Aisha to tear up the curtain but only to remove it from the place where it hung facing the entrance; he disliked seeing it there because it brought to his mind the world and its attractions. This is not strange, since the Prophet (peace be on him) used to perform the *sunnah* and *nafil* (voluntary) *salat* at home. Curtains and bedspreads or statues perhaps would have distracted him from concentration in his *salat* and complete attention in his supplications. Al-Bukhari also reported Anas as saying, "Aisha had covered a part of her apartment with a drape. The Messenger of Allah (peace be on him) told her, 'Take it away from my sight because its figures keep distracting me from my *salat*.' "

It is quite clear from the preceding *ahadith* that the Prophet (peace be on him) did not disapprove of having a curtain with a picture of a bird and a drape with figures in his house. On the basis of this and other similar *ahadith* scholars of earlier times have commented, "What is prohibited are figures which cast shadows (meaning those which are solid) and not those which do not cast shadows (meaning on plane surfaces)."[1]

In further support of this position we again quote the *hadith qudsi* in which Allah Ta'ala says,

---

[1] Al-Nawawi mentions this opinion in his *Sharh Muslim* but rejects it, saying that it represents a wrong position. In *Fath al-Bari*, al-Hafiz has traced this opinion on sound authority back to al-Qasim ibn Muhammd ibn Abu Bakr, who was a jurist of Madinah and the best of his time.

> Who does greater wrong than he who desires to create
> the like of what I create? Let them create an atom! Let
> them create a grain of barley!

As is evident, Allah's creation does not consist of two-dimensional drawings on a plane surface, for He fashions three-dimensional corporeal beings. As he says,

> It is He Who fashions you in the wombs as He
> pleases....(3:6)

There is only one *hadith*, narrated by both al-Bukhari and Muslim on the authority of 'Aisha, which poses some difficulty. 'Aisha said that she bought a cushion with pictures on it. When the Messenger of Allah (peace be on him) saw it, he stopped at the door and did not enter her apartment. She saw signs of displeasure on his face and said, "O Messenger of Allah, I turn to Allah and His Messenger in repentance. What have I done wrong?" He said, "What is this cushion?" She said, "I bought it for you to sit on or to rest your head." The Messenger of Allah (peace be on him) then said,

> The makers of such figures will be punished and will be
> told, 'Bring to life what you have created.' He
> continued, 'The angels do not enter a house in which
> there are figures.'

In the version of Muslim there is the addition, " 'Aisha said that she then cut it and made two pillows to recline upon."

However, this *hadith* is objectionable on several counts:

1. The content of this hadith has been transmitted in many versions which appear to be mutually contradictory. Some of them say that the Prophet (peace be on him) used the curtain with pictures after it was cut and made into cushions. In other versions there was no curtain to begin with.

2. According to some versions, only his disapproval of covering walls with printed curtains is establishsed, the reason for his disapproval being that they were a sign of luxury. In the version by Muslim he is reported to have said, "Allah has not commanded us to clothe stone and clay."

3. Then there is the *hadith* from 'Aisha herself, transmitted by Muslim, about the curtain with the picture of a bird on it and

113

the Prophet's saying, "Remove it from here. When I enter and see it, I am reminded of this world." This statement does not say anything concerning its prohibition.

4. There is also the *hadith* concerning the drape in 'Aisha's house which distracted the Prophet's attention from his prayers, whereupon he instructed her to remove it. Al-Hafiz says, "There is a problem in reconciling this *hadith* and the *hadith* of the *cushion*, both of which are ascribed to 'Aisha. This *hadith* indicates that he had allowed the drape to remain in the house as long as it had not distracted his attention from prayer; he did not have any particular objection to the pictures on it." Al-Hafiz then tries to reconcile the two *ahadith* by saying that the cushion had a picture of a living creature while the drape had pictures of inanimate objects. However, his attempt at reconciliation fails with respect to the *hadith* concerning the curtain with the picture of the bird on it.

5. The *hadith* concerning the cushion contradicts the *hadith* reported by Abu Talhah in which figures on cloth were exempted. Al-Qurtabi says, "Reconciliation is possible between the two (*ahadith*), as '*Aisha's hadith* indicates the disapproval of the Prophet (peace be on him), while Abu Talhah's *hadith* indicates absolute permissibility, and these two are not contradictory." Al-Hafiz ibn Hajar agreed with this statement.

6. The transmitter of the *hadith* of the cushion from 'Aisha was her nephew al-Qasim ibn Muhammad ibn Abu Bakr. Al-Qasim himself permitted pictures on a plane surface. Ibn 'Awm said, "I entered al-Qasim's house, which was in the outskirts of Makkah, and I saw a cloth canopy with figures of a beaver and a phoenix."[1] Al-Hafiz explains, "He probably adhered to the generality of the Prophet's saying, 'Except if it is made on cloth,' and understood the Prophet's stand toward 'Aisha's curtain as a special case. That is, the Prophet (peace be on him) dispproved of the combination of

---

[1] *Fath al-Bari*, reported on the authority of Ibn Abi Shaybah, who quotes al-Qasim ibn Muhammad ibn Abu Bakr. The transmitters are sound.

draping the wall and of the cloth having pictures on it. This is supported by the remark, "Allah has not commanded us to clothe stone and clay." Al-Qasim ibn Muhammad ibn Abu Bakr was one of the seven jurists of Madinah and the best of his time; it was he who transmitted the *hadith* of the cushion. Consequently, if he had not been convinced of the permissibility of this cloth canopy he would not have had it.[1]

There is another way of reconciling these *ahadith*. Probably in the early period of Islam the Prophet (peace be on him) was very strict in prohibiting all pictures, as the Muslims had only recently come out of the state of polytheism and idol-worship, and were prone to sanctifying figures and statues. As the belief in the Oneness of Allah became deeply rooted in their hearts and minds, he allowed them two-dimensional figures, that is, drawings and prints. As for himself, he disliked having curtains or drapes with figures and pictures in his house, not exempting even drawings or prints on cloth, paper, or the wall.

One of the great Hanafi jurists, al-Tahawi, says,

"In the beginning the Prophet (peace be on him) prohibited all types of figures, even if they were two dimensional, since the Muslims had only recently converted from the worship of images. Accordingly, everything of this type was prohibited. Later he lifted the prohibition from cloth with prints because of the necessity of wearing clothes. He also permitted figures which were not treated in a respectful manner,[2] since there was no danger that the ignorant would venerate what was debased. The prohibition of figures which are not debased was never lifted."[3]

[1] See the section on "Figures and Artists" in *Fath al-Bari*.
[2] As is evident from these *ahadith*, this would include figures which are made into pillows or cushions on which to sit or recline, figures in rugs or carpets which are trod upon and the like. (Trans.)
[3] This has been reported by Sheikh Bakhit in *Al-Jawab al-Shafi*.

115

The Permissibility of a Debased Figure

Any change in a figure which keeps it from being treated with respect and renders it debased transfers it from the sphere of detestability into that of permissibility. It is reported in the *hadith* that Jibril sought permission of the Prophet (peace be on him) to enter; when he bade him come in, Jibril said, "How can I enter while there is a curtain with figures in your house? If you have need of it, cut off the heads (of the figures), or cut it into pieces and make cushions, or use it as a floor-mat."[1] These words explain why, on observing the Prophet's dislike of the cushion with the pictures, 'Aisha changed it into smaller cushions for reclining upon, in order that by such use there would not be the slightest imputation of respect for what was depicted.

We have evidence that the early generations of Muslims used objects with pictures on them but only in a way which did not denote respect. 'Urwah used arm cushions with pictures of birds and men on them. 'Ikrimah said, "We detested seeing figures in the upright position but did not mind if they were in rugs or mats, since to tread on them was to debase them."

Photographs

Thus far the word *picture (suar)* has been used in reference to what is drawn, painted, or imprinted on a flat surface. Photography is a recent invention which was obviously non-existent in the time of the Prophet (peace be on him) and the early generations of Muslims. Thus, the question naturally arises whether the Islamic rulings concerning pictures and artists apply to photographs and photographers.

Those jurists who consider the prohibition to be restricted to statues alone do not see anything objectionable in photographic

---

[1]Al-Nisai, as well as Ibn Hibban in his *Sahih*.

pictures, especially if they are not of the full figure. Others raise many questions. Are photographs similar to drawings? Is it not true that the reason stated in some *ahadith* concerning the punishment of figure-makers, namely, imitation of Allah's attribute of Creatorship, does not apply in the case of photographic pictures? Does not the absence of the cause of prohibition nullify the prohibition?

The late Sheikh Muhammad Bakhit, the Egyptian jurist, ruled that since the photograph merely captures the image of a real object through a camera, there is no reason for prohibition in this case. Prohibited pictures are those whose object is not present and which is originated by the artist, whose intention is to imitate Allah's animal creation, and this does not apply to taking photographs with a camera.[1]

Even those who are very strict in classifying all kinds of figures, including photographs, as detestable, exempt, according to necessity, pictures retained for identity cards, passports, keeping a record of suspects and criminals, pictures for instructional purposes, and so on, with the proviso that there is no intention of respect or sanctification of these pictures which would affect Islamic belief. The need for such pictures is definitely greater than the "prints" on cloth which were exempted by the Prophet (peace be on him).

The Subject Matter of Photographs

Accordingly, if any kind of photograph is to be prohibited, the subject matter will be the determing factor. No Muslim would disagree concerning the prohibition of photographing subjects whose portrayal is against the beliefs, morals, and laws of Islam. Thus there cannot be any doubt concerning the prohibition of photographs, drawings, and paintings of nude or semi-nudes, of those parts of the male or female body which excite lust, or of pictures of men and women in sexy poses such as one sees in various magazines, newspapers, and on the billboards of movie theaters. It is *haram* to make such pictures, to publish them, to buy them, to take

---

[1] See the pamphlet, *Al-Jawab al-Shafi fi Ibahat al-Taswir al-Fotografi.*

them into homes, offices or shops, or to hang them on walls. It is *haram* to have the intention of looking at them.

The above applies to pictures of tyrants. The Muslim is required to detest such people and to feel enmity toward them for the sake of Allah. A Muslim is not permitted to make or acquire a picture of a "great" man or leader who is an atheist and denies the existence of God; of an idolator who worships cows, fire, or anything else; of a Jew or Christian who denies the Messengership of Muhammad (peace be on him); or of a professed Muslim who does not decide matters according to what Allah has revealed. Likewise, a Muslim should not make or acquire pictures of immoral individuals who propagate obscenity and lewdness in society, such as singers, actors, and other entertainers.

Similar is the case of pictures which portray polytheistic rituals or symbols of other religions abhorrent to the Islamic teachings, such as idols, crosses, and the like. Probably during the time of the Prophet (peace be on him) a great majority of rugs, curtains, and cushions bore these types of pictures. Al-Bukhari reported that the Prophet (peace be on him) broke everything in his house which was made in the shape of a cross. [1]

Ibn Abbas narrated that, during the conquest of Makkah, the Messenger of Allah (peace be on him) did not enter the Sacred House (the *Ka'aba)* until all the figures in it were destroyed. [2] There is no doubt that these figures and images represented the idolatrous practices of the Makkans and were the legacy of generations of unbelief and error.

'Ali ibn Abu Talib narrated,

> The Messenger of Allah (peace be on him) was attending a funeral and he said, 'Who among you is capable of going to Madinah and leaving no idol unbroken, no grave unlevelled, and no picture undefaced?' A man said, 'O Messenger of Allah, I am able to do it.' He went, and after a time returned and reported, 'O Messenger of Allah, I left no idol unbroken, no grave unlevelled, and no picture undefaced.' Then

---

[1] Reported by al-Bukhari.
[2] Reported by al-Bukhari.

the Messenger of Allah declared, 'Anyone who returns to this sort of practice will have rejected what was revealed to Muhammad.'[1]

What could these pictures have been which the Prophet (peace be on him) commanded to have defaced and mutilated except a representation of the idolatry of the period of *jahiliyyah?* The Prophet (peace be on him) was determined to purify Madinah of the remnants of idolatry, and that is why he described a return to any such practice as rejection of the message revealed to him.

A Summary of the Rulings Pertaining to Figures and Their Makers

We summarize here the rulings pertaining to figures and figure-makers.

1. The most strictly prohibited figures are those which are made to be worshiped in the place of or in addition to Allah Subhanahu wa Ta'ala. If the one who makes them does it intentionally for this purpose, he is going in the direction of unbelief (*kufr*). The most detestable among such figures are statues. Anyone who has a share in propagating or glorifying them will bear the sin proportional to his part.

2. Next to this in sinfulness are figures which are not made to be worshiped but which are intended to imitate Allah's creation. If the artist claims that he originates and creates as Allah does, he is an unbeliever. This matter pertains solely to the intention of the artist.

3. After this are statues which are erected in public places in order to commemorate great personalities such as kings, leaders and celebrities; this applies equally to full-length statues and to busts.

4. Next are statues of living beings which are neither worshipped nor reverenced. There is general agreement that

---

[1] Reported by Ahmad. Al-Mondhari commented, "It has *insha'Allah* good transmitters." Muslim reported on the authority of Hayyan ibn Hasein that the latter said, " 'Ali told me, 'I shall tell you what the Messenger of Allah (peace be on him) told me: "Do not leave any figure without mutilating it or any grave without levelling it." ' "

they are *haram*, except those which are not treated in a manner indicative of respect. Dolls or figures made of chocolate or sugar are clear exceptions.

5. Next are portraits of great people such as rulers and political leaders, especially when they are displayed or hung on walls. Strongly prohibited among these are portraits of tyrants, atheists, and immoral individuals, for to respect them is to degrade Islam.

6. Next are pictures of people or animals which are not accorded respect but constitute a display of luxury and high living, as, for example, when they cover a wall or the like. These are classified as detestable only.

7. Making and acquiring drawings or paintings of trees, lakes, ships, mountains, and landscapes of this sort is permitted. However, if they distract from worship or lead toward extravagant living, they are disapproved.

8. Photographic pictures are basically permissible. They become *haram* only when the subject matter is *haram*, as, for example, in the case of idols, individuals who are revered either because of their religious or worldly status, especially the leaders of idolators, Communists or other unbelievers, or immoral individuals such as actors and entertainers.

9. Finally, if the prohibited statues and pictures are defaced or degraded, their use becomes permissible; an example of this are figures on a rug or carpet, because they are walked upon.

Keeping Dogs Without Necessity

Keeping dogs inside the house without any necessity merely as pets was forbidden by the Prophet (peace be on him). When we observe how lavishly the well-to-do treat their dogs while despising their relatives, and how much attention they give their dogs while neglecting their neighbors, we realize the wisdom of this prohibiton. Moreover, the presence of a dog makes the household utensils unhygienic due to their licking of them. The Prophet (peace be on him) said,

120

"If a dog licks a plate (or pot), clean it seven times, of which one time should be with sand (or earth)."[1]

Some scholars are of the opinion that the reason for prohibiting the keeping of dogs may be because they bark at visitors, scare away the needy who come to ask for charity, and chase and try to bite passers-by.

The Prophet (peace be on him) said,

Jibril came to me and said, 'I came to you yesterday but what stopped me from entering was that there was a statue at the door, a curtain with figures on it in the house, and a dog inside the house. So order that the head of the statue be broken off so that it resembles the trunk of tree, that the curtain be cut and made into two pillows to recline on, and that the dog be taken out.'[2]

This prohibition is limited to keeping dogs without need or benefit.

The Permissibility of Keeping Hunting Dogs and Watch Dogs

Dogs which are kept for a purpose, such as hunting, guarding cattle or crops and the like are exempted from the above ruling. In a *hadith* reported by both al-Bukhari and Muslim, the Prophet (peace be on him) said,

Whoever keeps a dog except for hunting or for guarding crops or cattle will lose one large measure (*qirat*) of his reward each day.

On the basis of this *hadith* some jurists argue that the keeping of dogs as pets can be classified as *makruh* rather than *haram*, as the *haram* is absolutely prohibited without regard to whether there is a decrease in reward or not.

However, the prohbition of keeping dogs in the house does not mean that dogs may be treated cruelly or that they should be eradicated. Referring to the following verse of the Qur'an,

There is not an animal on the earth, nor a bird flying

---

[1]Reported by al-Bukhari.
[2]Reported by Abu Daoud, al-Nisai, al-Tirmidhi, and by Ibn Hibban in his *Sahih*.

121

upon two wings, but comprise nations like yourselves. (6:38),

the Prophet (peace be on him) said,

"If dogs were not a nation (*ummah*) among nations, I would have ordered that they be killed." [1]

The Prophet (peace be on him) told his Companions a story concerning a man who found a dog in the desert panting and licking the dust due to thirst. The man went to a well, filled his shoes with water, and relieved the dog's thirst. Said the Messenger of Allah (peace be on him),

"Allah appreciated this and forgave him all his sins." [2]

The Findings of Scientific Research Relative to Keeping Dogs

Some lovers of the West in Muslim countries claim to be full of love and compassion for all living creatures and they wonder why Islam warns against this "best friend" of man. For their benefit, we quote here a lengthy excerpt from an article by the German scientist, Dr. Gerard Finstimer, [3] in which the author sheds light on the dangers to human health resulting from keeping dogs or coming in contact with them. He says:

The increasing interest shown by many people in recent times in keeping dogs as pets has compelled us to draw public attention to the dangers which result from this, especially because pet dogs are hugged and kissed and permitted to lick the hands of the young and the old, and what is worse, to lick the plates and utensils which are used by human beings for eating and drinking.

Besides being unhygienic and uncouth, this practice is bad manners and abhorrent to good taste. However, we are not concerned with such matters. leaving them to be addressed by teachers of etiquette and good taste.

---

[1]Reported by Abu Daoud and al-Tirmidhi. (This was said by the Prophet following Jibril's remark that angels do not enter a house in which there is a dog. Trans.)
[2]Reported by al-Bukhari.
[3]Translated from the German magazine *Kosinos*.

Rather this article is intended to present some scientific observations.

From the medical point of view, which is our main concern here, the hazards to human health and life from keeping and playing with dogs are not to be ignored. Many people have paid a high price for their ignorance, as the tapeworm carried by dogs is a cause of chronic disease, sometimes resulting in death.

This worm is found in man, in cattle, and in pigs, but it is found in fully-developed form only in dogs, wolves and rarely in cats. These worms differ from others in that they are minute and invisible, consequently, they were not discovered until very recently.

He continues,

Biologically the developmental process of this worm has some unique characteristics. In the lesions caused by them, one worm gives rise to many heads which spread and form other and varied kinds of lesions and abscesses. These heads develop into full-grown worms only in dogs' tonsils. In humans and in other animals they appear as lesions and abscesses completely different from the tapeworm itself. In animals the size of an abscess may reach that of an apple, while the liver of the infected animal may grow from five to ten times its normal size. In human beings the size of the abscess may reach that of a clenched fist or even the head of an infant; it is filled with yellow fluid weighing from ten to twenty pounds. In the infected human it may cause diverse kinds of inflammations in the lungs, muscles, spleen, kidneys, and brain, and appears in such different forms that specialists, until very recently, had difficulty in recognizing it.

In any case, wherever this inflammation is found, it poses great danger to the health and life of the patient. What is worse is that, in spite of our knowledge of its life history, origin, and develoment, we have not been able to devise a cure for it, except that in some instances these parasites die out, possibly because of antibodies produced in the human body. Unfortunately, cases in

which such parasites die without causing damage are
rare indeed. Moreover, chemotherapy has failed to
produce any benefit, and the usual treatment is surgical
removal of the abscessed parts of the body. For all these
reasons we should use all possible resources to fight
aginst this dreadful disease and save man from its
dangers.

Professor Noeller, through post-mortem dissection of
human bodies in Germany, found that the incidence of
infection with dogs' worms is at least one percent. In
some places such as Dalmatia, Iceland, southeastern
Australia, and Holland, where dogs are used for pulling
sleds, the incidence rate of tapeworm among dogs is 12
percent. In Iceland the number of people who suffer
from the inflammation caused by this worm has
reached the rate of 43 percent. If we add to this the
human suffering, the loss of meat because of infection
of cattle, and the permanent danger to human health
because of the presence of tapeworms, we cannot be
very complacent toward this problem.

Perhaps the best way to combat the problem is to limit
the worms to dogs and not let them spread, since in
actuality we need to keep some dogs. We should not
neglect to treat dogs when necessary by getting rid of
the tapeworms in their tonsils and perhaps repeating
this process periodically on shepherd dogs and watch-
dogs.

Man can protect his life and health by keeping a safe
distance from dogs. He should not hug them, play with
them, or let them come close to children. Children
should be taught not to play with dogs or to fondle
them. Dogs should not be permittd to lick children's
hands or come to places where they play.
Unfortunately, dogs are allowed to roam about
everywhere, especially in places where children play,
and their bowls are scattered throughout the house.
Dogs must have their own separate bowls, and they
must not be allowed to lick bowls and plates used by
humans. They should not be allowed inside grocery

124

stores, restaurants, or marketplaces. In general, great care must be taken that they do not come in contact with anything which is used by people for eating and drinking.

We already know that the Prophet (peace be on him) forbade mixing with dogs, and that he warned against their licking plates and against keeping them without necessity. How is it possible that the teachings of an unlettered Arab, Muhammad, should agree with the latest findings of scientific research? Truly, we cannot say anything except to repeat the words of the Qur'an:

Nor does he speak from (his own) desire. It is nothing other than a revelation sent down. (53:3-4)

4. Work and Earning Livelihood

It is He Who has made the earth submissive to you; so traverse its paths and eat of what He provides you....(67:15)

The fundamental attitude of Islam toward man's position in the world is that Allah Subhanahu wa Ta'ala has made the earth for the benefit of man, to whom He has given control over it. It is the duty of man to profit from this favor and to exert himself to seek Allah's bounties throughout the earth.

The Obligation to Work If One Is Able

It is not permitted to the Muslim to avoid working for a living on the pretext of devoting his life to worship or trust in Allah, as gold and silver certainly do not fall from the sky. It is also not permissible for him to depend on charity while he is able to earn what is sufficient for his own and his family's needs through his own efforts. In this regard, the Prophet (peace be on him) has said,

"Charity is *halal* neither for the rich nor for the able-bodied."[1]

The Prophet (peace be on him) made it *haram* for the Muslim to

---

[1]Reported by al-Tirmidhi.

beg from others without dire necessity thus losing his honor and his dignity. He said,

> "He who begs without need is like a person holding a burning coal in his hand."[1]

He also said,

> Anyone who begs from people in order to increase his wealth will have his face scratched on the Day of Resurrection, and will eat burning stones from hell; so let him reduce it (his punishment) or let him increase it as he pleases.[2]

Again, he said,

> "A person keeps on begging until he meets Allah (on the Day of Resurrection) with no flesh on his face."[3]

By such strong admonitions, the Prophet (peace be on him) intended to train the Muslim to safeguard his dignity, to develop self-reliance, and to be far-removed from dependance on others.

When Begging is Allowable

The Prophet (peace be on him) was, however, aware of situations of necessity. If, under the pressure of need, one is forced to ask for financial help from the government or from individuals, he is blameless. Said Allah's messenger (peace be on him):

> Begging is similar to scratching the flesh off your face; so if someone wants to save his face he should avoid it, except for asking from the ruler or asking in case of dire need.[4]

In his *Sahih*, Muslim reported Abu Bishr Qubaysah ibn al-Makharaf as saying, "I agreed to pay *himlah* (an amount of money paid to two quarreling parties in order to make peace between them)

---

[1] Reported by al-Bayhaqi and by Ibn Khazimah in his *Sahih*.
[2] Reported by al-Tirmidhi. (The meaning here is that it is up to him to decrease his punshment by not begging,and vice-versa. Trans.)
[3] Reported by al-Bukhari and Muslim.
[4] Reported by Abu Daoud and al-Nisai.

and came to the Messenger of Allah (peace be on him) asking for help. Thereupon the Prophet (peace be on him) said,

> 'Wait until alms (*sadaqah*) are brought to us and we will give you from that. Qubaysah,' he continued, 'asking for money is not permissible except in three cases: for a man who takes it upon himself to pay *himalah*, he may ask people for help until the designated amount is received and then he should stop asking. For a man who suffers calamity and loses his property, it is permissible for him to ask until he is able to stand on his own feet. For a man who is starving, until three reliable persons from his community say, "That man is reduced to hunger; it is permissible for him to ask until he is able to stand on his own feet." Except for these, Qubaysah, begging is fire, it is eating fire.'[1]

Dignity of Work

Some people regard certain kinds of work or professions as contemptible. However, the Prophet (peace be on him) denied the validity of this notion. He taught his Companions that the whole of a human being's dignity is tied up with his work — any sort of work — and that real disgrace and humiliation consist of depending on other people's help. He said,

> It is better that a person should take a rope and bring a bundle of wood on his back to sell so that Allah may preserve his honor, than that he should beg from people, (regardless of) whether they give to him or refuse him.[2]

The Muslim can earn his livelihood by agriculture, trade, or industry or by any profession or employment as long as it does not involve doing, supporting, or propagating anything *haram*.

---

[1]Reported by Abu Daoud and al-Nisai.
[2]Reported by al-Bukhari and Muslim.

Earning Through Agriculture

In the Qur'an, while referring to His bounties and favors to man, Allah Ta'ala mentions the principles required for the pursuit of agriculture. He has spread out the earth and made it suitable and fertile for cultivation and production; this is a bounty to human beings which they ought to recall and to be thankful for:

> And Allah has spread out the earth for you, so that you may make your way through its spacious paths. (71:19-20)

> And He has spread out the earth for (His) creatures. In it is fruit, and date palms with spathes, and husked corn, and scented herbs. Then which of the favors of your Lord will you deny? (55:10-13)

He has also provided water in abundance. He sends it down as rain and makes it flow in streams to revive the earth after it is dead.

> And it is He Who sends down water from the sky. With it We then bring forth vegetation of all kinds; from some We produce green (crops) out of which We produce grain heaped up at the harvest....(6:99)

> Then let man look at his food, how We pour forth water in abundance, then We split the earth into fragments and produce therein corn and grapes and nutritious plants. (80:24-28)

Further, He sends the winds, with "good tidings" to drive the clouds and scatter the seeds:

> And We have spread out the earth and placed firm hills therein, and produced in it all kinds of things in due balance. And We have made means of sustenance in it for you and for those whom you are not the providers. And there is not a thing but its sources are with Us, and We send it down only in appointed measures. And We send the fertilizing winds, and send down the rain from the sky and give it to you to drink, although you are not the guardians of its stores. (15:19-22)

In all these Qur'anic verses there is encouragement for man to

128

engage in agricultural activity, for it has been made easy for him as a divine favor.

The Prophet (peace be on him) said,

> When a Muslim plants a plant or cultivates a crop, no bird or human being eats from it without its being accounted as a (rewardable) charity for him.[1]

He also said,

> When a Muslim plants a plant, anything eaten of it or stolen from it, until the Day of Ressurection, is accounted as a charity for him.[2]

The implication of these *ahadith* is that the reward of the person who plants a tree or a crop continues as long as the produce of this tree or crop is eaten or used, even though he may have sold it to someone else. The scholars have said,

> It is Allah's generosity that He continues to add to the reward of a person even after his death, just as when he was alive, for six things: for the charity whose benefits continue, for knowledge which is used, for righteous children who pray for him, for the trees he planted, for the crops he sowed, and for territorial borders he guarded.

Once a man passed Abu al-Darda while he was planting a walnut tree. The man said, "Are you planting this even though you are a very old man? This tree will not bear fruit for many years." "What of it?" Abu al-Darda replied. "Others will eat of its fruit, and the reward will be mine."

One of the Companions of the Prophet (peace be on him) said that he had heard the Messenger of Allah say,

> If anyone plants a tree, patiently protects it, and looks after it until it bears fruit, Allah the Mighty and Glorious will count as charity for him anything for which its fruits are used.[3]

On the basis of these sayings of the Prophet (peace be on him), some scholars have argued that agriculture is the best of

---

[1]Reported by al-Bukhari and Muslim.
[2]Reported by Muslim.
[3]Reported by Ahmad.

occupations. Others say that manufacturing and working with the hands are best, while still others consider trade to be the best.[1] In trying to reconcile these positions, some reseachers say that it all depends upon circumstances: if food is scarce, agriculture is the best; if people need goods, trade is the best; while if manufactured goods are needed, industry is the best. This conditional preference seems to be in the closest agreement with modern scientific thought.

Prohibited Crops

It is *haram* to cultivate a plant, such as hashish and the like, which is *haram* for eating or which has no other known use except what is harmful. The case of tobacco is of this nature; whatever be the classification of smoking, whether *haram* or *makruh*, the growing of tobacco is similarly classified. We ourselves prefer to classify smoking as *haram*.

It is not a valid excuse for the Muslim to say that he is growing the *haram* crop in order to sell it to non-Muslims, for the Muslim is never permitted to be a party to the propagation of what is *haram*. This is similar to a Muslim's raising pigs in order to sell them to Christians, which is clearly unlawful. As we have seen, even a *halal* item such as grapes cannot be sold to others if it is known that they will use them to make wine.

Industries and Professions

Agriculture is essential, and Islam persuades people to engage in it by pointing to the benefits in this world, and the rewards in the Hereafter resulting from it. However, from the Islamic point of view it would be extremely undesirable if people limited their economic efforts solely to agriculture, a situation analagous to supposing that the inexhaustible oceans had no use other than the extraction of pearls from their depths. Warning Muslims that confining their activity only to agriculture and pastoral pursuits would expose them to various dangers such as defeat, humiliation, and the loss of religious freedom, the Prophet (peace be on him) said,

[1]See al-Qastalani's commentary on al-Bukhari.

If you deal in usury, calling it by other names, and hang onto the tails of cows, being satisfied with cultivation and ceasing to perform *jihad*,[1] Allah will inflict a disgrace upon you which will not be removed until you return to your religion.[2]

Thus, in addition to agriculture, the Muslim must develop such industries, crafts, and professions as are essential for the life of a community, for the strength of a free and powerful nation, and for the posterity and wealth of a country. As the great scholars and jurists have explained, the essential industries and professions are not merely permitted by the Islamic *Shari'ah*, they are in fact an obligation on the Muslim community as a whole. Such obligations are termed "the obligations of sufficiency" *(fard kifiyah)*; that is to say, the Muslim community must include among its members people engaged in every essential science, industry, and profession in numbers sufficient to meet its needs. If there is a shortage of qualified persons in some field of essential science or industry, the entire Muslim community is blameworthy, especially those in positions of authority. Imam al-Ghazzali says:

> Sciences whose knowledge is deemed *fard kifayah* comprise every area which is indispensible for the welfare of this world, such as the following: medicine, which is necessary for the life of the body; arithmetic, for daily transactions and the division of legacies and inheritances, as well as others besides. These are the sciences without which, because of their absence, a community would be reduced to narrow straits. But should one who can practice them arise in the community, it would suffice, and the obligation to acquire their knowledge would cease to be binding upon the rest of the community.
>
> No one should be surprised when we say that medicine as well as arithmetic are of the sciences which are *fard kifayah*, as are the basic industries, such as agriculture,

---

[1]Striving or fighting in the cause of Allah. (Trans.)
[2]Reported by Abu Daoud.

weaving, politics, and even cupping and tailoring. For if a town should lack a cupper, extinction would overtake its people and they would be driven to expose themselves to destruction. Has not He Who has sent down the malady also sent down the remedy, given guidance for its use, and prepared the means for administering it? It is not, therefore, permissible to expose oneself to destruction by neglecting the remedy.[1]

The Qur'an mentions many industries, terming them Allah's favor and bounty. Allah Ta'ala says concerning David (Daoud),

...And We made iron soft for him (commanding): Make thou coats of mail and balance the links.... (34:10-11)

And We taught him the art of making garments (of mail) to protect you from your violence. Will you then be thankful? (21:80)

He says about Solomon:

...And We made a fountain of molten copper flow for him ; and of the *jinn* there were those who worked in front of him by his Lord's permission. And if any of them turned aside from Our command, We made him taste the penalty of the blazing fire. They worked for him as he desired, (making) synagogues and statues, basins as large as reservoirs and boilers built into the ground. Give thanks, O House of David....(34:12-13)

And He says about Duhl-Qarnayn and his building the high dam:

He said, 'That in which my Lord has established me is better (than tribute). Therefore, (if you) help me with your strength, I will erect a barrier between you and them. Give me blocks of iron.' Then when he had filled up the space between the two cliffs, he said, 'Blow (with your billows).' Then when he had set it afire, he said, 'Give me molten copper to pour on it.' Thus, they were unable to scale it, nor were they able to dig through it.' (18:95-97)

---

[1]*Ihya 'Ulum al-Din*, vol. 1 (*The Book of Knowledge)* translated by Nabih Amin Faris, Sh. Muhammad Ashraf, Lahore, Pakistan, 1966, p. 37

Allah mentions the story of Noah (Nuh) and the construction of the ark, and He also mentions great ships the size of mountains which sail the seas:

And among His signs are the ships on the sea, like mountains. (42:32)

The Qur'an also mentions hunting in all its varied forms, from the catching of fish and the pursuit of land animals to diving in the deep for pearls, coral, and the like.

In addition to this, the Qur'an has informed us about the value of iron in such emphatic terms as are apt to be found in any other previous book, religious or secular. After mentioning the sending of prophets to the people and revealing the scriptures, Allah Ta'ala says:

...And We send down iron, in which there is great strength and benefits for mankind....(57:25)

It is not surprising that the *surah* containing this verse was given the title of *Al-Hadid* (Iron).

Any sort of work which fills a need in the society or brings real benefit is regarded as good, provided the person performs it in a proper manner, as is required by Islam. Islam gave dignity to many professions which people considered lowly and degrading — for example, the occupation of shepherding. Although people do not usually look upon shepherds with esteem or honor, the Prophet (peace be on him) said,

'Allah did not send a prophet without his having tended sheep', They asked, 'You too, O Messenger of Allah? He replied, 'Yes. I tended sheep for wages for the people of Makkah'.[1]

Muhammad (peace be on him), the Messenger of Allah and the Seal of the Prophets, used to tend sheep! Moreover they were not even his own sheep but belonged to the people of Makkah, and he tended them for fixed wages. He told his Companions this in order to teach them that honor belongs to those who work, and not to thsoe who sit idle and are parasites.

The Qur'an tells the story of the Prophet Moses (Musa) (peace be on him) who worked for eight years as a hired man to gain the hand

---

[1]Reported by al-Bukhari.

of an old man's daughter in marriage. Moses was an excellent worker and employee; the old man's daughter had displayed real insight into his character. She said,

O my father, employ him; truly, the best for thee to employ is the strong and trustworthy one.   (28:26)

Ibn 'Abbas said, "David was a maker of coats of mail and sheilds, Adam was a farmer, Noah a carpenter, Idris a tailor, and Moses a shepherd."[1] Since every prophet of Allah had some occupation, the Muslim should derive satisfaction in his occupation or profession. A *hadith* states:

No one earns his food better than the one who worked with his hands, and the prophet of Allah, David earned his food by working with his hands.[2]

Industries and Professions Condemned by Islam

Islam has prohibited certain professions and industries to its followers because they are harmful to the beliefs, morals, honor ,or good manners of the society.

Prostitution: Prostitution, for example, is legal in many countries of the West; permits and licenses are issued to those who ply this trade, and prostitutes enjoy rights similar to other professionals. Islam absolutely rejects and condemns this practice, and forbids any female, free or slave, to earn money by selling her sexuality.

During the period of *jahiliyyah* some people used to exact a daily tribute from their female slaves without caring in what manner they earned this money to pay their masters. A majority of them had to resort to prostitution; some masters even forced their slave-girls to prostitution in order to earn a paltry fee. When Islam came, it lifted this disgraceful burden from its sons and daughters. Allah Ta'ala revealed,

...And do not force your slave-girls to prostitution if

---

[1]Reported by al-Hakim.
[2]Reported by al-Bukhari and others.

they desire chastity, in order that you may seek the pleasures of this world's life....(24:33)

Ibn 'Abbas narrated that Ibn Ubayy, the chief of the hypocrites of Madinah, came to the Prophet (peace be on him), bringing with him a very beautiful slave-girl named M'uadhah, and saying, "O Messenger of Allah! She belongs to such and such orphans. Will you not allow her to commit fornication so that they may receive the price of it?" "No!" replied the Prophet (peace be on him).[1]

Thus the Messenger of Allah (peace be on him) forbade this abominable profession, regardless of who might derive benefit from it, rejecting any claim concerning need, distress, or any other worthy purpose in order that Muslim society might remain pure of such degrading practices.

Dancing and Other Erotic Arts: Similarly, Islam does not permit sexually exciting dancing or any other erotic activity, such as suggestive or obscene songs, provocative dramas, and every type of rubbish which some people today term "art" and "progress."

The fact is that Islam prohibits every sort of sexual contact and sexual relationship outside marriage. This is the secret behind the significant words of the Qur'an prohibiting fornication and adultery (both of which are known as *zina* in Arabic).

And do not come near *zina;* indeed, it is an abomination and an evil way. (17:32)

This indicates that not only is *zina* forbidden, but likewise anything which brings one near to it. Everything to which we have referred above, as people are well aware, for example, provocative dances and songs, constitutes "coming near *zina;*" these things are certainly intended to tempt, excite, and lead one toward such sin. And what havoc they wreak in the lives of people!

Making Statues and Similar Articles: As we have already seen, Islam prohibits the acquisition of statues and even more strongly the making of them. Al-Bukhari reported on the authority of Sa'id ibn Abu al-Hasan that the latter said, "I was with Ibn 'Abbas when a man came and said to him, 'O Ibn 'Abbas, I earn my living with my

---

[1] *Tafsir* of Fakhr al-Deen al-Razi, vol. 23, p. 320.

own hands. I make these figures.' 'I shall tell you,' said Ibn 'Abbas, 'only what I heard from the Mesenger of Allah (peace be on him). I heard him say,

'Allah will punish anyone who makes figures until he breathes spirit into them, which he can never do.'

Seeing the man extremely upset, Ibn 'Abbas added, 'What ails you? If you must make figures, then make them of trees or of something which has no soul.' "[1] And the same obviously applies to the making of idols and the like.

As for drawing, painting, or photography, we stated previously that they are either permitted or at worst disapproved, depending on what comes closest to the spirit of the Islamic legislation. Of course, as was explained earlier, their subject matter should not be sexually provocative, as, for example, the erotic parts of the female body or a man and woman in a state of intimacy, and should not be of someone sacred or respected, such as the angels or the prophets.

Manufacturing Intoxicants and Drugs: Earlier we saw that Islam prohibits any participation in the promotion of alcoholic beverages, whether it be in their manufacture, distribution, or consumption, and that anyone who participates in any of these is cursed by the Messenger of Allah (peace be on him). The case of other intoxicants and drugs, such as hashish, cocaine, and the like, is the same; manufacturing, distributing, or consuming any of them is *haram*. In short, Islam prohibits the Muslim to work in any industry, business or profession which deals in, or promotes, anything which is *haram*.

Trade

The Qur'an and the *Hadith* of the Prophet (peace be on him) urge Muslims to engage in trade and commerce, and to undertake journeys for what the Qur'an refers to as "seeking the bounty of Allah." In fact, Allah mentions those who travel for the purpose of trade side by side with those who fight in His cause:

---

[1]Reported by al-Bukhari.

...Others travel through the land, seeking the bounty of Allah, and still others fight in the cause of Allah....(73:20)

Allah mentions merchant ships, which are the principal means of transporting goods throughout the world, as one of His favors to mankind, encouraging people to engage in exports and imports. He says:

...And thou seest the ships in it (the ocean), cleaving the waves, that you may seek of His bounty and that you may be thankful. (35:12)

In other places He describes the winds, associating them with the movement of ships:

And among His signs is that He sends the winds as heralds of good tidings and in order that you may taste His mercy, and that the ships may sail by His command and that you may seek of His bounty, and in order that you may be thankful. (30:46)

The Qur'an mentions this at other places as a reminder of Allah's power and wisdom:

Verily, in the creation of the heavens and the earth, and the alternation of night and day, and in the ships which sail upon the ocean with what is of benefit to mankind...are signs....(2:164)

And among His signs are the ships on the sea, like mountains. (42:32)

Allah reminds the people of Makkah that He caused their city to become a commercial center of the Arabian peninsula:

...And have We not established for them a secure sanctuary, to which is brought produce of all kinds, provision from Ourselves...? (28:57)

Thus was answered Abraham's prayer:

Our Lord! Verily, I have settled some of my progeny in a valley without cultivation by Thy Sacred House, Our Lord, in order that they may establish *salat*. Then incline the hearts of some of the people with love toward them, and provide them with fruits in order that they may be grateful. (14:37)

Allah counted it as His favor upon the Quraish that He facilitated for them their two commercial journeys each year, the journey to Yemen in winter and to Syria in summer; they traveled in security because of their guardianship of the House (Ka'aba). Accordingly, they should show their gratitude to the Lord of the House by acknowledging and worshipping Him alone:

> For the security of the Quraish, their security in journeying by winter and summer, let them worship the Lord of this House, Who provides them with food against hunger and makes them safe against fear. (106:1-4)

Islam has provided a great opportunity for international trade each year. The annual *Hajj* season brings together at one place millions of Muslims from all over the world:

> ...They will come to thee (Makkah) on foot and on every (kind of) lean camel; they will come from every deep ravine, in order that they may witness the benefits (provided) for them and celebrate the name of Allah....(22:27-28)

Commercial activity is unquestionably one of these benefits. Al-Bukhari reported that the Musims were reluctant to do business during the *hajj*, fearing that this might compromise the sincerity of their intentions or the purity of their worship. The verses of the Qur'an were then revealed, stating clearly and distinctly that

> It is no sin for you to seek the bounty of your Lord (during the *hajj*)....(2:198)

The Qur'an lauds those who go to the mosques often, glorifying their Lord morning and evening:

> Men whom neither business nor sale can divert from the remembrance of Allah, nor from regularity in *salat* or from giving *zakat*....(24:37)

In the view of Islam, the true believers are not those who remain in the mosques, nor the mystics or recluses in their places of retreat. The true Believers are men of action, whose distinguishing characteristic is that the affairs of the busy world do not make them forget their obligations to their Creator. These are some of the teachings of the Qur'an concerning trade and commerce.

138

The Prophet (peace be on him), by his words and deeds, delineated the rules of trade, encouraging, indeed, urging the Muslims to engage in it. Among some of his sayings are the following:

> "An honest and trustworthy merchant will be with the martyrs on the Day of Resurrection."[1]

> "An honest and trustworthy merchant will be with the prophets, the truthful, and the martyrs."[2]

It is not surprising that the Prophet (peace be on him) held the status of an honest merchant to be equal to that of a soldier or a martyr in the cause of Allah. His evaluation is confirmed by the experiences of life, since striving in the cause of Allah is not limited to the battlefield but extends to the economic front as well.

The Prophet (peace be on him) promised merchants a high status with Allah and a great reward in the Hereafter. We observe that the motivating force behind much trading activity is greed and profit-making by any means; "Money makes money" and "Business begets business" are the motives of much trading activity. Any merchant who remains within the bounds of honesty and fair-dealing in such an atmosphere is a fighter against his desires, meriting the status of a warrior in the cause of Allah.

The lure of business is great, and it can turn a businessman's attention exclusively to numbers, counting his capital and the profits of his business. Even during the Prophet's own lifetime the following incident occurred: while the Prophet (peace be on him) was addressing a gathering, the news came that a caravan of merchandise had arrived. The people rushed out, leaving the Prophet (peace be on him) behind, upon which Allah Ta'ala admonished them:

> But when they see some business or amusement, they disperse to it and leave thee standing. Say: 'What is with Allah is better than amusement and than business; and Allah is the best of providers.' (62:11)

Accordingly, a person who, in a vortex of commercial activity, can remain steadfast, with the fear of Allah in his heart and the mention of Him on his lips, most certainly deserves to be in the company of

---

[1]Reported by Ibn Majah and al-Hakim, who classified it as "sound."
[2]Reported by al-Hakim and al-Tirmidhi, with good transmitters.

the favored of Allah: the prophets, the witnesses to the truth, and the martyrs in His cause.

The example of the Prophet (peace be on him) in relation to business and trade is sufficient in itself. On the other hand he was eager to nurture the spiritual aspect; thus,he built the mosque in Madinah on the foundation of piety and seeking the pleasure of Allah, as a gathering place for worship, as a university for teaching and learning, as the headquarters for the call toward Islam, and as the seat of the government. On the other hand, he was equally eager to develop the economic aspect; thus, he established an Islamic marketplace in which the Jews had not the authority they had previously possessed in the marketplace of Banu Qaynqa'. The Prophet (peace be on him) himself organized the rules of business dealing, explaining and teaching its various aspects. There was to be no cheating nor misrepresentation, nor hoarding, nor undercutting, and the like. These topics will form the subject of our discussion under the heading of "Human Affairs" in the chapter entitled "The *Halal* and the *Haram* in the Daily Life of Muslims."

Among the Companions of the Prophet (peace be n him) we find skilled traders as well as craftsmen, farmers, and every other kind of professional person and worker. In their midst was the Messenger of Allah (peace be on him) to whom the Speech of Allah came down, who was visited by Jibril, the Trustworthy Spirit, bringing the revelations from Allah, and who guided the people by the Light of these heavenly messages. Each of the Companions loved this noble Messenger (peace be on him) from the depths of his being; he wished nothing more than to be in his company and disliked nothing more than being parted from him. Yet we find that each of them was busy with his work, this one journeying over the earth on a business trip, that one working in his palm-grove and farm, and yet another busy with his craft. Anyone who missed any part of the teaching of the Messenger (peace be on him) asked his friends about whatever he could, and the Prophet told those who listened to him to pass on his insructions to those who were absent. Among his Companions, the Helpers (*Ansar*, or people of Madinah) were, by and large, farmers and growers of date-palms, while the majority of the Immigrants from Makkah *(Muhajireen)* were engaged in trade and business.

Here is 'Abdur Rahman ibn 'Auf, the *Muhajir*, and here is Sa'd ibn al-Rabi', the *Ansar*, who were made brothers-in-Allah by the

140

Prophet (peace be on him) when the Muslims of Makkah migrated to Madinah. S'ad offered 'Abdur Rahman half of his property, one of his two houses, and asked him to choose one of his two wives so that he might divorce her. This noble sacrifice was gratefully declined by a noble excuse. "May Allah bless you in your wealth and your family," said 'Abdur Rahman to Sa'd. "I have no need for them. Only tell me which market has the most trading activity." "The Bani Qaynqa' Market," said Sa'd. 'Abdur Rahman went to the market with some cheese and butter, and spent the day buying and selling. He continued his trading activity until he became one of the wealthiest men among the Muslims, leaving behind a huge estate when he died.

And here is Abu Bakr al-Siddiq who was a trader. Even on the day on which he was elected caliph by the Muslims, he had been planning to go to the market. And here is 'Umar, who said about himself, "Going to the market kept me from listening to the *hadith* of Allah's Messenger (peace be on him)." And here are also 'Uthman and great many others who were engaged in trade and commerce.

Prohibited Kinds of Trade

Islam does not prohibit any trade except those which involve injustice, cheating, making exorbitant profits, or the promotion of something which is *haram.*

It is *haram* to do business in alcoholic beverages, intoxicants, drugs, swine, idols, statues, or anything of this sort whose consumption and use Islam has prohibited. Any earnings from such business are sinful earnings, and the Fire is likely to be the abode for the flesh which has been nourished on such earnings. Honesty and trustworthiness in such businesses will not be counted as meritorious, for Islam came to fight and destroy such practices.

However, there is no objection to trading in gold and silk because they are permitted to women, except if something is made of these materials exclusively for the use of men.

Even if the trading is in entirely *halal* things, a merchant must still adhere to many moral considerations so that he may not join the ranks of the wicked, for "Indeed, the wicked will be in hell."

141

(83:14). One day when the Prophet (peace be on him) was going to the mosque, he saw some people engaged in selling. "O merchants," he called out to them. When they turned their faces toward him, some of them craning their necks to listen to what he had to say, he said,

> Merchants will be raised up on the Day of Resurrection as wicked people, with the exception of those who fear Allah, do righteous deeds, and are truthful.[1]

Waithelah ibn al-Asqa' said, "We were business people. The Prophet (peace be on him) frequently came to us, and he would say,

> "Merchants, beware of lying."[2]

Thus, he warned them against lying about their merchandise, since this is the weakness of merchants. Lying leads to wrong-doing, and that in turn leads to the Fire. The Prophet (peace be on him) warned in general against swearing and, in particular, against swearing to a lie, saying,

> On the Day of Ressurection Allah will not look at three (kinds of) persons nor purify them. One of them is the person who swears (to the truth) while lying about his merchandise.[3]

Abu Sa'id narrated, "An Arab with a sheep passed by me and I said, 'Will you sell it for three dirhams?' He replied, 'No, by Allah!' but then he sold it to me. I mentioned this to the Messenger of Allah (peace be on him), who remarked,

> He sold his Hereafter for this world.[4]

The merchant should beware of cheating, for the cheater is outside the community of Islam; he should beware of tampering with the scales when weighing; beware of hoarding lest he forfeit the protection of Allah and His Messenger (peace be on him); and beware of dealing in usury or interest (*riba*), for Allah has prohibited it, and the Prophet (peace be on him) has said,

> "A dirham of *riba* which a person consumes knowingly is worse than commiting *zina* thirty-six times."[5]

---

[1] Reported by al-Tirmidhi, Ibn Majah, Ibn Hibban, and al-Hakim.
[2] Reported by al-Tabarani.
[3] Reported by Muslim and others.
[4] Reported by Ibn Hibban in his *Sahih*.
[5] Reported by Ahmad on the authority of sound transmitters.

We will elaborate on all these matters when we come to the topic "Human Affairs."

Salaried Employment

The Muslim is free to seek employment in the service of the government, an organization, or an individual as long as he is able to do his work satisfactorily and carry out his duties. However, he is not permitted to seek a job for which he is unfit, especially if the job carries judicial or executive authority. Abu Hurairah reported the Prophet (peace be on him) as saying,

> Woe to the rulers, the leaders, and the trustees! On the Day of Resurrection some people will wish that they could be suspended between heaven and earth rather than having had the burden of their responsibilities.[1]

Abu Dharr narrated, "I said, 'Messenger of Allah! Will you not appoint me?' The Prophet (peace be on him) patted me on the shoulder and then said, Abu Dharr, you are a weak person, and this is a trust; and on the Day of Resurrection it will be a cause of regret and shame except for the one who qualifies for it and fulfills his responsibilities."[2]

The Prophet (peace be on him) said,

> There are three classes of judges, one of whom will be in the Garden and the other two in the Fire. The one who will be in the Garden is a man who knew the truth and judged accordingly. The one who knew the truth but misjudged and the one who judged for the people in ignorance will be in the fire.[3]

It is better for the Muslim not to aspire to a high position, even though he may be suited for it, and to seek for something else; for whoever considers the position as a means of lording it over others is a slave of that position, and whoever turns his face toward worldly

---

[1]Reported by Ibn Hibban in his *Sahih*, and by al-Hakim who authenticated its transmitters.
[2]Reported by Muslim.
[3]Reported by Abu Daoud, al-Tirmidhi, and Ibn Majah.

glories will not receive guidance from heaven. Narrated 'Abdur Rahman ibn Samrah, "The Messenger of Allah (peace be on him) told me,

> Abdur Rahman, do not ask for governorship, for if you are appointed to it without asking, you will be helped, while if you are appointed to it at your request, you alone will be held responsible.[1]

Anas narrated that the Prophet (peace be on him) said,

> He who seeks the office of a judge, collecting recommendations, is left to himself, but for him who is compelled to accept it, Allah sends an angel to guide him.[2]

If, however, a person knows that there is no one else qualified to do a particular job except himself, and that if he does not come forward to take it, public interests will be damaged, he should come forward. The Qur'an tells us the story of the prophet Joseph in which Joseph tells the ruler,

> Set me over the storehouses of the land; I am surely a knowledgeable custodian. (12:55)

These are the Islamic guidelines in relation to seeking positions in government and the like.

Prohibited Types of Employment

What we have said above concerning the permissibility of working as an employee of a government, organization, or individual, excludes those jobs which are injurious to the cause of Islam or which harm Muslims. Accordingly, it is not permissible for a Muslim to be an officer or soldier in an army which is fighting against Muslims, nor to work in a corporation or factory which manufactures armaments to be used against Muslims, nor in an organization which is hostile to Islam and fights its adherents.

Similarly, any service rendered in support of injustice or in promoting what is *haram* is itself *haram*. For example, it is

---

[1]Reported by al-Bukhari and Muslim.
[2]Reported by Abu Daoud and al-Tirmidhi.

144

prohibited to the Muslim to be an employee in an organization which deals in interest, in a bar or liquor shop, nightclub, dance hall, and the like.

It is not a valid excuse to say that one is neither using what is *haram* nor directly involved with it. As we have stated previously, it is a basic principle of Islam that whatever aids and assists the *haram* is itself *haram*. For this reason, the Prophet (peace be on him cursed the person who writes the document of interest and the person who witnesses it, as well as the person who consumes it. Similarly cursed is the person who brings the wine, the one who serves it, as well as the one who drinks it.

Again, under the compulsion of unavoidable necessity, the Muslim may seek temporary employment in such activities to the extent of what is required, but he should in the meantime be searching for other gainful employments until Allah opens a way for him, for indeed Allah does open the door for those who sincerely seek to avoid what is *haram*.

The Muslim is always to be on guard against temptation which may lead him toward doubtful activities, thereby weakening his faith and compromising his religion, no matter how large a profit or gain may be involved. The Prophet (peace be on him said),

> "Leave alone what puts you in doubt and turn toward what does not put you in doubt."[1]

He also said,

> "A person does not reach the rank of the God-fearing (*muttaqeen*) until he abandons what is harmless out of fear that it may be harmful."[2]

A General Rule in Earning a Living

The general rule in regard to earning a living is that Islam does not permit its followers to earn money in any way they like, rather it differentiates between lawful and unlawful methods based on the criterion of the overall well-being of the society. One may formulate

---

[1]Reported by Ahmad, al-Tirmidhi, al-Nisai, al-Hakim, and Ibn Hibban in his *Sahih*.
[2]Reported by al-Tirmidhi.

as a general rule that any transaction in which one person's gain results in another's loss is unlawful, while any transaction which is fair and beneficial to all the parties concerned and which is transacted by mutual consent is lawful.

> O you who believe, do not consume your property among yourselves wrongfully, but let there be trade by mutual consent, and do not kill yourselves; indeed, Allah is ever merciful to you. And whoever does so in enmity and injsutice, we shall cast him into the Fire; and that is easy for Allah. (4:29-30)

This verse lays down two conditions for a transaction: first, that the transaction should be with the mutual consent of the two parties; second, that the benefit to one party should not be a loss to the other. In explaining the meaning of "Do not kill yourselves," scholars give two interpretations, both of which are generally applicable here. The first is, "Do not kill each other," and the second is, "do not kill yourselves by your own hands." In either case, a person who makes someone else suffer for his own benefit is, in effect, shedding his blood and opening the door for others to do the same to him, thus leading to his own eventual ruin. Theft, bribery, gambling, cheating, fraud, misrepresentation, and interest, although some of these may be carried out by mutual consent, do not satisfy the second condition implied in the saying of Allah Ta'ala, "And do not kill yourselves."[1]

---

[1] See Abul 'Ala Maududi's book, *Asas al-Iqtisad (Economic Principles)*, p.152.

CHAPTER THREE
THE *HALAL* AND THE *HARAM* IN MARRIAGE AND FAMILY LIFE

1. The Physical Appetites

2. Marriage

3. The Relationship Between Husband and Wife

4. Contraception

5. Divorce

6. The Relationship Between Parents and Children

1. The Physical Appetites

Allah Subhanahu wa Ta'ala created man as His vicegerent on earth in order that he might populate and rule it. Obviously this purpose cannot be realized unless the human species perpetuates itself, living, thriving, cultivating, manufacturing, building, and worshipping its Creator. Accordingly, the Creator has placed certain appetites and impulses in man so that he is impelled toward the various activities which guarantee the survival of the species.

Among the appetites which an individual must satisfy for his personal survival is that of food and drink. The sexual appetite, however, is for the purpose of the survival of the species. Sex is a strong driving force in the human being which demands satisfaction and fulfillment. Human beings have responded to the demands of the sexual appetite in three different ways:

1. One way is to satisfy ones sexual need freely with whomever is available and whenever one pleases, without any restraints of religion, morality, or custom. This is the position of the advocates of free sex, for they do not believe in any religion. This philosophy reduces the human being to the status of an animal, and, if practiced universally, would result in the destruction of the family structure and of all society as we know it.

2. The second approach is to suppress, and try to annihilate, the sexual drive; this approach is advocated by ascetic religions and other-worldly philosophies, approaches which lead toward monasticism and an escape from the world. Such advocacy of suppression of a natural appetite, or rather annihiliation of its functioning, is contrary to Allah's plan and purpose, and is in conflict with the course of the natural order which requires the use of this appetite for the continuity of life.

3. The third approach is to regulate the satisfaction of this urge, allowing it to operate within certain limits, neither suppressing nor giving it free rein. This is the stand of the revealed religions, which have instituted marriage and have prohibited fornication and adultery. In particular, Islam duly recognizes the role of the sexual drive, facilitates its

148

satisfaction through lawful marriage, and just as it strictly prohibits sex outside of marriage and even what is conducive to it, it also prohibits celibacy and the shunning of women.

This is the just and intermediate position. If marriage were not permitted, the sexual instinct would not play its role in the continuation of the human species; while if fornication and adultery were not prohibited, the foundation of the family would be eroded. Unquestionably, it is only in the shade of a stable family that mercy, love, affection, and the capacity to sacrifice for others develop in a human being, emotions without which a cohesive society cannot come into being. Thus, if there had been no family system, there would have been no society through which mankind would be able to progress toward perfection.

The Prohibition of Approaching *Zina*

It is not surprising that all the revealed religions[1] have prohibited fornication and adultery (*zina*) and have fought against these crimes against society. Islam, the last of the divinely revealed religions, is very strict in prohibiting *zina,* for it leads to confusion of lineage, child abuse, the breaking-up of families, bitterness in relationships, the spread of veneral diseases, and a general laxity in morals; moreover, it opens the door to a flood of lusts and self-gratifications. Assuredly, the command of Allah Ta'ala,

> And do not come near *zina*; indeed, it is an abomination
> and an evil way, (17:32), is just and true.

As we know, when Islam prohibits something, it closes all the avenues of approach to it. This is achieved by prohibiting every step and every means leading to the *haram*. Accordingly, whatever excites passions, opens ways for illicit sexual relations between a man and a woman, and promotes indecency and obscenity, is *haram.*

---

[1]See footnote [1], page 5.

Khulwah[1]

Islam prohibits *khulwah* between a man and a woman who are outside the degree of a *mahrem* relationship.[2] The reason for this is not a lack of trust in one or both of them; it is rather to protect them from wrong thoughts and sexual feelings which naturally arise within a man and a woman when they are alone together without the fear of intrusion by a third person. The Prophet (peace be on him) said:

> Whoever believes in Allah and the Last Day must never be in privacy with woman without there being a *mahrem* (of hers) with her, for otherwise Satan will be the third person (with them).[3]

Allah Ta'ala tells the Companions of the Prophet (peace be on him),

> ...And when you ask them (the Prophet's wives) for anything, ask them from behind a curtain; that is purer for your hearts and for their hearts....(33:35)

In an explanation of this verse, Imam al-Qurtabi says, "This means such thoughts as occur to men regarding women and to women regarding men. This will remove any possibility of suspicion and accusation, and will protect (their) honor. This command implies that no one should trust himself to be in privacy with a non-*mahrem* woman; the avoidance of such situations is better for one's purity of heart, strength of soul, and perfection of chastity."[4]

The Prophet (peace be on him) particularly warned women concerning *khulwah* with male-in-laws such as the husband's brother or cousin, since people are quite negligent in this regard,

---

[1]Privacy or *khulwah* denotes a man and woman's being alone together in a place in which there is no fear of intrusion by anyone else, so that an opportunity exists for sexual intimacy such as touching, kissing, embracing or even for intercourse.
[2]*Mahrem* denotes a relationship either by marriage or by close blood ties of such degree that marriage is permanently prohibited. With reference to a woman, a *mahrem* is either her husband or any male relative with whom marriage is permanently forbidden, such as her father, grandfather, son, brother, uncle or nephew. For the purposes of this discussion, all other relationships will be referred to as "non-*mahrem*." (Trans.)
[3]Reported by Ahmad on the authority of 'Amir ibn Rabi'ah.
[4]*Tafsir* of al-Qurtabi, vol. 14, p. 228.

sometimes with disastrous consequences. It is obvious that a relative has easier access than a stranger to a woman's quarters, something concerning which no one would question him. The same is true of the wife's non-*mahrem* relatives, and it is prohibited for any of them to be in *khulwah* with her. The Prophet (peace be on him) said:

'Beware of entering where women are.' A man from the Ansar asked, 'O Messenger of Allah, what about the in-law?' He replied, 'The in-law[1] is death.'[2]

He meant that there are inherent dangers and even destruction in such privacy: religion is destroyed if they commit sin; the wife is ruined if her husband divorces her out of jealousy; and social relationships are torn apart if relatives become suspicious of each other.

The danger lies not merely in the possibility of sexual temptation. It is even greater in relation to the possibility of gossip about what is private and personal between the husband and wife by those who cannot keep secrets to themselves and relish talking about others; such talk has ruined many a marriage and destroyed many a home. In explaining the meaning of "The in-law is death," Ibn al-Atheer says, "It is an Arabic figure of speech like, 'The lion is death' or 'The king is fire,' which means that meeting a lion is similar to facing death and a confrontation with a king is like being in the fire. Thus privacy between an in-law and a woman is far more dangerous than in the case of a stranger because he might persuade her to do things against her husband's wishes, such as asking him for things he cannot afford, nagging him, and the like."

Looking With Desire at the Opposite Sex

What Islam prohibits in the sphere of sex includes looking at a member of the opposite sex with desire; for the eye is the key to the

---

[1] Al-Nawawi explains, "The in-law here means a relative of the husband other than his father and sons (who are *mahrem* to his wife), such as his brother, nephew, and cousins, etc., with whom marriage would be permissible for her, if she were to be divorced or widowed." Al-Mazari is of the opinion that it includes the husband's father as well. See *Fath al-Bari*, vol. 11, p. 344.

[2] Reported by al-Bukhari and Muslim.

feelings, and the look is a messenger of desire, carrying the message of fornication or adultery. A poet of ancient times has said,

"All affairs begin with the sight;
The raging fire a spark can ignite,"
while a contemporary poet declares,
"A look, then a smile, then a nod of the head,
Then a talk, then a promise, then the warmth of a bed."

This is why Allah Subhanahu wa Ta'ala has commanded the believing men and the believing women alike to lower their gaze, together with His command to guard their sexual parts:

Tell the believing men that they should lower their gazes and guard their sexual organs; that is purer for them. Indeed, Allah is well-acquainted with what they do. And tell the believing women that they should lower their gazes and guard their sexual organs, and not display their adornment, except that which is apparent of it; and that they should draw their head-coverings over their bosoms, and not display their adornment except to their husbands or their fathers or their husbands' fathers, or their sons or their husbands' sons, or their brothers or their brothers' sons or their sisters' sons, or their women, or those whom their right hands possess, or male servants who lack sexual desire, or children who are not aware of women's nakedness; and that they should not strike their feet in order to make known what they hide of their adornment.... (24:30-31)

Several divine injunctions are contained in these two verses. Two of them pertain to both men and women, namely, the lowering of the gaze and the guarding of the sexual organs, while the rest are addressed exclusively to women.

A difference is to be noted here between the expressions, "lower their gazes" and "guard their sexual organs," signifying that while the sexual organs must be totally guarded without any leeway, the lowering of the gaze is only partial, because necessity and the general interest of the people require that some looking at members of the opposite sex be allowed.

152

"Lowering the gazes" does not mean that in the presence of the opposite sex the eyes should be shut or that the head should be bowed toward the ground, since this would be impossible; in another place the Qur'an says, "Lower thy voice" (31:19), which does not mean sealing the lips. Here "lowering of the gazes" means to avert one's gaze from the faces of the passers-by and not to caress the attractive features of the members of the opposite sex with one's eyes. The Prophet (peace be on him) told 'Ali ibn Abu Talib,

> "Ali, do not let a second look follow the first. The first look is allowed to you but not the second."[1]

The Prophet (peace be on him) considered hungry and lustful looks at a person of the opposite sex as "the *zina* of the eye," according to his saying,

> "The eyes also commit *zina*, and their *zina* is the lustful look."[2]

He termed the lustful look *zina* because it gives sexual pleasure and gratification in an unlawful way. This is also what Jesus (peace be on him) is reported to have said in the Gospel of Matthew:

> You have heard that it was said, 'You shall not commit adultery'. But I say to you that everyone who so much as looks at woman with evil desire for her has already committed adultery with her in his heart. (Matt. 5:27-28)

Indeed, such hungry and lustful looks are not merely a danger to chastity but they also result in agitation of the mind and disturbed thoughts. The poet says,

> If you let your looks go a-wandering,
> Many charming sights will make your heart pine.
> The one you see cannot belong to you altogether,
> Nor will your heart remain content with the little you saw.

---

[1]Reported by Ahmad, Abu Daoud, and al-Tirmidhi.
[2]Reported by al-Bukhari and others.

The Prohibition of Looking at the 'Awrah[1] of Others

Looking at the *'awrah* of another person must be avoided. The Prophet (peace be on him) forbade that any person should look at the *'arwah* of another, whether of the same or the opposite sex, and whether with or without desire, saying,

A man should not look at the *'arwah* of another man, nor a woman of a woman, nor should a man go under one cloth with another man, nor a woman with another woman.[2]

The *'awrah* of a man referred to in this *hadith* is from his navel to his knee, although some scholars, such as Ibn Hazm and some Maliki jurists, do not include the knee. With respect to a man who is not her *mahrem*, a woman's *'awrah* is her entire body excepting only her face and hands, while with respect to a *mahrem* such as her father or brother it is different. This we will discuss later.

What it is *haram* to look at is also of course *haram* to touch with the hands or with any other parts of the body.

What we have said concerning the prohibition of looking at or touching the parts of the body which must be covered becomes void in case of need or necessity such as first aid or medical treatment. At the same time, what we have said about the permissibility of looking becomes void in case of lust, as the ways leading to sin must be blocked.

What May Be Seen of the Man or Woman

It is clear from the above discussion that a woman may look at a man's body, apart from his *'awrah*, which is from the navel to the knee, provided that her looking is free of lust and that no temptation is feared. The Prophet (peace on him) let 'Aishah watch the

---

[1] *'Awrah* (lit., that which is to be hidden) denotes those parts of the body which Islam requires to be covered in front of others, whether of the same or the opposite sex. (Trans.)

[2] Reported by Muslim, Abu Daoud, and al-Tirmidhi. Scholars have inferred from this that two men, or two women, should not lie under the same covering so that parts of their bodies touch.

154

Abyssinians while they were engaging in spear play in the courtyard of the Prophet's mosque; she watched their performance until she had enough and retired.[1]

Similarly, a man is permitted to look at a woman's face and hands, since they are not part of her 'awrah, provided that the looking is without lust and that no temptation is feared. 'Aishah narrated that her sister Asma once came to the Prophet (peace be on him) clad in transparent clothes which revealed her body. The Prophet (peace be on him) averted his gaze and told her,

> 'Asma, when a woman begins to menstruate, nothing should be seen of her except this and this,' and he pointed to his face and hands.[2]

This *hadith* is classified as weak, but there are other sound *ahadith* which support the thesis that only the face and hands may be seen if they can be viewed without temptation.

In summary, the innocent look at what is other than the 'awrah of a man or a woman is permissible as long as it does not become an intent look or is repeated with perhaps a taint of pleasure and lust. It is the reasonableness of the Islamic *Shari'ah* that a glance which accidentally falls on something which it is not permissible to see is forgiven. Jarir ibn 'Abdullah narrated, "I asked the Messenger of Allah (peace be on him) about the unexpected glance. He replied, 'Avert your eyes,' meaning, do not look back deliberately."[3]

The Display of Women's Adornment: What Is Permissible and What Is Not

Thus far we have discussed the subject of the lowering of the gaze, which is commanded for both men and women in the two verses cited. These verses also contain other divine instructions. Says Allah Subhanahu wa Ta'ala:

> That they should...not display their adornment, except that which is apparent of it. (24:31)

---

[1] Reported by al-Bukhari and Muslim.
[2] Reported by Abu Daoud.
[3] Reported by Ahmad, Abu Daoud, Muslim, and al-Tirmidhi.

The adornment of women includes both natural features such as the face, hair, and other attractive parts of the body, and artificial enhancement of beauty, such as the dress, ornaments, make-up, and the like. In this noble *ayah* Allah Ta'ala commands women not to show their adornment "except that which is apparent of it."

There is some difference of opinion among scholars concerning the extent of this exception. Does it mean what is exposed by necessity and without intention, for example, if the wind exposes some part? Or does it mean what is customarily, or instinctively, or by its very nature exposed?

The majority of the early Muslim jurists accept the latter meaning. Ibn 'Abbas interprets "except what is apparent of it" to mean *kohl* and a ring, and Anas has said something similar; the permissibility of showing the face and hands is implicit in the permissibility of showing *kohl* and a ring. Sa'id ibn Jubayr, 'Ata and al-Awzai have stated explicitly that the showing of the face and hands is permissible. 'Aishah, Qatadah, and others have added bracelets to what may be shown of the adornments; this interpretation implies that a part of the arm may also be shown. Various scholars have allowed the exposure of the lower part of the arm up to a length varying between about four inches to one-half of the arm.

On the other hand, others such as 'Abdullah ibn Mas'ud, have restricted the application of "what is apparent" to what necessarily appears, such as the outer garment (*abaya, jilbab, chaddor, burqa,* and the like). My own preference lies with that group of the Companions and their immediate followers[1] who include the face, the hands, and their ordinary adornments, such as *kohl* and a ring in the application of the Qur'anic phrase, "except that which is apparent of it."

This permissibility, however, excludes such cosmetics which women today use for their cheeks, lips and nails. We consider these cosmetics to be excessive, and they must not be used except within a woman's own home when non-*mahrem* men are present. The aim of women in using these cosmetics when going out of the house is

---

[1] This is the preferred opinion of al-Tabari, al-Qurtabi, al-Zamakhshari, al-Razi, and others from among the interpreters of the Qur'an; one may refer to their explanations of this verse of *Surah al-Nur.*

obviously to attract the attention of men, which is *haram*. At the same time, however, the interpretation of "what is apparent" as being the outer garment or covering is not acceptable, for this is not something which can possibly be concealed so that an exemption must be made; similarly, what the wind blows cannot be controlled, whether an exemption is made or not. What strikes the mind is that the purpose of the exemption was to provide some concession for the believing woman by permitting her to show something which it is possible to conceal. Reason would indicate that it is the face and hands which are exempted from covering.

Assuredly a woman is permitted to show her face and hands because covering them would be a hardship on her, especially if she must go out on some lawful business. For example, a widow may have to work to support her children, or a woman who is not well-off may have to help her husbnad in his work; had covering the face and hands been made obligatory, it would have occasioned such women hardship and distress. Al-Qurtabi says,

> It seems probable that, since the face and hands are customarily uncovered, and it is, moreover, required that they be uncovered during acts of worship such as *salat* and *hajj*, the exemption (referred to in the verses of *Surah al-Nur)* pertains to them. This conclusion is supported by what Abu Daoud has transmitted on the authority of 'Aishah. She said that 'Asma, the daughter of Abu Bakr, once came to the Prophet (peace be on him) wearing transparent clothes. The Prophet (peace be on him) turned his face away from her and told her, 'Asma, when a woman begins to menstruate, nothing should be seen of her except this and this,' and he pointed to his face and hands.

In addition to this, we may infer from Allah's words, "Tell the believing men that they should lower their gazes," that the faces of the women of the Prophet's time were not veiled. Had the entire body including the face been covered, it would have made no sense to command them to lower their gaze, since there would have been nothing to be seen.

In spite of all this, however, because of the widespread immorality and laxity in obeying the Islamic injunctions in our time, the best thing for the Muslim woman is to conceal all her adornments, including her face if she can. Obviously, more caution in this regard is necessary for a woman who is beautiful. Allah Ta'ala also says,

...That they should draw their head-coverings over their bosoms....(24:31)

It is obligatory for the Muslim woman to cover her head, breasts, and neck completely so that nothing of them can be seen by onlookers. In addition, Allah Ta'ala says,

...And not display their adornment except to their husbands or their fathers....(24:31)

This injunction prohibits women to show their concealed adornments, such as the ears, hair, neck, breasts, or ankles, to men who are outside the *mahrem* relationship, before whom they are permitted to expose only the face and hands (of "that which is apparent").

Twelve categories of persons are exempted from this prohibition:

1. "Their husbands:" The husband and wife can see whatever they please of each other. A *hadith* states

   "Guard your nakedness *('awrah)* except in front of your wife."

2. "Their fathers," including the grandfathers from both mother's and father's sides as well.
3. "Their husbands' fathers," for these are regarded as fathers to women.
4. "Their sons," as likewise the grandsons from both sons and daughters.
5. "Their husbands' sons (stepsons)," a necessity for normal interaction, since the woman is regarded as their mother.
6. "Their brothers," including half - and step-brothers.
7. "Their brothers' sons," since marriage is permanently prohibited between a man and his paternal aunt.
8. "Their sisters' sons," since marriage is permanently prohibited between a man and his maternal aunt.
9. "Their women," Meaning female relatives and sisters-in-faith, that is, other Muslim women. As for non-Muslim women, they are not allowed to see the Muslim woman's

158

adornments other than what is allowed for non-*mahrem* men, and the correctness of this opinion is verified.

10. "Those whom their right hands possess," refers to bond-servants, because in Islam they are considered as members of the family. Some scholars restrict this permission to female bond-servants only.

11. "Male servants who lack sexual desire," refers to hired hands or household servants who, because of some physical or mental condition, are devoid of sexual desire. This is applicable only under the following two conditions: that they are the servants of those into whose houses they are given entry and that they lack sexual desire.

12. "Children who are not aware of women's nakedness." These are small children whose consciousness of sex is not yet developed. But if evidence of the sexual urge is noted among them, a woman should treat them like non-*mahrem* men even though they may not have reached puberty.

This verse does not mention maternal and paternal uncles because they customarily occupy the same status as the father. A *hadith* states,

"The man's uncle is like his father."[1]

Women's 'Awrah

Whatever of the woman's body is not allowed to be shown constitutes her *'awrah*. It must be covered, for exposing it is *haram*.

Consequently, with respect to non-*mahrem* men and non-Muslim women, a woman's *'awrah* is her entire body with the exception of her face and hands, according to the interpretation we have preferred. We agree with al-Razi's argument that Islam has permitted her to expose those parts of the body, the face and hands, which need to be exposed in order to carry out daily business and for giving and taking; it has commanded her to cover what it is not necessary to expose, and has forgiven her accidental, inadvertant

---

[1] Reported by Muslim.

exposures or such exposures as are required by necessity. All this is in accordance with the flexibility of Islam. Says al-Razi, "Since the showing of the face and hands is necessary, the jurists had no choice but to agree that they are not 'awrah, and since the showing of the feet is not necessary, they have differed concerning whether or not they are 'awrah."[1]

With respect to the above-mentioned twelve categories of mahrem relatives, a woman is permitted to expose her hair, ears, neck, upper part of the chest, arms, and legs. Other parts of her body, such as the back, abdomen, thighs and two private parts, are not to be exposed before anyone, man or woman, excepting her husband.

The above interpretation of the ayah is closer to its intent than that of some other scholars who say that, with respect to her muharramah[2] and other Muslim women, the woman's 'awrah is the area between her navel and knee. Rather, the intent of the ayah seems to support the opinion of some scholars who say that with respect to her muharramah the woman's 'awrah is that part which is not exopsed while she is doing her housework; that is, whatever is exposed during the course of her daily chores may be seen by men who are her muharramah.

That is why Allah Subhanahu wa Ta'ala commands the believing women to cover themselves with a loose over-garment whenever they go out, for in this way they may be distinguished from non-believing and loose women. Allah Ta'ala commanded His Prophet (peace be on him) to convey to the whole ummah of Islam this divine message:

> O Prophet! Tell thy wives and daughters and the believing women that they should put on their outer garments (jalabeebihinna);[3] that is most convenient in order that they may be recognized (as Muslims) and not be molested....(33:59)

During the period of jahiliyyah some women used to go out with the attractive parts of their bodies, such as the neck, upper part of the breast and hair, exposed, and the loafers and lechers would

---

[1] Tafsir of Fakhr al-Deen al-Razi, vol. 20, pp. 205-206.
[2] Plural of mahrem. (Trans.)
[3] That is, whenever they are outside the home or inside it when non-mahrem men are present. (Trans.)

160

follow them about. Accordingly, this noble *ayah* came down, commanding the believing woman to cover herself with her garment so that no provocative part of her body would be visible; because her appearance would make it clear to everyone that she is a chaste, believing woman, no lecher or hypocrite would dare to molest her.

It is clear from this verse that the reason for this injunction is not the fear of women's misbehavior or mistrust of them, as some people claim, but the danger to them from lecherous and evil men; for the woman who decks herself out, walks seductively, or talks invitingly always attracts men who lust after her. This verifies the Qur'anic verse,

> ...Then do not be too pleasant of speech, lest one in
> whose heart there is a disease should feel desire (for
> you)....(33:32)

Accordingly, Islam insists that the Muslim woman cover, and so protect herself; no concession is made in this except to reduce it somewhat for old women. Says Allah Ta'ala:

> And the elderly among women who are past (the
> prospect) of marriage — there is no blame on them if
> they lay aside their (outer) garments without
> displaying their adornment; but it is better for them to
> be modest. And Allah is Hearing, Knowing. (24:60)

By "the elderly among women" is meant such post-menopausal women as have no desire for mariage or sex, and to whom men are not attracted. Allah has made this concession for them so that they can put aside their covering garments, such as the *chaddor, abaya, burqa, jilbab,* and the like. However, the Qur'an makes the condition that this should not be for the purpose of displaying their adornment but only for ease and comfort. Despite this concession, it is preferable and better for them to be more perfect in their dignity and far removed from any suspicion: "but it is better for them to be modest." (24:60)

Concerning Women Going to Public Baths

In consideration of Islam's concern for women's *'awrah* and its proper covering, the Prophet (peace be on him) warned the Muslim

161

woman against entering public baths and disrobing in front of other women, who might subsequently make her physical characteristics a topic of their gossip and vulgar comments.

Similarly, the Prophet (peace be on him) warned the Muslim man against entering public baths without a waist wrapper. Jabir narrated that the Messenger of Allah (peace be on him) said,

> Whoever believes in Allah and the Last Day must not enter the public bath without a lower garment (to cover his private parts), and whoever believes in Allah and the Last Day must not let his wife go to the public bath.[1]

And 'Aishah said,

> At first the Messenger of Allah (peace be on him) prohibited people from going to public baths, but later allowed men to enter them wearing a lower garment.[2]

Exception to this prohibition is made for the woman who suffers from some illness for which warm baths are beneficial and for women following childbirth. 'Abdullah ibn 'Amr narrated that the Prophet (peace be on him) said concerning public baths that

> Men must not enter them without a lower garment. Prevent women from entering them except when sick or after childbirth.[3]

There is some weakness in the transmission of this *hadith*, but it is supported by the rules of the *Shari'ah* which makes concessions in worship and other obligations for a sick person, and by the well-known principle that what is prohibited as a precaution becomes permissible in the case of need or benefit. It is also supported by a *hadith* reported by al-Hakim on the authority of 'Abdullah ibn 'Abbas, who narrated that the Prophet (peace be on him) said,

> 'Beware of a building called the Public Bath.' Some people said, 'O Messenger of Allah, it certainly removes dirt and benefits the sick.' He then said, 'Then whoever enters should cover his nakedness.'[4]

---

[1] Al-Mondhari in *Al-Targheeb* says that this was reported by al-Nisai and by al-Tirmidhi, who classified it as "good." Al-Hakim reported it and called it "sound."
[2] The wording is from the report of Abu Daoud; also reported by al-Tirmidhi and Ibn Majah.
[3] Reported by Ibn Majah and Abu Daoud. One of the transmitters is Abdur-Rahman Ziyadah ibn 'An'am al-Ifriqi.
[4] Reported by al-Hakim, who classifies it as "sound."

162

If a woman enters a public bath without a valid reason or need, she has commited a *haram* act and deserves the censure of the Prophet (peace be on him). Abul Malih al-Hadhali reported that some women from Homs or Damascus came to visit 'Aishah and she said, "Are you from a place where women go to the public baths? I heard the Messenger of Allah (peace be on him) saying,

> A woman who removes her clothes (i.e., goes naked) outside her husbands's house tears doen the veil (*hijab*) between herself and her Lord."[1]

And Umm Salmah narrated that the Prophet (peace be on him) said,

> "If any woman takes off her clothes outside her own house, Allah will tear His covering from her."

When Islam takes such a strict view of women's entering public baths which are, after all, buildings with four walls in which only women are allowed, imagine its judgement concerning the nearly-nude women lying about on beaches and the swimming pools, exposing their nakedness to the hungry and lustful eyes of every passer-by without any sense of shame. Assuredly they have torn down every veil between themselves and their most Merciful Lord. And their men are partners in their sin, since they are responsible protectors of their women. If only they knew!

The Prohibition of the Display of Women's Attractions

The morals and manners of the Muslim woman are quite different from those of non-Muslim women and the women of the time of *jahiliyyah*. The Muslim woman is chaste, dignified, self-respecting, and modest, while the woman who is ignorant of the divine guidance may be vain, showy and anxious to display her attractions. Such display includes exposing the attractive parts of the body, walking or talking in a seductive manner, displaying her ornaments, wearing revealing and sexy clothes, and the like.

The variety of ways in which women display their attractions is no secret to people, ancient or modern. In commenting on the verse concerning the women of the Prophet's household,

---

[1]Reported with this wording by al-Tirmidhi; also reported by Abu Daoud, Ibn Majah, and al-Hakim, who classified it as "sound" (*al-targheeb*).

And be in your houses, and do not make a display of
yourselves in the manner of display of
jahiliyyah....,(33:33)

Mujahid remarks, "Women used to walk about among men.
Qatadah says, 'They used to walk in a seductive and sensuous
manner;' while Maqatil says, 'The displaying of attractions means
putting a cloth on the head without tying it, and toying with the
necklace, earrings, and other ornaments in a provocative fashion.'"

The ways in which women displayed themselves during the
period of pre-Islamic *jahiliyyah* included mingling freely with men,
walking seductively, and wearing a head-covering in a manner
which exposed the ornaments and beauties of the head and neck.
But during the present period of ignorance of the divine guidance
the display of feminine attractions has gone to such vulgar extremes
that the women of the pre-Islamic era appear in contrast to be
models of chastity and dignity!

How a Muslim Woman Should Conduct Herself

The correct Islamic behavior required of Muslim women which
keeps them from wantonly displaying their attractions is
characterized by the following:

(A) Lowering the gaze: Indeed, the most precious ornament of a
woman is modesty, and the best expression of modesty is in the
lowering of the gaze, as Allah Subhanahu wa Ta'ala says,

...And tell the believing women that they should lower
their gazes....(24:31)

(B) Not intermingling with men in such way that their bodies
come in contact or that men touch women, as happens so
often today in movie theaters, university classrooms,
auditoriums, buses, streetcars, and the like. Ma'qal ibn
Yasar narrated that the Messenger of Allah (peace be on
him) said,

It is better for one of you to be pricked in the head with

164

an iron pick than to touch a woman whom it is unlawful to touch[1]

(C) Her clothing must conform to the standards laid down by the Islamic *Shari'ah*, which are as follows:

(1) Her dress must cover her entire body with the exception of "that which is apparent," which, according to the most preferable interpretation, refers to the face and hands.

(2) It must not be transparent, revealing what is underneath it. The Prophet (peace be on him) has informed us that,

Among the dwellers of hell are such women as are clothed yet naked, seduced and being seduced. These shall not enter the Garden, nor shall (even) its fragrance reach them.

Here the meaning of "clothed yet naked" is that their light, thin, transparent garments do not conceal what is underneath. Once some women of Bani Tamim, who were clad in transparent clothes, came to see 'Aishah, and she remarked, "If you are Believers, these are not the clothes which befit believing women." On another occasion, when a bride wearing a sheer and transparent head-covering was brought into her presence, she commented, "A woman who dresses like this does not believe in *Surah al-Nur*."[2]

(3) Her dress must not be too tight so as to define the parts of her body, especially its curves, even though it may not be transparent. This describes many of the styles of clothing current in the sensuous, materialistic civilization of the Western world, whose fashion designers compete with one another in devising clothing for women which tantalizingly emphasizes the bustline, waist, and hips, etc., in order to elicit the lustful admiration of men. Women who wear such clothes likewise fall under the definiton of "clothed yet naked," since

---

[1]Al-Mondhari says, "It (this *hadith)* is reported by al-Tabarani and al-Bayhaqi, and al-Tabarani's transmitters are authentic and sound.
[2]*Surah* 24, which together with *Surah* 33 (*al-Ahzab*) contains many injunctions concerning purity and propriety, man-woman relations, and dress. (Trans.)

165

such a dress is often more provocative than one which is transparent.

(4) She must not wear clothes which are specifically for men, such as trousers in our time. The Prophet (peace be on him) cursed women who try to resemble men and men who resemble women, and prohibited women from wearing men's clothing and vice-versa.

(5) In her choice of clothing she should not imitate non-Muslims, whether they are Jews, Christians, or pagans, for Islam disapproves of conformity to non-Islamic modes and desires its followers to develop their own distinctive charcteristics in appearance, as well as in beliefs and attitudes. This is why Muslims have been asked to be different from non-Muslims in many aspects, and why the Prophet (peace be on him) has said,

"Whoever imitates a people is one of them."

(D) The Muslim woman walks and talks in a dignified and business-like manner, avoiding flirtatiousness in her facial expressions and movements. Flirting and seductive behavior are characteristics of wrong-minded women, not of Muslims. Allah Ta'ala says:

...Then do not be too pleasant of speech, lest one in whose heart there is a disease should feel desire (for you)....(33:32)

(E) She does not draw men's attention to her concealed adornment by the use of perfume or by jingling or toying with her ornaments or other such things. Allah says:

They should not strike their feet in order to make known what they hide of their adornment....(24:31)

The women of the time of *jahiliyyah* used to stamp their feet when they passed by men so that the jingling of their ankle-bracelets might be heard. The Qur'an forbade this, both because it might tempt a lecherous man to pursue her and also because it demonstrates the evil intention of the woman in attempting to draw the attention of men to herself. Similar is the Islamic ruling

166

concerning the use of fragrant perfumes, since here again the intention is to attract men by exciting their desire. A *hadith* states,

> The woman who perfumes herself and passes through a gathering is an adulteress.[1]

From all this we know that Islam does not require, as some people claim, that a woman should remain confined to her house until death takes her out to her grave. On the contrary, she may go out for *salat*, for her studies, and for her other lawful needs, both religious and secular, as was customary among the women of the families of the Companions and the women of later generations. Moreover, this early period of Islam is considered by all Muslims to be the best and most exemplary period in the history of Islam. Among the women of this time were those who took part in battles in the company of the Prophet himself (peace be on him), and after that under the caliphs and their commanders. The Messenger of Allah (peace be on him) told his wife Saudah,

> "Allah has permitted you to go out for your needs."[2]

He also said,

> "If someone's wife asks his permission to go to the mosque, he should not deny it to her."[3]

On another occasion he said,

> "Do not prevent the bond-maids of Allah from (going to) Allah's mosques."[4]

Some very strict scholars are of the opinion that a woman is not allowed to see any part of a man who is not her *mahrem*. They base their ruling on a *hadith* reported by al-Tirmidhi on the authority of Nabhan, the slave of Umm Salmah, that the Prophet (peace be on him) told Umm Salmah and Maymunah, his wives, to veil themselves when Ibn Umm Maktum entered. "But he is blind," they said. The Prophet (peace be on him) replied,

---

[1]Al-Mondhari says, "This is reported by Abu Daoud and al-Tirmidhi, who classifies it as sound and good." It has also been reported by al-Nisai, Ibn Khazimah, and Ibn Hibban in the following words: "Any woman who perfumes herself and passes by a group of people so that her scent reaches them is an adulteress." Al-Hakim also reported this and said, "It has sound transmitters."

[2]Reported by al-Bukhari in his book *Marriage* in the chapter entitled "Women May Go Out For Their Needs," on the authority of 'Aishah.

[3]Reported by al-Bukhari, on the authority of 'Umar.

[4]Reported by Muslim.

"But are you blind, too? Do you not see him?"

However, researchers say that the manner in which this *hadith* has been transmitted renders it unsound. While the narrator here is Umm Salmah, the transmitter is her slave Nabhan, who had no concern with the incident nor any need to report it. Even if the *hadith* is sound, it simply shows that the Prophet (peace be on him) was very strict in respect to his wives because their exceptional status required greater modesty on their part; Abu Daoud and other great scholars have commented on this exceptional position of the wives of the Prophet (peace be on him). In any case, the significance of the following well-established and sound *hadith* remains uncontested: The Prophet (peace be on him) instructed Fatimah bint Qais to spend the required period of confinement (*'iddah)* following the death of her husband at the house of Umm Sharik. But he later changed his mind, saying,

> My Companions gather in her house. Go and stay with Ibn Umm Maktum, since he is a blind man. If you uncover yourself he will not see you.[1]

A Woman's Serving Male Guests

A woman may serve her husband's guests in his presence as long as she adheres to the Islamic standards in her dress, movements, and speech. They will naturally see her and she will see them, and there is no harm in this as long as there is no danger of involvement on either side.

Al-Bukhari, Muslim, and others have reported Sahl ibn Sa'd al-Ansari as saying,

> Abu Usayd al-Sa'adi invited the Prophet (peace be on him) and his Companions to his wedding. The food was prepared and served by none other than his wife, Umm Usayd. She had soaked some dates in milk in a stone pot overnight. When the Prophet (peace be on him) had finished his meal, she mashed the dates and brought the drink to him.

Shaikh al-Islam Ibn Hajar commented that, "From this *hadith* we

---

[1] *Tafsir* of al-Qurtabi, vol. 11, p. 228.

168

conclude that a woman is permitted to serve her husband and his male visitors, just as the husband is permitted to serve his wife. It is evident that her serving the visitors is allowed only if there is no fear of temptation and if she is properly dressed; if the wife is not properly dressed (as is the case with a majority of women in our time) her appearing in front of men is *haram.*"

Sexual Perversion: A Major Sin

We must be aware that in regulating the sexual drive Islam has prohibited not only illicit sexual relations and all ways which lead to them, but also the sexual deviation known as homosexuality. This perverted act is a reversal of the natural order, a corruption of man's sexuality, and a crime against the rights of females.[1]

The spread of this depraved practice in a society disrupts its natural life pattern and makes those who practice it slaves to their lusts, depriving them of decent taste, decent morals, and a decent manner of living. The story of the people of the prophet Lut (Lot) as narrated in the Qur'an should be sufficient for us. Lut's people were addicted to this shameless depravity, abandoning natural, pure, lawful relations with women in the pursuit of this unnatural, foul and illicit practice. That is why their prophet, Lut (peace be on him), told them,

> What! Of all creatures, do you approach males and
> leave the spouses whom your Lord has created for you?
> Indeed, you are people transgressing (all limits)!
> (26:165-166)

The strangest expression of these peoples' perversity of nature, lack of guidance, depravity of morals, and aberration of taste was their attitude toward the guests of the prophet Lut (peace be on him) who were angels of punishment in human form sent by Allah to try these people and to expose their perversity. The Qur'an narrates the story thus:

> And when Our messengers came to Lut, he was grieved
> on their account and did not know how to protect them.

---

[1] The same applies equally in the case of female homosexuality. (Trans.)

169

He said, 'This is a day of distress.' And his people, who had long since been practicing abominations, came rushing toward him. He said, 'O my people, here are my daughters. They are purer for you, so fear Allah and do not disgrace me in front of my guests. Is there not a single upright man among you?' They said, 'Thou knowest well that we have no right to thy daughters, and certainly thou knowest what we want.' He said, 'If only I had strength to resist you or had some powerful support!' Said (the angels) 'O Lut, truly, we are messengers of thy Lord; they shall not reach thee....'(11:77-81)

The jurists of Islam have held differing opinions concerning the punishment for this abominable practice. Should it be the same as the punishment for fornication, or should both the active and passive participants be put to death? While such punishments may seem cruel, they have been suggested to maintain the purity of the Islamic society and to keep it clean of perverted elements.

A Ruling Concerning Masturbation

The pressing need to relieve himself of sexual tension may drive a young man to masturbation.

The majority of scholars consider it *haram*. Imam Malik bases his judgement on the verse,

Those who guard their sexual organs except with their spouses or those whom their right hands possess, for (with regard to them) they are without blame. But those who crave something beyond that are transgressors, (23:5-7)

arguing that the masturbator is one of those who "crave something beyond that."

On the other hand, it is reported that Imam Ahmad Ibn Hanbal regarded semen as an excretion of the body like other excreta and permitted its expulsion as blood letting is permitted. Ibn Hazm holds the same view. However, the Hanbali jurists permit masturbation only under two conditions: first, the fear of

170

committing fornication or adultery, and second, not having the means to marry.

We are inclined to accept the opinion of Imam Ahmad in a situation in which there is sexual excitation and danger of committing the *haram*. For example, a young man has gone abroad to study or work, thereby encountering many temptations which he fears he will be unable to resist, may resort to this method of relieving sexual tension provided he does not do it excessively or make it into a habit.

Yet better than this is the Prophet's advice to the Muslim youth who is unable to marry, namely, that he seek help through frequent fasting, for fasting nurtures will-power, teaches control of desires, and strengthens the fear of Allah. The Prophet (peace be on him) said,

> Young men, those of you who can support a wife should marry, for it keeps you from looking at women (lit., lowers your gaze) and preserves your chastity; but those who cannot should fast, for it is a means of cooling sexual passion.[1]

2. Marriage

No Monastacism in Islam

The stand of Islam is, on the one hand, against sexual license; consequently, it prohibits fornication and adultery, and blocks all ways leading to them. On the other hand, Islam is also against suppressing the sexual urge; accordingly, it calls people toward marriage, prohibiting renunciation and castration.[2]

As long as he possesses the means to marry, the Muslim is not permitted to refrain from marriage on the grounds that he has dedicated himself to the service or the worship of Allah and to a life of monastacism and renunciation of the world.

---

[1]Reported by al-Bukhari.
[2]Renunciation means remaining celibate and renouncing worldly activity for the sake of devoting oneself to the worship of God. Castration denotes suppressing sexual desire by removing the testicles.

171

The Prophet (peace be on him) noted a tendency toward monastacism among some of his Companions. Declaring this to be a deviation from the straight path of Islam and a rejection of his *sunnah* (recommended practice), he thereby rid Islam's conceptual framework of such a Christian notion. Abu Qulabah narrated, "Some of the Companions of the Prophet (peace be on him) decided to relinquish the world, forsake their wives, and become like monks. The Prophet (peace be on him) told them with asperity,

> People before you perished because of their asceticism; they made excessive demands on themselves until Allah brought hardships on them: you can still see a few of them remining in monastaries and temples. Then worship Allah and do not associate anything with Him, perform the *hajj* and the *'umrah*, be righteous, and all affairs will be set right for you."[1]

Abu Qulabah said the following verse was revealed concerning them:

> O you who believe! Do not make *haram* the good of things which Allah has made *halal* for you, and do not transgress; indeed, Allah does not like transgressors. (5:90 (87))

Mujahid narrated, "Some people, including 'Uthman ibn Maz'un and 'Abdullah ibn 'Umar, intended to renounce their wives, castrate themselves, and wear coarse clothing. Then the above verse and the verse following it were revealed."[2]

It is reported by al-Bukhari and others that three people came to the Prophet's wives and asked how the Prophet (peace be on him) conducted his worship. When they were told about it, they seemed to consider it but little, saying, "What a difference there is between us and the Messenger of Allah (peace be on him), whose past and future sins have been forgiven him by Allah!" One of them said, "As for me, I will always pray during the night." The other said, "I will have nothing to do with women and will never marry." When the Prophet (peace be on him) heard about this, he explained to them their error and deviation from the straight path, saying,

---

[1] Reported by 'Abdur Razzaq, Ibn Jarir, and Ibn al-Mundhir.
[2] Reported by Ibn Jarir in his *Tafsir*.

I am the one who fears Allah the most among you, yet I
fast and I break my fast, I pray and I sleep, and I marry
women. He who turns away from my *sunnah* has
nothing to do with me.

S'ad ibn Abi Waqqas said,

Allah's Messenger (peace be on him) objected to
'Uthman ibn Maz'un living in celibacy. If he had given
him permission (to do so), we (others) would have had
ourselves castrated.[1]

Addressing the young men of all times, the Prophet (peace be on
him) said,

'Young men, those of you who can support a wife should
marry, for it keeps you from looking at women and pre-
serves your chastity.'[2]

From this statement some scholars have inferred that marriage is
obligatory for the Muslim who is able to support a wife and that the
avoidance of it is not permisible, while other scholars add the
further condition for its obligatoriness that he should be afraid of
falling into sin.

In fact, it is not befitting that a Muslim should refrain from
marriage out of fear of poverty or of not being able to meet his
obligations. He should make every possible attempt to find
employment, seeking help from Allah, for He has promised to help
those who marry in order to protect their chastity and purity. Says
Allah Ta'ala:

And marry those among you who are single and the
virtuous ones among your slaves, male or female. If
they are in poverty, Allah will enrich them out of His
bounty....(24:33)

And the Messenger of Allah (peace be on him) said,

There are three who have a right to the help of Allah:
the one who marries out of the desire to live a chaste life,
the slave whose master has agreed to his buying his
freedom when he wishes to pay the sum, and the one
who fights in the cause of Allah.[3]

---

[1] Reported by al-Bukhari and Muslim.
[2] Reported by al-Bukhari.
[3] Reported by Ahmad, al-Nisai, al-Tirmidhi, Ibn Majah, and al-Hakim.

Seeing the Woman to Whom One Proposes Marriage

It is permissible for a Muslim man to see the woman to whom he intends to propose marriage before taking further steps so that he can enter into the marriage knowing what is ahead for him. Otherwise, if he has not seen her before marriage, he may not find her looks to his liking and may have regrets after he is married to her.

The eye is the messenger of the heart; when the eyes meet, the hearts and the souls of man and woman may meet as well. Muslim reported Abu Hurairah as saying that a man came to the Prophet (peace be on him) and told him that he had contracted to marry a woman of the Ansar. "Did you look at her?" the Prophet (peace be on him) asked. "No," he said,

> 'Then go and look at her,' said the Prophet (peace be on
> him), 'for there is something in the eyes of the Ansar,'

meaning that some of them have a defect of their eyes.

Al-Mughira ibn Shu'bah said,

> I asked for a woman in marriage and Allah's Messenger (peace be on him) asked me whether I had looked at her. When I replied that I had not, he said, 'Then look at her, for it may produce love between you.'
> I went to her parents and informed them of the Prophet's advice. They seemed to disapprove of the idea. Their daughter heard the conversation from her room and said, 'If the Prophet (peace be on him) has told you to look at me, then look.' I looked at her, and subsequently I married her.[1]

The Prophet (peace be on him) did not specify either to Mughirah or to the other man how much of the woman they were permitted to see. Some scholars are of the opinion that looking is limited to seeing the face and hands. However, it is permissible for anyone to see the face and hands as long as no desire is involved; therefore, if asking for woman in marriage is an exemption, obviously the man making the proposal should be able to see much more of the woman than that. The Prophet (peace be on him) said,

---

[1]Reported by Ahmad, Tirmidhi, Ibn Majah, Ibn Hibban, and Darimi.

When one of you asks for woman in marriage, if he is able to look at what will induce him to marry her, he should do so.[1]

Some scholars have gone to one extreme or another in relation to this permission, but the best course seems to be the middle one. One researcher considers it quite appropriate in our time that the man who is proposing be allowed to see the woman as she normally appears before her father, brother, and other *muharramah*. He says:

In the context of the above *hadith*, he may even accompany her, together with her father or some other *mahrem* as chaperone, on her usual visits to relatives or to public places, while clad in full *hijab*.[2] In this way he will have the opportunity to get an insight into her reasoning, behavior, and personality. this is a part of the meaning of the *hadith*, "...to look at what will induce him to marry her."[3]

If the man's intention of marriage is sincere, he is permitted to see the woman with or without her and her family's knowledge. Jarir ibn 'Abdullah said concerning his wife, "(Before marriage) I used to hide under a tree to see her."

From the *hadith* concerning al-Mughira we understand that the father of a girl cannot, out of deference to custom and tradition, prevent a suitor who is in earnest from seeing her, for customs and traditions must be governed by the *Shari'ah*. How is it possible that the Divine Law should be subjected to the whims of human beings? On the other hand, however, neither the father, the suitor, or the fiancee' can stretch this permission to such an extent that the young man and woman, under the pretext of bethrothal or engagement, go to movie theaters, clubs, and shopping places together without being accompanied by a *mahrem* of hers, a practice which has become common today among Muslims who are fond of imitating Western civilization and its customs.

---

[1]Reported by Abu Daoud.
[2]*Hijab* denotes the proper Islamic dress. (Trans.)
[3]Al-Bahee al-Khooly, *Al-Mar'ah Bain al-bayn al-bait wal-Mujtamah'*.

175

Prohibited Proposals

It is *haram* for a Muslim man to propose to a divorced or widowed woman during her *'iddah* (that is, the waiting period during which she is not allowed to remarry), for this waiting period is part of the previous marriage and may not be violated. Although one may, during this period, convey his desire for marriage through indirect hints or suggestions, it may not be done through an explicit proposal. Says Allah Ta'ala:

> And there is no blame on you in what you proclaim or hide in your minds concerning betrothal to women....(2:235)

It is likewise forbidden to the Muslim to propose to a woman who is already betrothed to a brother Muslim; the one whose proposal has already been accepted has acquired a right which must be safeguarded in consideration of goodwill and affection among people, especially among his brother Muslims. However, if the first suitor terminates his bethrothal or gives the second suitor his permission, there is no harm in proceeding with it.

Muslim reported that the Messenger of Allah (peace be on him) said,

> A Believer is a brother to another Believer. It is therefore not lawful for him to outbid his brother in buying something or to propose to a woman when his brother has done so, unless he gives him permission.

And al-Bukhari reported that the Prophet (peace be on him) said,

> A man must not propose to anther man's bethrothed unless he withdraws or gives him permission.

The Consent of the Girl

It is the girl's right to make a decision concerning her marriage, and her father or guardian is not permitted to override her objections or ignore her wishes. The Prophet (peace be on him) said,

> A woman who has been previously married has more right concerning her person than her guardian, and a

176

virgin's consent must be asked about herself, her consent being her silence.[1]

Ibn Majah and some other transmitters report the following *hadith:*

A girl came to the Prophet (peace be on him) and informed him that her father had married her to her cousin against her wishes, whereupon the Prophet (peace be on him) allowed her to exercise her choice. She then said, 'I am reconciled to what my father did but I wanted to make it known to women that fathers have no say in this matter.'

The father of a girl must not delay marriage of his daughter if a proposal is received from a man of equal status who is of sound religion and character. The Prophet (peace be on him) said,

Three matters should not be delayed: *salat* when its time comes, burial when the funeral has arrived, and the marriage of a single woman when a man of equal status has proposed.[2]

He further said

When someone with whose religion and character you are satisfied asks for your daughter in marrige, accede to his request. If you do not do so there will be corruption and great evil on the earth.[3]

Women To Whom Marriage is Prohibited

It is permanently *haram* for a Muslim to marry a woman who belongs to one of the following categories:

(1) The father's wife, whether divorced or widowed. During the period of *jahiliyyah* such marriages were allowed. Then Islam prohibited them, for once a woman is married to a man's father she acquires the status of his mother, and this prohibition is out of honor and respect for the father. Moreover, as this inviolable prohibition leaves no room for sexual attraction between the

---

[1]Reported by al-Bukhari and Muslim.
[2]Reported by al-Tirmidhi.
[3]Reported by al-Tirmidhi.

son and his step-mother, they are able to develop a relationship of respect and honor.

(2) The mother, including the grandmothers on both sides.
(3) The daughter, including the granddaughters from the son or daughter.
(4) The sister, including the half- and step sisters.
(5) The paternal aunt, whether she is the real, half, or step-sister of the father.
(6) The maternal aunt, whether she is the real, half, or step-sister of the father.
(7) The brother's daughter, i.e., his niece.
(8) The sister's daughter, i.e., his niece.

All these female blood-relatives are a man's *muharramat* and he is *mahrem* to his corresponding female relatives. Marriage to any *mahrem* whomsoever is permanently prohibited. The reasons for this prohibiton are as follows.

(A) Entertaining any sexual thoughts concerning such close relatives as one's mother, sister, and daughter is instinctively abhorrent to human nature; there are even certain animals which avoid mating with such closely-related animals. The respect a man feels for his aunts is like the respect he has for his mother, and likewise uncles are regarded as fathers.

(B) Since the family must live together in intimacy and privacy but without incestuous relations, the *Shari'ah* intends to cut at the roots of any sexual attraction among such close relatives.

(C) Since there is natural love and affection among such close blood relatives, the intent of the *Shari'ah* is to expand the circle of love and kinship by prohibiting incest and thereby directing the man's search for women outside the family. Thus each marriage extends the sphere of love, bringing new people within this ever-expanding network of affection: "And He has put love and mercy between you." (30:21)

(D) The natural sentiments of love and affection between a man and the above-mentioned female relatives must be kept strong forever. If marriage were permitted between such relatives, it would cause jealousies, dissensions, and the disruption of families, destroying the very sentiments of love and affection

178

which give cohesiveness and permanence to the family structure.

(E) The offspring of marriages to such close blood relatives would most probably be defective and weak. Moreover, if physical or mental defects are present in the members of a family, they would become more pronounced among the children of such marriages.

(F) The woman needs someone to champion her rights and support her case against her husband, especially when relations between the two of them become strained. If those women who could defend her became rivals, how would this be possible?

Marriages Prohibited by Reason of Fosterage:

(9) *The foster mother*: It is *haram* for a Muslim to marry a woman who has suckled him during his infancy, for suckling makes her like his real mother, since milk has gone into the making of his flesh and bones. Nursing consciously or unconsciously produces feelings of motherhood in a woman and of kinship in a child, and although these feelings might seem to disappear as the child grows and becomes a man, they remain hidden in the unconscious.

However, the prohibtion of marriage based on fosterage is effective only if the suckling occured before the time of weaning; that is, when milk was the primary source of food. Another condition is that the child has suckled his fill on five separate occasions, a fill being defined as when the child leaves off suckling of his own accord. After a survey of all the *ahadith* on this subject, the fixing of five sucklings as the minimum seems to be the preferred view.

10. *Foster sisters*: Just as a woman becoms a mother to a child by virtue of suckling, likewise her daughters become his sisters, her sisters his aunts, and so on. The Prophet (peace be on him) said:

"What is *haram* by reason of genealogy is *haram* by reason of fosterage."[1]

---

[1]Reported by al-Bukhari and Muslim.

179

Thus the foster-sisters, foster-aunts, and foster-nieces are all *muharramat* and marriage to them is permanently prohibited.

In-Law Relationships:

11. *The mother-in-law*: Marriage to the wife's mother is permanently prohibited from the time a man enters into a marriage contract with a woman, whether he and his wife have engaged in sexual intercourse or not. The act of marriage itself gives the mother-in-law the same status as the mother.

12. *The step-daughter*: A man cannot marry his step-daughter (his wife's daughter by a previous marriage) if sexual intercourse has taken place with her mother, his wife. However, if a man divorces his wife without having had intercourse with her, it is permissible for him to marry her daughter by a previous marriage.

13. *The daughter-in-law*: That is, the wife of the real son, not that of the adopted son. In fact, Islam abolished the permissibility of the system of legal, formalized adoption, because this is contrary to fact and to reality, resulting in the prohibiting of what is essentially *halal* and the permitting of what is essentially *haram*. Allah Ta'ala says:

    ...Nor has He made your sons by adoption your (real) sons. Those are simply words from your mouths....(33:4)

    meaning that it is merely an expression of the language which does not alter reality nor transform an outsider to the family into a blood relative.

These three types of female relatives are forbidden in marriage in order that peaceful relationships may be maintained among the in-laws.

Sisters as Co-Wives

14. As opposed to the practice of the period of *jahiliyyah*, Islam forbade taking two sisters as co-wives, at the same time because the feeling of love and sisterliness which Islam wants to maintain betwen sisters would be destroyed if one sister became

the co-wife of the same husband. While the Qur'an mentioned the two sisters, the Prophet (peace be on him) added,

A man may not be married to a woman and her paternal aunt (at the same time), nor to a woman and her maternal aunt.[1]

and he said,

If you do this, you will sever your ties of kinship,[2]

and how could Islam permit the breaking of such kinship ties when it places so much importance on them?

Married Women

15. As long as a woman is married, her marriage to any other man is prohibited. She may marry another man only when two conditions are fulfilled:

   (1) Her marriage tie is broken either because of the death of her husband or because of divorce;
   (2) She has completed the period of waiting (*'iddah*) ordained by Allah. For a pregnant woman this period ends when she delivers the baby. If she is widowed but not pregnant, the period of *'iddah* is four months and ten days, while if she is divorced and it is not known whether or not she is pregnant, the *'iddah* is three menstrual cycles. This *'iddah* relates to the woman who has menstrual periods; for a woman who does not menstruate, the *'iddah* is three months. Allah Ta'ala says:

   And divorced women shall wait concerning themselves for three monthly periods. And it is not permissible for them to conceal what Allah has created in their wombs, if they believe in Allah and the Last Day.   (2:228)

and

---

[1] Reported by al-Bukhari and Muslim.
[2] Reported by Ibn Hibban.

As for those who have no further expectation of menstruation among your women, if you are in doubt, the waiting period is three months, as well as for those who have no menses. And for those who are pregnant, their period is until they deliver their burdens,(65:4)

and,

For those of you who die and leave behind widows, they shall wait concerning themselves for four months and ten days....(2:234)

Of these fifteen categories of female relatives to whom marriage is prohibited, fourteen are mentioned in *Surah al-Nisa:*

And do not marry those women whom your fathers married, except what is past; indeed, it was an indecency and an abomination, and an evil path. Forbidden to you are your mothers and your daughters, and your sisters and your father's sisters and your mothers's sisters, and your brothers' daughters and your sisters' daughters, and your foster mothers and your foster sisters, your wives' mothers, your step-daughters under your guardianship born of your wives to whom you have gone in — and if you have not gone into them there is no blame on you — and the wives of your sons proceeding from your loins, and that you should marry two sisters at one time, except what is past; indeed Allah is Forgiving, Merciful. (4:22-23)

The prohibition against being married to a woman and any of her aunts at the same timne is derived from the *hadith* cited above.

Mushrik Women [1]

16. A woman who is *mushrik*, that is, who worships idols or associates other deities with Allah, is also among those who are prohibited. Allah Ta'ala says,

---

[1] *Mushrik* denotes someone who commits *shirk*, or ascribes partners to Allah by his polytheistic beliefs or idolatrous practices. (Trans.)

And do not marry *mushrik* women until they believe, for a believing bondmaid is better than a *mushrik* woman, even though you may admire her. And do not marry (your girls) to *mushrik* men until they believe, for a believing bondsman is better than a *mushrik*, even though you may admire him. They (*mushrikeen*) invite you to the Fire, but Allah invites you to the Garden and to forgiveness by His grace....(2:221)

This verse proclaims that a Muslim man may not marry a *mushrik* woman nor may a Muslim woman marry a *mushrik* man, because there is a great, unbridgeable gulf between the two systems of belief. Islam invites people to the Garden of Paradise, while *shirk* (idolatry or polytheism) leads them to the Fire of Hell. While Muslims believe in God, His messengers, and the Hereafter, *mushrikeen* associate others with God, reject His messengers, and deny the Hereafter. Marriage means living under one roof in harmony and love; how then would it be possible for such conflicting beliefs and practices to co-exist peacefully together in one abode?

Marriage to the Women of the People of the Book

Islam has made marriage to Jewish or Christian women lawful for Muslim men, for they are *Ahl al-Kitab*, that is, People of the Book, or people whose tradition is based upon a divinely revealed Scripture. Although they have distorted and altered it, they do possess a religion of divine origin, and hence Islam has made some exceptions in dealing with them. The Qur'an says:

...And the food of those who were given the Scripture (before you) is permitted to you and your food is permitted to them. And (lawful to you in marriage are) chaste women from the Believers and chaste women from those who were given the Scripture before you, when you give them their due dowers, desiring chastity, not lewdness or secret intrigues....(5:6: (5))

Tolerance of such a degree is a characteristic of Islam which is

183

hardly to be found among other faiths and nations. Despite the fact that Islam takes the People of the Book to task for their unbelief and error, it permits the Muslim to marry a Christian or Jewish woman, who may, as his consort, the mistress of his house, the mother of his children, the source of his repose, and his companion for life, retain her own faith — all this, while the Qur'an says concerning marriage and its mystique,

> And among His signs is that He created for you mates
> from among yourselves, that you may dwell with them
> in tranquility, and He has put love and mercy between
> you....(30:21)

However, a warning is in order here. In order of preference, a believing, practicing Muslim woman who loves her religion is preferable to a nominal Muslim woman who has inherited Islam from her parents. The Prophet (peace be on him) said,

> "Get the one who is religious and prosper." [1]

It is also obvious that a Muslim woman, regardless of who she is, is better suited to a Muslim man than a woman of Christian or Jewish faith, regardless of her merits. If a Muslim man has the slightest suspicion that a non-Muslim wife might affect the beliefs and attitudes of his children, it becomes obligatory on him to exercise caution.

If the number of Muslims in a country is small — for example, if they are immigrants residing in a non-Muslim country — their men ought to be prohibited from marrying non-Muslim women because, since Musilm women are prohibited from marrying non-Muslim men, their marriage to non-Muslim women means that many Muslim girls will remain unmarried. Since this situation is injurious to the Muslim society, this injury can be avoided by temporarily suspending this permission.

The Prohibition of a Muslim Woman's Marrying a Non-Muslim Man

It is *haram* for a Muslim woman to marry a non-Muslim man,

---

[1]Reported by al-Bukhari.

regardless of whether he of the People of the Book or not. We have already mentioned the saying of Allah Ta'ala,

> ...And do not marry (your girls) to idolaters until they believe....(2:221)

And He said concerning the immigrant Muslim women,

> ...Then if you know them to be Believers, do not send them back to the unbelievers. They are not *halal* for them (as wives), nor are they *halal* for them (as husbands). (60:10)

No text exists which makes exceptions for the People of the Book; hence, on the basis of the above verses, there is a consensus among Muslims concerning this prohibition.

Thus, while a Muslim man is permitted to marry a Christian or Jewish woman, a Muslim woman is not allowed to marry a Christian or Jewish man. There are many sound reasons for this difference. First, the man is the head of the household, the one who maintains the family, and he is responsible for his wife. And while Islam guarantees freedom of belief and practice to the Christian or Jewish wife of a Muslim, safeguarding her rights according to her own faith, other religions, such as Judaism and Christianity, do not guarantee the wife of a different faith freedom of belief and practice, nor do they safeguard her rights. Since this is the case, how can Islam take chances on the future of its daughters by giving them into the hands of people who neither honor their religion nor are concerned to protect their rights?

A marriage between a man and woman of different faiths can be based only on the husband's respect for his wife's beliefs; otherwise a good relationship can never develop. Now, the Muslim believes that both Judaism and Christianity originated in divine revelation, although later distortions were introduced into them. He also believes that God revealed the *Taurat* to Moses and the *Injeel* to Jesus,[1] and that both Moses and Jesus (peace be on them) were among the messengers of Allah who were distinguished by their steadfast determination. Accordingly, the Christian or Jewish wife

---

[1] *Taurat* refers to the original scripture revealed to the Prophet Moses by God, and *Injeel* to the Prophet Jesus. These are not to be confused with either the existing Torah or Old Testament, or the four Gospels of the New Testament. (Trans.)

185

of a Muslim lives under the protection of a man who respects the basic tenets of her faith, her scripture, and her prophets, while in contrast to this the Jew or Christian recognizes neither the divine origin of Islam, its Book, or its Prophet (peace be on him). How then could a Muslim woman live with such a man, while her religion requires of her the observance of certain worships, duties, and obligations, as well as certain prohibitions. It would be impossible for the Muslim woman to retain her respect for her beliefs as well as to practice her religion properly if she were opposed in this regard by the master of the house at every step.

It will be realized from this that Islam is consistent with itself in prohibitng the Muslim man to marry a *mushrik* woman, for since Islam is absolutely opposed to *shirk*, it would obviously be impossible for two such people to live together in harmony and love.

Fornicatresses

17. Here "fornicatresses" (*al-zaniyah*) denotes women who earn money through prostitution. It is reported that Marthad ibn Abu Marthad asked the Prophet's permission to marry a prostitute named 'Anaq with whom he had relations during the pre-Islamic period. The Prophet (peace be on him) did not give him an answer until Allah revealed,

    The fornicator shall not marry anyone except a fornicatress or an idolatress, and the fornicatress shall not marry anyone but a fornicator or an idolator, and that (marrying them) is *haram* for the Believers. (24:3)

    The Prophet (peace be on him) then recited this verse to Marthad and said,

    "Do not marry her."[1]

    Allah Subhanahu wa Ta'ala has permitted Muslims to marry chaste believing women or chaste women of the People of the Book. Similarly, He has made marriage lawful to men on the condition that they seek it "in honest wedlock, not in lust." (4:24). Accordingly, if someone does

---

[1]This story is reported by Abu Daoud, al-Nisai, and al-Tirmidhi.

not accept this command from the Book of Allah, nor considers it binding, he is a *mushrik*[1], and no one will agree to marry him except another *mushrik*. If someone accepts this command as binding, but despite this he marries a fornicatress to whom marriage has been prohibited, he becomes a fornicator himself.

This *ayah* just cited comes after the *ayah* prescribing the punishment of flogging for fornicators:[2]

Flog the woman and the man guilty of fornication each with a hundred stripes....(24:2)

While this is a corporal punishment, the punishment mentioned in 24:3 is a civil punishment, for depriving fornicators of the right to marry chaste women is like depriving someone of citizenship, nationality, or some other civil right as a punishment for a crime.

Ibn al-Qayyim, after explaining the meaning of the previously-cited verse goes on to say:

This explicit injunction of the Qur'an is what human nature and reason demand. Allah Ta'ala prohibits His slave (the Muslim man) to become a pimp to his wayward wife, as He made man's nature with an instinctive abhorrence and contempt for acting as a pimp. This is why, when people want to abuse someone in the most disparaging manner, they call him 'the husband of a whore;' and Allah does not permit the Muslim to be like that.

Further light is thrown on this prohibiton by considering the crime of the woman against her husband and society. She defiles the bed of her husband and perverts the lineage which Allah desires to preserve for the integrity and smooth functioning of society, which He counts as one of His favors upon

---

[1] As we saw in Chapter One in the discussion concerning Allah's sole right to legislate the *halal* and *haram* for His servants, anyone who disobeys or disregards this explicit command of Allah Ta'ala is considered a *mushrik* or an associator.

[2] This punishment has been prescribed for the unmarried fornicator and his partner, while the punishment of death by stoning, if the crime is proved either by four male adult eye witnesses to the act or by self-confession, has been prescribed for the married adulterer and his partner. (Trans.)

mankind. Adultery leads to the confounding and doubting of parentage. It is thus one of the beauties of the Islamic *Shari'ah* that it prohibits marriage to a prostitute until she repents and demonstates that she is not pregnant (that is, until she has a menstrual period in order to ascertain that she is not carrying a child).[1]

Moreover, a prostitute is a vile and degraded woman. Allah has ordained that marriage be a source of affection and mercy between the spouses. How then could a vile woman be the object of love of a virtuous man, since the partners in a marriage must be akin in their ideas, attitudes, and characters if true love and understanding are to develop between them. As vileness and virtue are antithetical to each other both by nature and by considerations of morality, there cannot even be a sympathy, much less love and affection, between the two. Indeed, Allah Subhanahu wa Ta'ala has spoken truly in His saying,

> Vile women are for vile men, and vile men are for vile women; virtuous women are for virtuous men and virtuous men are for virtuous women. (24:26)

Temporary Marriage (Mut'ah)

Marriage in Islam is a strong bond, a binding contract, based on the intention of both partners to live together permanently in order to attain, as individuals, the benefit of the repose, affection, and mercy which are mentioned in the Qur'an, as well as to attain the social goal of the reproduction and perpetuation of the human species:

> And Allah has made for our spouses of your own nature, and from your spouses has made for you sons and grandsons....(16:72)

Now, in temporary marriage (known in Arabic as *mut'ah*), which is contracted by the two parties to last for a specified period of time

---

[1] *Ighathat al-Lahfan*, vol. 1, pp. 66-67.

in exchange for a specified sum of money, the above-mentioned purposes of marriage are not realized. While the Prophet (peace be on him) permitted temporary marriage during journeys and military campaigns before the Islamic legislative process was complete, he later forbde it and made it forever *haram.*

The reason for it was permitted in the beginning was that the Muslims were passing through what might be called a period of transition from *jahiliyyah* to Islam. Fornication was very common and wide-spread among the pre-Islamic Arabs. After the advent of Islam, when they were required to go on military expeditions, they were under great pressure as a result of being absent from their wives for long periods of time. Among the Believers were some who were strong in faith and others who were weak. The weak ones feared that they would be tempted to commit adultery, a major sin and an evil course, while the strong in faith, on the other hand, were ready to castrate themselves, as stated by Ibn Mas'ud:

> We were on an expedition with the Messenger of Allah (peace be on him) and did not have our wives with us, so we asked Allah's Messenger (peace be on him), 'Should we not castrate ourselves?'[1] He forbade us to do so but permitted us to contract marriage with a woman up to a specified date, giving her a garment as a dower *(mahr)*[2]

Thus temporary marriage provided a solution to the dilemma in which both the weak and the strong found themselves. It was also a step toward the final legalization of the complete marital life in which the objectives of permanence, chastity, reproduction, love, and mercy, as well as the widening of the circle of relationships through marriage ties were to be realized.

We may recall that the Qur'an adopted a gradual course in prohibiting intoxicants and usury, as these two evils were widespread and deeply rooted in the *jahili* society. In the same manner, the Prophet (peace be on him) adopted a course of gradualism in the matter of sex, at first permitting temporary marriage as a step leading away from fornication and adultery, and at the same time coming closer to the permanent marriage

---

[1]The reason for this request was the desire to maintain their purity of mind and body, which was in danger of being affected by their unmet needs. (Trans.)
[2]Reported by al-Bukhari and Muslim.

relationship. He then prohibited it absolutely, as has been reported by 'Ali and many other Companions. Muslim has reported this in his *Sahih*, mentioning that al-Juhani was with the Prophet (peace be on him) at the conquest of Makkah and that the Prophet (peace be on him) gave some Muslims permission to contract temporary marriages. Al-Juhani said, "Before leaving Makkah the Messenger of Allah(peace be on him) prohibited it." In another version of the *hadith* we find the Prophet's own words,

> "Allah has made it *haram* until the Day of Resurrection."

The question then remains—Is temporary marriage (*mut'ah*) absolutely *haram*, like marriage to one's own mother or daughter, or is it like the prohibition concerning the eating of pork or dead meat, which becomes permissible under real necessity, the necesity in this case being the fear of commiting the sin of *zina?*

The majority of the Companions held the view that after the completion of the Islamic legislation, temporary marriage was made absoulutely *haram*. Ibn 'Abbas, however, held a different opinion, permitting it under necessity. A person asked him about marrying women on a temporary basis and he permitted him to do so. A servant of his then asked, "Is this not under hard conditions, when women are few and the like?" and he replied, "Yes."[1] Later, however, when Ibn 'Abbas saw that people had become lax and were engaging in temporary mariages without necessity, he withdrew his ruling, reversing his opinion.[2]

Marrying More Than One Woman

Islam is a way of life consonant with nature, providing human solutions to complex situations and avoiding extremes. This characteristic of Islam can be observed most clearly in its stand concerning the taking of more than one wife. Islam permits the Muslim to marry more than one woman in order to resolve some very pressing human problems, individual as well as social.

---

[1] Reported by al-Bukhari.
[2] *Zad al-Mi'ad*, vol. 4, p. 7. Bayhaqi transmitted it and Muslim as well.

Many peoples and religions prior to Islam permitted marriage to a host of women, whose number reached tens and sometimes hundreds, without any condition or restriction. Islam, on the other hand, laid down definite restrictions and conditions for polygamy.

With regard to the restriction, it limited to four the maximum number of wives a man might have. When Ghailan al-Thaqafi accepted Islam, he had ten wives.

"Choose four of them and divorce the rest,"[1]

the Prophet (peace be on him) told him. Similarly, some men who had eight[2] or five[3] wives at the time of embracing Islam were told by the Prophet (peace be on him) to retain only four.

The case of the Prophet (peace be on him), who himself had nine wives, was exempted from this by Allah for the sake of *da'wah* (the propagation of the message of Islam) during his lifetime and because of the need of the Muslim *ummah* after his death.

Justice Among Wives - A Condition

The condition which Islam lays down for permitting a man to have more than one wife is confidence on his part that he will be able to deal equitably with his two or more wives in the matter of food, drink, housing, clothing and expenses, as well as in the division of his time between them. Anyone who lacks the assurance that he will be able to fulfill all these obligations with justice and equlity is prohibited by Allah Ta'ala from marrying more than one woman, for Allah Ta'la says:

...But if you fear that you will not be able to do justice (among them), then (marry) only one....(4:3)

And the Prophet (peace be on him) said,

Anyone who has two wives and does not treat them equally will come on the Day of Resurrection dragging one part of his body which will be hanging down.[4]

[1]Reported by al-Shafi'i, Ahmad, al-Tirmidhi, Ibn Majah, Ibn Abi Shaybah, al-Darqutni, and Bayhaqi.
[2]Reported by Abu Daoud in his *Musnad*.
[3]Reported by Ahmad, al-Darimi, Ibn Hibban, al-Hakim, and the compilers of *Sunan* (Abu Daoud, al-Nisai, and Ibn Majah).
[4]Reported by the compilers of *Sunan* and by Ibn Hibban and al-Hakim.

The equal treatment mentioned here pertains to the *rights* of the wives, not to the love the husband feels towad them, for equality in the division of love is beyond human capacity and any imbalance in this regard is forgiven by Allah Ta'ala who says:

> And you will not be able to do justice among (your) wives, however much you may wish to. But do not turn away (from one of them) altogether....(4:139)

This is why the Prophet (peace be on him) used to divide his time among his wives equally, saying,

> O Allah, this is my division in regard to what I can control. Then do not take me to task regarding what Thou controllest and I do not control,[1]

referring to the attachment and affection which he felt for one particular wife. And when he planned to go on a journey, Allah's Messenger (peace be on him) would cast lots among his wives, and the one who was chosen by lot would accompany him.[2]

Why Marraige to More Than One Woman is Permitted in Islam

Islam is the last and final word of Allah Subhanahu wa Ta'ala, ending the series of His messages to mankind. It therefore came with a general law suitable for all times and places, and for the whole of humanity. It did not legislate for the city dweller only, while neglecting the nomad, nor for the cold regions while ignoring the hot ones, nor for one particular period of time, forgetting later times and the generations to come.

Islam recognizes the needs and interests of all people, of individuals as well as groups. And among human beings one finds that individual who has a strong desire for children but whose wife is barren, chronically ill, or has some other problem. Would it not be more considerate on her part and better for him that he marry a second wife who can bear him children, while retaining the first wife with all her rights guaranteed?

Then there may also be the case of a man whose desire for sex is

---

[1]Reported by the compilers of *Sunan*.
[2]Reported by al-Bukhari and Muslim.

192

strong, while his wife has little desire for it, or who is chronically ill, has long menstrual periods, or the like, while her husband is unable to restrain his sexual urge. Should it not be permitted to him to marry a second wife instead of his hunting around for girlfriends?

There are also times when women outnumber men, as for example after wars which often decimate the ranks of men. In such a situation, it is in the interests of the society and of women themselves that they become co-wives to a man instead of spending their entire lives without marriage, deprived of the peace, affection, and protection of marital life and the joy of motherhood for which they naturally yearn with all their hearts.

Only three possible alternatives exist for such surplus women who are not married as first wives:

(1) to pass their whole lives in bitter deprivation,
(2) to become sex objects and playthings for lecherous men; or
(3) to become co-wives to men who are able to support more than
     one wife and who will treat them kindly.

Unquestionably, the last alternative is the correct solution, a healing remedy for this problem, and that is the judgement of Islam:

> And Who is better than Allah in judgement, for a people
> who have certain faith? (5:53 (50))

For this is the Islamic "polygamy" which people in the West consider so abhorrent and to which they react with such hostility, while their own men are free to have any number of girlfriends, without restriction and without any legal or moral accountability, either in respect to the woman or to the children she may bear as a result of this irreligious and immoral plurality of extra-marital relationships. Let the two alternatives — plurality of wives or plurality of illicit affairs — be compared, and let people ask themselves which is the proper course of action, and which of the two groups is correctly guided!

3. The Relationship Between Husband and Wife

The Qur'an emphasizes the spiritual objectives of marriage, making them the foundations of marital life. These objectives are realized in the peace of mind which comes through wholesome sexual experience with the spouse whom one loves, in the enlargement of the circle of love and affection between the two families united through marriage, and in the nurturing of affection and tenderness among the children under the loving care of their parents. These are the objectives mentioned by Allah Ta'ala:

> And among His signs is that He created for you mates
> from among yourselves, that you may dwell with them
> in tranquility, and He has put love and mercy between
> you. Indeed, in this are signs for those who reflect.
> (30:21)

The Sexual Relationship

At the same time, the Qur'an does not neglect the sensual aspect and the physical relationship between husband and wife. It guides human beings to the best path, fufilling the demands of the sexual urge while avoiding harmful or deviant practices.

It is reported that the Jews and Zoroastrians used to go to extremes in avoiding any physical contact with menstruating women, while the Christians continue to have sexual relations with them without regard to the flow of blood. The Arabs of the period of *jahiliyyah* would not eat, drink, or sit with women who were menstruating and would send them to separate dwelling just as the Jews and Zoroastrians did.

Accordingly, some Muslims asked the Prophet (peace be on him) about what is permitted and what is forbidden in relation to menstruating women. The following verse was then revealed:

> And they ask thee about menstruation. Say: It is a hurt,
> so refrain from women during their menstruation and
> do not approach them until they are cleansed. And
> when they have cleansed themselves you may go in to
> them in the manner ordained by Allah; indeed, Allah
> loves those who turn to Him and He loves those who are
> clean. (2:222)

Some people understood the phrase, "Refrain from women," as meaning that they should not live together in the same house during the menstrual periods. The Prophet (peace be on him) then explained the correct meaning of this verse, saying,

194

I ordered you only to refrain from having intercourse
with menstruating women and did not tell you to send
them out of the house as the foreigners do.

When the Jews of Madinah heard this they said, "This man does not
like to leave any part of what we do unchanged, but does the
opposite."[1]

Thus the Muslim can fondle and enjoy his menstruating wife,
avoiding only the place of hurt. The Islamic position in this regard
is, as always, a middle one, between the one extreme of expelling the
menstruating woman from the house and the other extreme of
having intercourse with her.

Recent medical researchers have discovered that the menstrual
flow contains a toxic substance which, if undischarged, may be
harmful to the body. Likewise, they have discovered the reason why
intercourse should be avoided during this time. The reproductive
organs become highly congested and the nerves very sensitive due
to the secretion of the internal glands; consequently, intercourse
may irritate them, possibly impeding the menstrual flow and
causing inflammation of the sexual organs.[2]

Prohibited Intercourse

Concerning the sensual relationship, these words of Allah Ta'ala
were revealed:

Your wives are a tillage to you, so go in to your tillage as
you will, and send (ahead something) for your souls;
and fear Allah and know that you will (one day) meet
Him, and give glad tidings to the Believers.   (2:223)

The Indian scholar, Waliullah Dehlavi, in explaining the
occasion of the revelation of this ayah and its significance says:

The Jews had unnecessarily restricted the postures of
sexual intercourse without any divine authority. The

---

[1] *Tafsir* of al-Razi, vol. 6, p. 66.
[2] See *Al-Islam wal-Tibb al-Hadith (Islam and Modern Medicine)* by the late 'Abdul
'Aziz Isma'il.

Ansar (of Madinah) being their friends, followed their practice and used to say, 'If a man has intercourse with his wife through the vagina while he is on her back, the child will have a squint.' Thus the verse, 'So go in to your tillage as you will' was revealed; that is, it is immaterial whether the husband is on top of his wife or on her back as long as intercourse is through the vagina, which constitutes the tillage. This is so because these matters have nothing to do with religious or social policy but are entirely a matter of personal taste. Such sayings were among the absurdities of the Jews and Allah Ta'ala abolished them.[1]

It is not a function of religion to define the postures of sexual intercourse. However, a Muslim who fears Allah in his relationship with his wife and possesses the certainty that he will meet Him avoids the anus because the Prophet (peace be on him) said,

"Do not approach women from the anus."[2]

Again, he referred to such an act as "minor sodomy."[3] A woman of the Ansar asked him concerning vaginal intercourse from the back; he then recited to her,

'Your wives are a tilth to you, so go in to your tilth as you will,' but with only one receptacle.[4]

'Umar came to him one day saying, "O Messenger of Allah, I am ruined!" "What has ruined you?" asked the Prophet (peace be on him). He replied, "Last night I turned my wife over," meaning that he had had vaginal intercourse with her from the back. The Prophet (peace be on him) did not say anything to him until the verse cited above was revealed. Then he told him,

"From the front or the back, but avoid the anus and intercouse during menstruation."[5]

---

[1] *Hujjat Allah al-Baligah*, vol. 2, p. 134.
[2] Reported by Ahmad, al-Tirmidhi, al-Nisai, and Ibn Majah.
[3] Reported by Ahmad and al-Nisai.
[4] Reported by Ahmad.
[5] Reported by Ahmad and al-Tirmdhi.

Guarding the Secrets Between the Husband and Wife

The Qur'an praises virtuous wives,

> ...Who are obedient, guarding in secret what Allah has guarded....(4:34)

Among those secrets which must be guarded is the intimate relationship with the spouse which it would be wrong to discuss in a gathering or speak about to friends. The Prophet (peace be on him) said:

> Among those who will occupy the worst position in the sight of Allah on the Day of Resurrection is the man who has intercourse with his wife and she with him, and then he spreads her secret. [1]

Abu Hurairah narrated,

> Allah's Messenger (peace be on him) led us in prayer, and when he had finished he turned toward us and said, 'Remain seated. Is there among you the man who comes to his wife, closes the door, and draws the curtain, and then goes out and speaks about it, saying, "I did this and I did that with my wife?" They remained silent. Then he turned toward the women and asked, 'Is there among you one who tells about such things?' A girl raised herself on her knees so that the Messenger of Allah (peace be on him) could see her and listen to what she said. She said, 'Yes, by Allah, the men talk about it and the women do, too.' Then the Prophet (peace be on him) said, 'Do you know what those who do this are like? The ones who do this are like a male and female devil who meet each other in the road and satisfy their desire while the people look on. [2]

This emphatic way of expressing the matter should be sufficient to turn the Muslim away from such ill-considered and degraded behavior, which would make him or her resemble a devil!

---

[1]Reported by Ahmad, Abu Daoud, and al-Bazzar.
[2]Reported by the compilers of *Sunan*.

4. CONTRACEPTION

The preservation of the human species is unquestionably the primary objective of marriage, and such preservation of the species requires continued reproduction. Accordingly, Islam encourages having many children and has blessed both male and female progeny. However, it allows the Muslim to plan his family due to valid reasons and recognized necessities.

The common method of contraception at the time of the Prophet (peace be on him) was *coitus interruptus*, or withdrawal of the penis from the vagina just before ejaculation, thus preventing the entrance of semen. The Companions of the Prophet (peace be on him) engaged in this practice during the period the Qur'an was being revealed to him. Narrated Jabir,

> We practiced *coitus interruptus* during the time of the Messenger of Allah (peace be on him) while the Qur'an was being revealed.[1]

In a version transmitted by Muslim, he said,

> We practiced *coitus interruptus* during the time of the Messenger of Allah (peace be on him). He came to know about it, but he did not prohibit it.

A man came to the Prophet (peace be on him), saying, "I have a slave girl. I desire what men desire, but I do not want her to become pregnant, so I practice *coitus interrputus* with her. The Jews say that this is a minor form of burying your children alive". The Prophet (peace be on him) said,

> "The Jews are wrong. If Allah wishes to create a child, you cannot prevent it,"[2]

meaning that despite the employment of *coitus interrputus*, a drop of semen might have been deposited in the vagina without his awareness, resulting in conception.

In a gathering at which 'Umar was present, someone remarked, "Some say that *coitus interruptus* is a minor form of burying a child alive." 'Ali then said, "This is not so before the completion of seven

---

[1]Reported by al-Bukhari and Muslim.
[2]Reported by Abu Daoud, Ibn Majah, al-Nisai, and al-Tirmidhi.

stages: being a product of the earth, then a drop of semen, then a clot, then a little lump of tissue, then bones, then bones clothed with flesh, which then become like another creation." [1] "You are right," said 'Umar. "May Allah prolong your life."

Valid Reasons for Contraception

The first valid reason for employing contraception is the fear that the pregnancy or delivery might endanger the life or health of the mother; past experience or the opinion of a reliable physician are the guides in determining this possibility. Allah Ta'ala says:

> ...And do not be cast into ruin by your own hands....(2:195)

> ...And do not kill yourselves; indeed, Allah is ever merciful to you. (4:29)

Another reason is the fear that the burden of children may straiten the family's circumstances so much that one might accept or do something *haram* to satisfy their needs. Allah says:

> ...Allah desires ease for you, and He does not desire hardship for you....(2:185)

> ...It is not Allah's desire to place a burden upon you....(5:7 (6))

Again, fear that the children's health or upbringing may suffer may be a valid reason. On the authority of Usama ibn Zayd, Muslim in his *Sahih* reported that a man came to the Messenger of Allah (peace be on him), saying, "I practice *coitus interruptus* with my wife." "Why do you do that?" asked the Prophet (peace be on him). He said, "I fear for her child," or he may have said, "for her children." The Messenger of Allah (peace be on him) then said,

> "If it (the pregnancy of a nursing mother) were harmful, it would have harmed the Persians and the Greeks."

Another valid reason is the fear that the new pregnancy or a new baby might harm a previous suckling child. The Prophet (peace be

---

[1] 'Ali was paraphrasing the Qur'an 23:12-14, considering the creation of Adam from wet earth as the first stage of development of evey human foetus. (Trans.)

on him) termed intercourse with a nursing mother, or rather the intercourse which results in pregnancy while the mother is still nursing a baby, "*gheelah*," thinking that pregnancy would ruin the milk and weaken the suckling infant. Since he was greatly concerned with the welfare of his *ummah*, he dissuaded them from what was harmful. Among his personal opinions [1] was the saying,

> "Do not kill your children secretly, for *gheelah* overtakes the rider and throws him from the horse." [2]

The Prophet (peace be on him) did not, however, go so far as to prohibit intercourse with a nursing mother, as he noted that the Persians and Greeks, the two most powerful nations of his time, practiced it without any resulting injury to their children. Moreover, he feared that it would be a great hardship for husbands to abstain from their wives during the period of suckling, which may last up to two years. He said,

> I intended to prohibit *gheelah*, but I considered the Persians and the Greeks and saw that they suckled their children during pregnancy without any injury being caused to their children as a result. [3]

Ibn al-Qayyim, in discussing the relationship of this *hadith* to the one quoted just before it, "Do not kill your children secretly..." says,

> The Prophet (peace be on him) saw that pregnancy harms the suckling infant in the same way as being thrown off a horse harms a rider: it is injurious, but not to the extent of killing the baby. He advised them to avoid intercourse leading to pregnancy while the woman is nursing an infant but did not prohibit it. He then intended to prohibit it in order to save the health of the suckling child but realized that the resulting hardship to the husband, especially for young ones, would be much more injurious to the society. On balancing these matters, therefore, he preferred not to prohibit it. Moreover, he saw that (in) the two most

---

[1] The Prophet sometimes expressed his personal opinions in worldly matters, which he distinguished from his binding judgments in matters of religion. (Trans.)
[2] Reported by Abu Daoud. It is said that the child who nurses from a pregnant mother will suffer from it in later life like a horseman who is thrown from his horse. (Trans.)
[3] Reported by Muslim.

powerful and populous nations of his time, (women) suckled their children during pregnancy without its affecting their strength or numbers, and accordingly he refrained from prohibiting it.[1]

In our time new methods of contraception are available which realize the objective intended by the Prophet (peace be on him), that of protecting the suckling infant from any possible harm which may occur due to the pregnancy of its mother,[2] while at the same time avoiding the hardship to the husband in abstaining from sexual relations with his nursing wife. From this we may conclude that from the Islamic point of view the ideal spacing between two children is thirty months, or, if one wants to nurse the baby for two full years,[3] thirty-three months.

Imam Ahmad bin Hanbal is of the opinion that contraception requires the consent of the wife, because she has a right both to sexual enjoyment and to decide whether or not she wants a child. It is reported that 'Umar fobade the practice of *coitus interruptus* without the consent of the wife. This was, on the part of Islam, a noteworthy step toward establishing the rights of women in an age in which they had no rights.

Abortion

While Islam permits preventing pregnancy for valid reasons, it does not allow doing violence to the pregnancy once it occurs.

Muslim jurists agree unanimously that after the foetus is completely formed and has been given a soul, aborting it is *haram*. It is also a crime, the commission of which is prohibited to the Muslim because it constitutes an offense against a complete, live human being. Jurists insist that the payment of blood money (*diya*) becomes incumbent if the baby was aborted alive and then died, while a fine of lesser amount is to be paid if it was aborted dead.

---

[1] *Miftah Dar al-Sa'adah* by Ibn al-Qayyim, p. 620; also see *Zad al-Mi'ad*, vol. 4 p. 26 and ff.

[2] Although the primary issue discussed here is the welfare of the child, the mother's health and well-being is also an object of concern here as well. (Trans.)

[3] Two full years is the maximum period for the suckling of an infant in Islam. (Trans.)

However, there is one exceptional situation. If, say the jurists, after the baby is completely formed, it is reliably established that the continuation of the pregnancy would necessarily result in the death of the mother, then, in accordance with the general principle of the *Shari'ah*, that of choosing the lesser of two evils, abortion must be performed.

> For the mother is the origin of the foetus; moreover, she is established in life, with duties and responsibilities, and she is also a pillar of the family. It would not be possible to sacrifice her life for the life of a feotus which has not yet acquired a personality and which has no responsibilities or obligations to fulfill.[1]

Imam al-Ghazzali makes a clear distinction between contraception and abortion, saying,

> Contraception is not like abortion. Abortion is a crime against an existing being. Now, existence has stages. The first stages of existence are the settling of the semen in the womb and its mixing with the secretions of the woman.[2] It is then ready to receive life. Disturbing it is a crime. When it develops further and becomes a lump, aborting it is a greater crime. When it acquires a soul and its creation is completed, the crime becomes more grevious. The crime reaches a maximum seriousness when it is committed after it (the foetus) is separated (from the mother) alive.[3]

5. DIVORCE

Marriage, as stated previously, is a strong bond by means of which Allah joins a man and a woman. While they are "single" as individual human beings, after marriage they are termed a "couple." Marriage makes of them a pair, and thus the sorrow and

---

[1] *Al-Fatawa* by Shaikh Shaltut, p. 164.
[2] It was then believed that the mingling of the semen with the secretions of the woman in the uterus caused pregnancy. (Trans.)
[3] *Al-Ihya*, book of "*Al-Nikah*" (*Marriage*), p. 74.

joy of the one are equally the sorrow and joy of the other. The Qur'an describes this bond in beautiful and vivid language:

> ...They (wives) are your garments and you are their garments....(2:187)

meaning that each is the protection, the covering, the support, and the adornment of the other.[1]

Each of the two spouses has rights in regard to the other which must be recognized and which are not to be diminished. These mutual rights are equivalent except in relation to what is particular to men by virtue of their natural position, as Allah says:

> ...And they (women) have (rights) similar to those (of men) over them in an honorable fashion, but men have a degree over them. (2:228)

This "degree" (*darajah*) is related to men's role as the maintainers and leaders of the family.

A man asked the Prophet (peace be on him), "O Messenger of Allah, what rights may a wife demand of her husband?" He replied,

> That you should feed her (with the same standard) as you feed yourself, clothe her as you clothe yourself, that you should never hit her face or put her down, or cut yourself off from her unless it occurs in the house.[2]

Accordingly, it is not permissible for the Muslim husband to neglect to provide his wife with food and clothing. A *hadith* states,

> "Wasting the sustenance of his dependents is sufficient sin for a man."[3]

Striking her on the face is also prohibited, since it is an insult to her human dignity as well as being a danger to the most beautiful part of her body. And if the Muslim is pushed to discipline his wife in the event of open rebellion, when all other methods have failed, he is not allowed to beat her in a manner which causes pain or injury, and he is most certainly not permited to touch her face or other easily

---

[1] Al-Tirmidhi transmitted that Abu Hurairah reported Allah's Messenger (peace be on him) as saying, "The Believers who show the most perfect faith are those who have the best disposition, and the best of you are those who are best to their wives." In a *hadith* narrated by 'Aishah, the last words are "and are kindest to their families," as transmitted by al-Tirmidhi. (Trans.)
[2] Reported by Abu Daoud and by Ibn Hibban in his *Sahih*.
[3] Reported by Abu Daoud, al-Nisai, and al-Hakim.

injured parts of her body. Similarly, the Muslim is not permitted to revile, curse, or say insulting words to his wife.

Concerning the rights of the husband, the Prophet (peace be on him) said,

> It is not lawful for a woman who believes in Allah to allow anyone in her husband's house while he dislikes it. She should not go out of the house if he dislikes it and should not obey anyone who contradicts his orders. She should not refuse to share his bed.[1] She should not beat him (in case she is stronger than he). If he is more in the wrong than she, she should plead with him until he is reconciled. If he accepts her pleading, well and good, and her plea will be accepted by Allah; while if he is not reconciled with her, her plea will have reached Allah in any case.[2]

Mutual Tolerance Between Husband and Wife

A husband must be patient with his wife if he sees something in her which he disapproves and dislikes. He should recognize that he is dealing with a human being with natural imperfections, and he should balance her good qualities with her failings. The Prophet (peace be on him) said,

> Let a believing man not dislike a believing woman. If something in her is displeasing to him, another trait may be pleasing.

And Allah Ta'ala says,

> ...And consort with them in kindness, for if you dislike them, it may be that you dislike something in which Allah has placed much good. (4:19)

While on the one hand Islam requires the men to be tolerant and patient with what he dislikes in his wife, on the other it commands the wife to try to please her husband as far as her ability and charm allow, and warns her not to let a night pass during which her husband remains angry with her. A *hadith* states:

---

[1] Meaning that she should not deny him sexual acess when he desires it. (Trans.)
[2] Reported by al-Hakim.

There are three (persons) whose *salat* does not rise even a single span above their heads: a man leading a congregational *salat* while the people hate him, a woman passing the night while her huysband is angry with her, and two quarreling brothers. [1]

Rebelliousness and Strife

Because of his natural ability and his resonsibility for providing for his family, the man is the head of the house and of the family. He is entitled to the obedience and cooperation of his wife, and accordingly it is not permissible for her to rebel against his authority, causing disruption. Without a captain the ship of the household will flounder and sink.   If the husband senses that feelings of disobedience and rebelliousness are rising against him in his wife, he should try his best to rectify her attitude by kind words, gentle persuasion, and reasoning with her. If this is not helpful, he should sleep apart from her, trying to awaken her agreeable feminine nature so that serenity may be restored and she may respond to him in a harmonious fashion. If this approach fails, it is permissible for him to beat her lightly with his hands, avoiding her face and other sensitive areas. In no case should he resort to using a stick or any other instrument which might cause pain and injury. Rather this "beating" should be of the kind which the Prophet (peace be on him) once, when angry with his servant, mentioned to him, saying,

> If it were not for the fear of retaliation on the Day of Resurrection, I would have beaten you with this *miswak* (tooth-cleaning stick). [2]

The Prophet (peace be on him) admonished men concerning beating their wives, saying,

> "None of you must beat his wife as a slave is beaten, and then have intercourse with her at the end of the day." [3]

---

[1] Reported by Ibn Majah and by Ibn Hibban in his *Sahih*.
[2] Reported by Ibn Sa'd in his *Tabaqat*.
[3] Reported by Ahmad; al-Bukhari has something similar to it.

It was reported to the Prophet (peace be on him) that some of his Companions beat their wives, whereupon he said,

"Certainly those are not the best among you."[1]

Says Imam al-Hafiz ibn Hajar,

The saying of the Prophet (peace be on him), 'The best among you do not beat,' could imply that beating wives is in general permissible. To be specific, one may beat only to safeguard Islamic behavior and if he (the husband) sees deviation only in what she must do or obey in relation to him. It is preferable to warn (her), or something of the sort, and as long as it is possible to achieve things through warning, any use of force is disallowed because force generates hatred, which is inimical to the harmony expected in marriage. Force is applied only when sin against Allah Ta'ala (*masiyah*) is feared. Al-Nisai has reported 'Aishah as saying, 'The Prophet (peace be on him) never beat any of his wives or servants; in fact, he did not strike anything with his hand except in the cause of Allah or when the prohibitons of Allah were violated, and he retaliated on behalf of Allah.'[2]

If all of these approaches fail, and the rift between the husband and wife deepens, the matter then devolves on the Islamic society for solution. Two individuals of good will and sound judgement, one from the wife's and one from the husband's side, should meet with the couple in order to try to resolve their differences. Perhaps the sincerity of their efforts may bear fruit and Allah may bring about reconciliation between the spouses.

These various approaches are stated by Allah Ta'ala in the following *ayah*.

...And as for those women on whose part you fear stubborness, (first) admonish them; then refuse to share their beds; and (finally) beat them (lightly). Then if they return to obedience, do not seek for a way against them; indeed, Allah is Most High, Great. And if you fear

---

[1] Reported by Ahmad, Abu Daoud and al-Nisai. Ibn Hibban and al-Hakim classify it as sound, as narrated by Iyas ibn 'Abdullah ibn Abu Dhiab.
[2] *Fath al-Bari*, vol. 9, p. 249.

breach between the two of them, appoint an arbiter from his family and an arbiter from her family. If they desire to set things aright, Allah will bring about reconciliation between them; indeed, Allah is Knowing, Aware. (4:34-35)

When Divorce Becomes Permissible

If all these efforts fail and every course tried proves to be of no avail, the husband may resort to the final solution permitted by the *Shari'ah* of Islam. In response to the bitter realities of life, when difficulties cannot be resolved except through the separation of the two parties in an honorable fashion, Islam has made the provision of divorce. Islam has permitted divorce reluctantly, neither liking nor commending it. Said the Prophet (peace be on him),

"Among lawful things, divorce is most hated by Allah."[1]

That a thing is lawful yet detested by Allah means that it is permissible under unavoidable circumstances, when living together becomes a torture, mutual hatred is deep-seated, and it becomes difficult for the two parties to observe the limits of Allah and to fulfill their marital responsibilities. In such a situation separation is better, and Allah Ta'ala says,

But if they separate, Allah will provide for each of them out of His abundance....(4:130)

Divorce in the Pre-Islamic Period

Islam is not alone among religions in permitting divorce. Prior to its advent, apart from a very few societies, divorce was allowed everywhere in the world. It was a common occurrence that when a man became angry with his wife, he would turn her out of the house, with or without a just cause, and the wife had no legal recourse

---

[1]Reported by Abu Daoud.

against him nor any claim on his property, nor even a right to support money or compensation.

Unconditional and unrestrained divorce was allowed among the ancient Greeks when their civlization was ascendant. Under Roman law a judge was empowered to annul a marriage even if the two parties had included a provision against divorce in their marriage contract, since the possibility of divorce was regarded as a part of the marrige contract. During the earlier period of Roman civilization the religious marriage made no provision for divorce, but at the same time the husband was given absolute power over his wife; for example, under certain circumstances it was lawful for him to kill her. As time passed, the religious law was brought into conformity with the civil law, which permitted divorce.

Divorce in Judaism

Judaism improved the status of the wife but it also broadened the scope of divorce. The religious law requires that the husband divorce the wife if moral deliquency is proved against her, even though he may prefer to forgive her; likewise, he is required to divorce her if she does not bear him children throughout a period of ten years of married life.

Divorce in Christianity

Christianity stands alone among the religions we have mentioned, in distinction even to Judaism, in prohibiting both divorce and marriage to divorced men and women. Jesus (peace be on him) is reported to have said, "It was also said, 'Whoever divorces his wife must give her a certificate of divorcement. But I tell you, whoever divorces his wife, except on the grounds of adultery, causes her to commit adultery; and whoever marries a woman who has been divorced commits adultery.[1] " (Matt. 5:31-32) "And he said to them, 'Whoever divorces his wife and marries another, commits

---

[1] *Al-Islam Din 'Am Khalid* by Farid Wajdi, p. 172.

208

adultery against her; and if a woman divorces her husband and marries another, she commits adultery.' " (Mark 10:11-12)

The reason for this is given in the Gospels in the words, "What therefore God has joined together, let no man put asunder."[1] This statement is correct in the sense that, since the husband and wife are married by God's permission and legislation, one may say that God has joined them together, although it is the man who enters into the marriage contract. In similar fashion, since God has permitted and legislated divorce in relation to certain reasons and circumstances, one may say that God has separated them, even though the man implements the divorce. It thus becomes clear that no man puts asunder what God has joined together, for joining together and putting asunder is in the hands of Almighty God, and is it not God Himself Who puts them asunder due to the reason of sexual immorality?

Differences Among Christian Denominations Regarding Divorce

The New Testament Gospels do make an exception with regard to the prohibition of divorce in the case of sexual immorality. Some Catholics, however, try to explain away even this exception by saying, "The meaning here is not that adultery is an exception in the case of which divorce is permitted, because in Christian law there is no divorce. The phrase, 'Except for unchastity,' means that the marrige itself is annulled, since its legality and correctness have been violated; thus, while it is seemingly a marriage, in actuality it is adultery. Consequently, in such a case it is permissible for the husband, or rather incumbent upon him, to leave the woman."[2]

The Protestant denominations permit divorce on the grounds of adultery, betrayal of the husband, and some other specified reasons, in addition to those mentioned in the text of the Gospels. However, some of these denominations prohibit the remarriage of a divorced man or woman.

---

[1]Matt. 19:6, Mark 10:9.
[2]In a commentary on the Gospel According to Matthew, Institute of Coptic Catholic Research.

209

The councils of the Orthodox Church in Egypt permit its followers the right of divorce on the grounds of adultery, as provided by the Gospels, and for some other reasons such as sterility extending over a period of three years, chronic illness, and prolonged dissension which appears to be irresolvable.

Consequences of the Christian Stand on Divorce

As a result of this uncompromising stand of Christianity with regard to divorce, people in Western countries were obliged to resort to civil legislation in order to legalize it. Unfortunately, many of them, the Americans, for example, went to an extreme of permissiveness in the matter of divorce so that it is granted for quite trivial reasons. Some Western philosophers warn that this ease in divorce will dilute the sanctity of the marital bond and erode the very foundations of family life. A well-known judge declared that the time is not too far off when, in Western countries, marriage will be replaced by a loose and tenuous relationship between men and women, similar to a commercial transaction, which can be broken for the most trivial reasons. Since there will be no bond of religion or love between such a pair, they will be united only by their lusts and the desire to experience a variety of pleasures, a type of relationship which is against the teachings of every religion:

> This phenomenon of regulating personal affairs through civil law is against the teachings of every religion and is not to be found anywhere in the world except among the peoples of the Christian West; even Hindus, Buddhists, and Zoroastrians observe religious injunctions in the ordering of their personal affairs. Although we may find among them those who have made innovations in the teachings of their religions in matters of public concern, such innovations are not undertaken in personal affairs, that is to say, in marriage, divorce, and what pertains to family life.[1]

[1] As quoted in *Huquq al-insan fil-Islam (Human Rights in Islam)*, by 'Abd al-Wahid Wafi, p. 88.

210

The Christian Stand on Divorce: A Temporary Injunction, Not a Permanent Law

A serious student of the Gospels cannot escape the conclusion that what Jesus (peace be on him) taught was intended to correct excesses introduced into the divine law by the Jews. His teachings, including his statements concerning divorce, were never intended to be taken as permanent law for the whole of mankind.

In the Gospel according to Matthew we find the following dialogue between Jesus and the Pharisees:

> And the Pharisees came to him and put him to the test by asking, 'Is it lawful to dismiss one's wife for any cause?' He replied, 'Have you never read that "He Who made them from the beginning made them male and female, and said, 'For this reason a man shall leave his father and mother and shall be joined inseparably to his wife, and the two shall become one flesh? ' " (Gen. 1:27, 2:24) So they are no longer two but one flesh. What therefore God has joined together, let not man put asunder.' They said to him, 'Why then did Moses command (us) to give a certificate of divorce, and thus to dismiss a wife?' (Deut. 24:1-4). He said to them, 'Because of the hardness of your hearts Moses permitted you to dismiss your wives; but from the beginning it has not been so (ordained). I say to you: whoever dismisses his wife, except for unchastity, and marries another, commits adultery, and he who marries a divorced woman commits adultery.' The disciples said to him, 'If the case of a man with his wife is like that, it is neither profitable nor advisable to marry.' (Matt. 19:3-10)

From this dialogue it is clear that by restricting the permissibility of divorce to the case of unchastity alone, Jesus intended to correct the excesses of the Jews in the indiscriminate application of divorce, which was permitted under Mosaic Law. This was obviously a temporary remedy, abrogated by the permanent and universal law of Islam brought by Prophet Muhammad (peace be on him).

To suppose that Jesus (peace be on him) intended to make this an

211

eternal law for all mankind does not appeal to reason. We see that his disciples, the most sincere of his followers, were aghast at such a harsh decree, saying, "If the case of a man with his wife is like that, it is neither profitable nor advisable to marry," that is, the moment a man marries a woman he puts a yoke around his neck which it is impossible to remove, regardless of how miserable their life together may become because of mutual hatred and incompatability of temperaments. As a wise man has aptly said, "The greatest torment in life is a companion who neither agrees with you nor leaves you alone."

The Islamic Limits for the Regulation of Divorce

The Islamic *Shari'ah* has placed a number of obstacles in the way of divorce in order to confine it within the narrowest possible compass. Divorce without lawful necessity and without first exhausting all the other means mentioned earlier of resolving the conflict is unlawful and is prohibited in Islam. Some jurists maintain, it is injurious to both husband and wife, unnecessarily damaging the interests of the two, which, like the wasting of property, is *haram*.

"Do not harm yourself or others,"[1]
the Prophet (peace be on him) has instructed us.

People who divorce their spouses and marry others in order to enjoy a variety of sexual partners are liked neither by Allah nor by His Messenger (peace be on him). The Prophet (peace be on him) called them "the tasters," saying,

"I do not like the tasters, men and women,"[2]
and,

"Allah does not like the tasters, men and women."[3]
Said 'Abdullah bin 'Abbas, "Divorce is (only) in the case of necessity."

---

[1] *Al-Mughni* by Ibn Qadamah, vol. 7, p. 77. This *hadith* is transmitted by Ibn Majah and al-Darqutni.
[2] Reported by al-Tabarani and al-Darqutni.
[3] Al-Tabarani in *al-Kabir*, on the authority of good transmitters.

The Prohibition of Divorcing During Menstruation

When divorce becomes necessary, it is not permissible for the Muslim to implement it any time he pleases; he must wait for a suitable time. According to the *Shari'ah*, this suitable time is when the woman is clean following her menstrual period or the period of puerperal discharge following childbirth and before her husband has resumed sexual relations with her, or when she is pregnant and her husband is aware of her pregnancy.

The reason for prohibiting divorce during menstruation or the period of puerperal discharge is that, since during such periods sexual intercourse is *haram*, the idea of divorce may come to a man's mind because of sexual frustration and nervous tension. He is therefore advised to wait until his wife is clean and to divorce her then, if he is intent on divorce, before the resumption of marital relations.

Just as divorce during menstruation is *haram*, it is likewise *haram* between menstruation periods (i.e., "the period of purity") if the husband has had intercourse with his wife following the termination of her previous period. Because it is possible that she may have become pregnant from this union, the husband may change his mind concerning divorce when he knows that his wife is carrying a child, desiring to stay married to her for the sake of the embryo in her womb. However, when the wife is in the period of purity but he has not had intercourse with her following the termination of her menses, or when she is pregnant and he is aware of it, he will be able to ascertain that his intention to divorce her is the result of deep-seated antipathy, and accordingly is permitted to carry through with the divorce.   In the *Sahih* of al-Bukhari, it is transmitted that 'Abdullah bin 'Umar divorced his wife during her menstrual period. When 'Umar mentioned the matter to the Messenger of Allah (peace be on him) he became angry, saying,

> He must take her back. If he still wishes to divorce her he may do so when she is clean of the menstrual discharge before having intercourse with her, for that is the period of waiting which Allah has prescribed for divorce, referring to the *ayah*, 'O Prophet, when you

213

(men) divorce women, divorce them during the prescribed periods.' (65:1)

Another version of this *hadith* reads,

Command him to take her back and then divorce her when she is clean from the menstrual dischage or (otherwise) is pregnant.

A question now remains: If a person does divorce his wife during these prohibited periods, does the divorce become effective or not? The prevailing opinion is that it does become effective, although the husband will be considered sinful. However, some jurists hold that, as Allah did not legislate it, it does not become effective, and whatever is not legal cannot be correct nor enforced. Abu Daoud, on sound authority, has transmitted that when 'Abdullah bin 'Umar was asked, "What would you say if a man were to divorce his wife during menstruation?" he related his own story of divorcing his wife during her period and the Prophet's commanding him to take her back, disregarding his pronouncement of divorce.

Taking an Oath of Divorce

It is not permissible for the Muslim to take an oath of divorce, vowing that if a particular event does not occur his wife will be divorced, or to threaten her by saying that if she does this or that particular thing she will be divorced. In Islam an oath may be expressed only in one specific manner, that is, in the name of Allah alone; apart from this, no other form of oath-taking is permitted. The Prophet (peace be on him) said,

"Anyone who swears by (anything) other than Allah has committed *shirk*,"[1]

and,

"Whoever wants to take an oath should take it in the name of Allah or keep silent."[2]

---

[1]Reported by Abu Daoud, al-Tirmidhi, and al-Hakim.
[2]Reported by Muslim.

Where the Divorcee Resides During the Waiting Period

The Islamic *Shari'ah* requires that the divorced woman remain in her home, that is to say, her husband's house, for the duration of her *'iddah* (waiting period). It is not permissible for her to move from the house, as it is likewise not permissible for her husband to evict her without a just cause. This requirement leaves the way open, during the *'iddah* following a first or second pronouncement of divorce,[1] for the husband to revert to his wife without the requirement of remarriage. Her presence in the same house with him makes it quite probable that the mutual sympathy and love between them may be rekindled, while if she is pregnant the passing of months will make her pregnancy obvious, which may be a further inducement to him to change his mind. In any case, ample time is at their disposal to reconsider the whole situation. With the healing effect of time, feelings of antipathy may give place to affection and reconciliation, and the revitalization of their love may occur.

> ...And fear Allah, your Lord. Do not turn them out of their houses, nor shall they leave (of their own accord) unless they commit some clear immorality; and these are the limits set by Allah. And whoever transgresses Allah's limits indeed wrongs his own soul. Thou knowest not; it may be that Allah will afterwards bring some new thing to pass. (65:1)

If then they must separate, it should be done with dignity and kindness, without mutual abuse, injury, recrimination, or infringement of rights. Says Allah Ta'ala:

> ...Either retain them in kindness or part with them in kindness....(65:2)

> ...Then (either) retain her in honor or release her with kindness....(2:229)

> For divorced women a provision (shall be made) in

---

[1] In the Islamic *Shari'ah* the pronouncement of divorce by the husband constitutes a complete act of divorce in itself, to be followed by the required *'iddah* or waiting period. In order to simplify the discussion, the word *divorce* is here used to denote the divorce pronouncement, i.e., the act of divorce itself (Trans.)

kindness, a duty for those who are conscious of Allah.
(2:241)

Repeated Divorce

The Muslim is allowed three chances, that is to say, three
pronouncements or acts of divorce on three different occasions,
provided that each divorce is pronounced during the time when the
wife is in the period of purity and he has had no intercourse with her.

A husband may divorce his wife once and let the *'iddah* pass.
During the period of *'iddah* the two have the option of being
reconciled without the necessity of remarriage. If, however, this
waiting period expires without reconciliation, they are now fully
divorced. Each of them is free to marry someone else or to remarry
each other; should they want to remarry each other, a new marriage
contract is required.

If after the first divorce the husband is reconciled with his wife but
later the hostility and conflict begin all over again, all efforts at
reconciliation and arbitration resulting in failure, he may divorce
her a second time in the same manner as described above. In this
case, too, he can return to her during the *'iddah* without remarriage,
or after the *'iddah* has expired through a new marriage contract.

But it may happen that although he is reconciled with his wife
again after the second divorce, he may later divorce her for the third
time. This will then be a clear proof that the hostility between the
two of them runs very deep and that they are incapable of living
together. If this third divorce takes place, it is not permissible for the
husband to return to his wife during her *'iddah*, nor may he remarry
her after the *'iddah* unless she has been married to another man, to
live with him as a permanent and true wife, and he then
subsequently divorces her. It is, however, totally prohibited for the
other man to marry and divorce her simply in order to make her
halal for her first husband.

Those Muslims who utter three divorce pronouncements at one
time or in one statement are rebels against Allah's law and are
deviating from the straight path of Islam. Once the Prophet (peace
be on him) was informed about a man who had pronounced three
divorces at one time. He got up in anger, saying,

216

Is sport being made of the Book of Allah while I am (yet) among you? As a result, a man stood up and said, O Messenger of Allah, shall I not kill him? [1]

Reconciling Honorably or Separating with Kindness

When the husband has divorced his wife and the period of *'iddah* is passing, he has two alternatives: either to reconcile with her honorably — that is, to return to her with the intention of living in peace and harmony, and not in order to torment or harm her — or to free her and part with her in kindness by allowing the *'iddah* to expire without arguments and harsh words, and without setting aside any of their mutual rights.

It is not lawful for him to return to her just before the *'iddah* is due to expire in order to torment her by prolonging the waiting period, thus depriving her of the oportunity to marry someone else. This was what was done in the period of *jahiliyyah*. Allah Ta'ala then prohibited this injury to women in a very decisive manner, using a style of expression which makes the heart quake:

> And when you have divorced women and they have fulfilled the term (of their *'iddah*), either retain them honorably or release them honorably; but do not retain them in order to injure them, for this is transgression, and whoever does this has wronged his own soul. And do not take the revelations of Allah in mockery, but remember Allah's favor upon you and what He has sent down to you of the Book and the Wisdom, to instruct you by means of it. And be conscious of Allah, and know that Allah is aware of everything. (2:231)

A little reflection upon this noble *ayah* of seven phrases, containing warning after warning, reminder after reminder, ought to be sufficient for anyone who has any feeling in his heart or any hearing when it is recited.

---

[1]Reported by al-Nisai.

The Divorced Woman's Freedom to Remarry

After the expiration of the divorced woman's *'iddah*, neither her ex-husband, guardian, nor anyone else can prevent her from marrying anyone she chooses. As long as she and the man who proposes to her follow the procedure required by the *Shari'ah*, no one has the right to interfere. What some men of today do in attempting to prevent their ex-wives from remarrying, intimidating them and their families, is in fact something pertaining to *jahiliyyah*; likewise, what some families or guardians of divorced women do to prevent them from returning to their husbands when they want to be reconciled, as indeed "Peace is better," (4:128) is also of *jahiliyyah*. Allah Ta'ala says:

> And when you divorce women and they complete their term (*'iddah*), do not prevent them from marrying their (former) husbands if they agree among themselves in an honorable manner. This is to instruct those among you who believe in Allah and the Last Day. That is more virtuous and pure for you; and Allah knows and you do not know. (2:232)

The Woman's Right to Demand Divorce

The woman who cannot bear to live with her husband has the right to free herself from the marriage bond by returning to her husband the *mahr* (required marrige gift) and gifts he has given her, or more or less than that according to their mutual agreement. It is, however, preferable that he should not ask for more than he has given her. Allah Ta'ala says:

> ...And if you (the judges) fear that the two may not be able to keep to the limits ordained by Allah, there is no blame on either of them if she redeems herself (from the marriage tie by returning all or part of the *mahr*)....(2:229)

The wife of Thabit bin Qais came to the Prophet (peace be on him) and said, "O Messenger of Allah, I do not approach Thabit bin Qais in respect of character and religion, but I do not want to be guilty of showing anger to him."[1] The Prophet (peace be on him) asked her about what she had received from him. She replied, "A garden." He asked, "Will you give him back his garden?" "Yes," she said. The Prophet (peace be on him) then told Thabit,

"Accept the garden and make one declaration of divorce."[2]

It is not permissible for woman to seek divorce from her husband unless she has borne ill-treatment from him or unless she has an acceptable reason which requires their separation. Said the Prophet (peace be on him),

If any woman asks her husband for a divorce without some strong reason, the fragrance of the Garden will be forbidden to her.[3]

The Prohibition of Ill-Treatment

It is *haram* for the husband to torment and mistreat his wife in order to compel her to seek a divorce so that she will return to him all or part of the property he has given her. Only if the wife is guilty of clear immorality may her husband demand the return of part of the *mahr*. In this regard Allah Ta'ala says:

...Nor should you treat them with harshness in order that you may take away part of what you have given them, (for you may not take it back) unless they are guilty of open lewdness. (4:19)

It is also *haram* for a husband to take back anything from his wife because he hates her and wants to divorce her so he can marry another woman. As Almighty Allah says,

But if you decide to take one wife in the place of another, even if you have given one of them a heap of gold, do not take (back) anything of it; would you take it back by

---

[1] Her meaning was that although Thabit was a good man, she was unable to get along with him and thus might not be able to show him the respect due to a husband. (Trans.)
[2] Reported by al-Bukhari and al-Nisai.
[3] Reported by Abu Daoud.

slander and a manifest wrong? And could you take it back, when each of you has been privately with the other, and they (the wives) have taken a solemn covenant from you? (4:20-21)

The Prohibition of the Oath of Desertion

One of the aspects of Islam's concern for the rights of women is that it prohibits a man to be so angry with his wife as to discontinue sexual relations with her for a period which she cannot bear. If this abandonment of sexual relations is accompanied by an oath on his part, he is given a limit of four months in which to calm down and revert to her. If he comes to his senses and resumes sexual relations before the expiration of the four months, it is possible that Allah may forgive him for his excess and open the door of repentance to him; however, he must still do the penance prescribed for a broken oath. If, on the other hand, this period expires and he has not returned to her, his wife is divorced from him as a just punishment for his neglect of her rights.

Some jurists hold that the divorce is automatic at the expiration of four months and that no judgement from a court is needed. Others, however, require that at the end of the period the matter should be referred to the judicial authority, who will then give them the option of reconciliation or divorce.

Such an oath of abstention from the wife is technically known in the *Shari'ah* as *eela*. Concerning it Allah Ta'ala says:

> For those who take an oath of abstention from their wives, a waiting period of four months (is ordained); if they return, indeed, Allah is Forgiving, Merciful. But if their intention is firm for divorce, then, indeed, Allah is Hearing, Knowing. (2:226-227)

This period of four months has been specified to give the husband ample time to calm himself and to restore the relationship of his own volition. Moreover, four months is normally regarded as the maximum period a woman can endure separation from her husband. Commentators on the Qur'an narrate the following incident in support of this opinion:

One nght during his caliphate, while 'Umar was making a round of Madinah, he heard a woman singing,

The night is long, the darkness all around me;
I am sleepless, for I have no friend to play with.
I swear by Allah that had there been no fear of Him,
This cot would be shaking from side to side.

Upon investigation, 'Umar found that the woman's husband had been gone on a military expedition for a long time. He then asked his daughter Hafsah, the widow of the Prophet (peace be on him), "How long can a woman endure separation from her husband?" She replied, "Four months." Subsequently, the caliph of the Believers decided that he would not send a married man away from his wife for a period exceeding four months.

6. PARENTS AND CHILDREN

The Protection of the Lineage

The child is an extension of his father and the bearer of his characteristics. During his lifetime he is the joy of his father's eyes, while after his death he represents a continuation of his existence and an embodiment of his immortality. He inherits his features and stature as well as his mental qualities and traits, both the good and the bad, the beautiful as well as the ugly, from his father. The child is a part of his father's heart and a piece of his body.

Allah Subhanahu wa Ta'ala has ordained marriage and has forbidden adultery so that paternity may be established without doubt or ambiguity and that the child may be referred to his father and the father to his sons and daughters. Through marriage a woman is reserved for one man; it is *haram* for her to be unfaithful to him or to let anyone else have access to what belongs exclusively to him. Thus, every child born to her in wedlock will be her husband's child, without any need for recognition or public proclamation of the fact by him or a corresponding claim on the part of the mother.

221

"The child is attributed to the one on whose bed it is born,"[1]

declared the Prophet of Islam (peace be on him).

The Prohibition of Denying Paternity

It is not permissible for the husband to deny his paternity of any child born to his wife as long as they are married to each other. Such a denial would bring the ugliest shame imaginable upon both the wife and the child. He is, therefore, not allowed to take such a step on the basis of a mere suspicion, a sudden notion, or an evil rumor. If, however, on the basis of evidence which has come to his attention, he is convinced that his wife has betrayed him, the *Shari'ah* of Islam has no desire to force him to raise a child whom he believes not to be his own or to let the child be his heir, or — at the very least — to allow him to suffer from suspicion and doubt the rest of his life.

A way out of this dilemma, known in Islamic jurisprudence as *li'an*, is provided by the *Shari'ah*. If a man is convinced or strongly suspects, although without having proof, that his wife has had sexual relations with another man and is carrying his child, he can take the case to a Muslim judge *(qadi)*. The *qadi* will ask the man and his wife to invoke the curse of Allah on one another in the manner prescribed in *Surah al-Nur:*

> As for those who accuse their wives but have no witnesses except themselves, the testimony of one of them shall consist of bearing witness by Allah four times that he is of the truthful, and a fifth (time) that the curse of Allah be upon him if he is one of those who lie. And it shall avert the punishment from her if she bear witness by Allah four times that he is indeed of those who lie, and a fifth (time) that the wrath of Allah be upon her if he is among the truthful. (24:6-9)

After this the two shall be separated permanently, and the child shall be identified by the name of his or her mother.

----

[1]Reported by al-Bukhari and Muslim. Literally: "The child belongs to the bed."

The Prohibition of Legal Adoption

Just as it is *haram* for a man to deny his paternity of a child born to his wife in wedlock, it is likewise *haram* for him to legally adopt a son of whom he is not the natural father. Like peoples of other societies during the course of history, the Arabs of *jahiliyyah* used to add anyone they wished to their lineage and family through adoption. A man would adopt (*tabanna,* "to make one's son") any boy of his liking as son (*mutabanna),* announce the fact to the public, and the boy would become like a son to him, sharing the responsibilities and rights of his adopted family and taking its name. The adoption was effective despite the fact that the adopted son might have a known father and come from a known lineage.

This practice was widespread in Arab society at the advent of Islam. Before receiving the call to prophethood, the Prophet (peace be on him) had himself adopted Zaid bin Harithah, who had been captured as a child during one of the raids on his tribe which were common occurrences during the period of *jahiliyyah.* Hakim bin Hizam had bought him for his aunt Khadijah, and after her marriage to the Prophet (peace be on him) Khadijah presented Zaid to him. When Zaid's father and uncle learned his place of residence, they came to the Prophet (peace be on him) to demand Zaid's return. The Prophet (peace be on him) gave Zaid a choice, and he chose to stay with the Prophet (peace be on him) in preference to his father and uncle. The Prophet (peace be on him) then set him free and adopted him as his son in the presence of others. He was thereafter called Zaid ibn Muhammad and became the first of the freed slaves to accept Islam.

Now what is the judgement of Islam concerning such a system of adoption? Islam rightly views this sort of adoption as a falsification of the natural order and of reality. Taking a stranger into the family as one of its members and allowing him privacy with women who are not his *muharrmat,* nor he theirs, is a deception, for the man's wife is not the adopted son's mother, nor is his daughter the boy's sister nor is his sister his aunt, since all of them are non-*mahrem* to him. Moreover, the adopted son acquires a claim on the inheritance of the man and his wife, depriving the rightful, deserving relatives of their inheritance. Such a situation arouses the anger of the real

223

relatives against the intruder who encroaches upon them and usurps their rights, depriving them of their full inheritance.[1] Frequently such anger leads to quarrels and to the breaking of relations among relatives. That is why the Qur'an abolished this *jahili* system, prohibiting it totally and eradicating all its consequences. Says Alla Ta'ala:

> ...Nor has He made your adopted sons your (real) sons; that is simply a saying of your mouths. But Allah speaks the truth, and He guides you to the (right way). Call them by (the names of) their fathers; that is more just in the sight of Allah. But if you do not know their fathers, they are your brothers-in-faith and your wards....(33:4-5)

Let us ponder the Qur'anic words, "He has not made your adopted sons your (real) sons; that is simply a saying of your mouths." This signifies that the declaration of adoption consists of words having no corresonding objective reality. A mere pronouncement does not change realities, alter facts, or make a stranger a relative, or an adopted individual a son. A mere verbal expression or figure of speech cannot make the blood of a man run in the veins of the adopted son, produce feelings of fatherly affection in the man's heart or filial emotions in the heart of the boy, or transfer either the genetic characteristics or physical, mental, or psychological traits.

Islam abolished all the effects of this system of adoption which relate to inheritance and to prohibition of marriage to the widowed or divorced wife of the adopted son. In matters of inheritance, the Qur'an does not recognize any claim except those based on relationship through blood and marriage:

> ...But blood relatives are nearer to each other in the ordinance of Allah....(8:75)

With regard to marriage, The Qur'an declared that only the wives of one's real sons, "the wives of your sons who are from your (own) loins" (4:23), not the wives of the adopted sons, are permanently forbidden in marriage. Accordingly, it is permissible for a man to

---

[1]Since the Islamic *Shari'ah* specifies the share of an individual's property to which each near blood relative is entitled, the legal adoption of a child who is not among such relatives, but who, by virtue of adoption, is one of the heirs would naturally create bitterness and hostility among the rightful heirs. (Trans.)

marry the divorced wife of his adopted son, since she has been, in actuality , the wife of a "stranger" not related by blood.

A Practical Example of the Abolition of Legal Adoption

The practice of adopting sons was very deeply rooted in the society of pre-Islamic Arabia, and it was not easy for people to give it up. But Allah Ta'ala wanted to eradicate it and its effects, not only by words but also by deeds. In order that all doubts concerning the matter might be dispelled, that the Believers might feel at ease with respect to marrying the ex-wives of their adopted sons, and, more importantly, that they might know with certainty that the *halal* is that which is permitted by Allah and that the *haram* is that which is forbidden by Him alone, Allah Ta'ala chose the Prophet (peace be on him) himself for this important task.

Now Zaid bin Harithah, who was known as Zaid ibn Muhammad, had married the Prophet's cousin, Zainab bint Zahsh. Zaid and Zainab were not happy together, and Zaid became increasingly dissatisfied with his wife, complaining frequently to the Prophet (peace be on him). Although the Prophet (peace be on him) knew, through divine revelation, that Zaid would divorce Zainab and that he would afterwards marry her himself, human weakness occasionally overcame him, and he was afraid of facing the people. Thus, whenever Zaid complained to him about his wife, the Prophet (peace be on him) would tell him, "Hold on to your wife and fear Allah."   At that point Allah Subhanahu wa Ta'ala revealed some verses of the Qur'an admonishing the Prophet (peace be on him) and at the same time fortifying his will to face society in demolishing the remnants of this ancient system, in this case, the established practice which prohibited a man from marrying the ex-wife of a stranger who had been adopted as a son. Says Allah Ta'ala:

> And when thou didst say to him who had received the favor of Allah and thy favor, 'Retain thy wife and fear Allah,' thou didst hide within thyself what Allah was about to make manifest, fearing the people; but Allah has more right that thou shouldst fear Him. Then, when Zaid had carried out the necessary formality (of divorce) from her, We gave her to thee in marriage so

225

that (in the future) there might be no difficulty for the Believers with respect to (marriage to) the wives of their adopted sons when the latter have carried out the necessary formality (of divorce) from them; and Allah's command must be fufilled.   (33:37)

The Qur'an goes on to support the Prophet (peace be on him) in this action, confirming its lawfulness and removing any stigma attached to it:

There is no fault in the Prophet in what Allah has made obligatory for him. That was Allah's practice with those of old who passed away, and the commnd of Allah is a decree determined — those who delivered the messages of Allah and feared Him, fearing none but Allah; and Allah suffices in keeping account. Muhammad is not the father of any man among you, but he is the Messenger of Allah and the Seal of the Prophets; and Allah is the Knower of all things. (33:38-40)

Adopting a Child to Rear and to Educate

As explained above, the type of adoption which has been abolished by Islam is that kind which makes a boy a member of the family, with all the rights of inheritance, the permissibility of mixing freely with other members of the household, the prohibition of marriage and so on.

But the word "adoption" is also used in another sense, one which is not prohibited by Islam—that is, when a man brings home an orphan or a foundling to rear, to educate, and to treat as his own child; he protects, feeds, clothes, teaches, and loves the child as his own. However, he does not attribute the child to himself, nor does he give him the rights which the Shari'ah reserves for natural children. This is a meritorious act in Allah's religion, and the man who does it will be rewarded by being admitted to Paradise. Said the Prophet (peace be on him),

"I, and the one who raises an orphan, will be like these two in the Garden",

226

and he pointed to his middle and index fingers with a slight gap between the two.

A foundling *(laqeet)* is regarded as an orphan *(yateem)*, and one may also apply the term *wayfarer (ibn al-sabeel)*,[1] one of those who must also be cared for, to him as well.

If a man has no children of his own, and he wishes to benefit such a child from his wealth, he may give him whatever he wants during his lifetime and may also bequeath to him up to one-third of his inheritance before his death.

Artificial Insemination

Islam safeguards lineage by prohbiting *zina* and legal adoption, thus keeping the family line unambiguously defined without any foreign element entering into it. It likewise prohibits what is known as artificial insemination if the donor of the semen is other than the husband. In such a case, as the well-known professor, Shaikh Shaltut, says,

> It is a despicable crime and a major sin, to be classified in the same category as adultery. Both (adultery and artificial insemination by anyone other than the husband) are similar in nature and in effects; that is, in both cases the tillage which belongs exclusively to the husband is intentionally inseminated by a stranger. Had the form of this crime not been of a lesser degree, such insemination would have been punishable by the same *hadd* punishment as is prescribed for adultery in the divinely revealed *Shari'ah*.
>
> There is, however, no doubt that insemination by a donor other than the husband is a more serious crime and detestable offense than adoption, for the child born of (such) insemination incorporates in itself the result

---

[1] The "Wayfarer" is one of several categories of people mentioned as deserving of charity in various Qur'anic verses, notably 2:176 and 9:60. A foundling or orphan can also be considered as belonging in this category and hence as doubly deserving of help and charity. (Trans.)

of adoption — the introduction of an alien element into the lineage — in conjunction with the offense of adultery, which is abhorrent both to the divinely revealed laws and to upright human nature. By this action the human being is degraded to the level of an animal, who has no consciousness of the noble bonds (of morality and lineage) which exist among the members of a human society.[1]

Attributing the Child to a Man Other Than the Child's Father

Just as Islam prohibits a father to deny his paternity of his own child without a justifiable reason, it likewise forbids the child to claim a lineage other than his own, or to claim as father someone who is not his real father. The Prophet (peace be on him) listed this practice among the abominable evils deserving the curse of both the Creator and His creatures. Once 'Ali, speaking from the pulpit, read from some pages on which he had written various *ahadith*. One of the Prophet's statements was the following:

> The one who claims descent from someone other than his (real) father, and the slave who attaches himself to someone other than his (real) master, are cursed by Allah, His angels, and the people. Allah will accept neither repentance nor ransom from such a person on the Day of Resurrection.[2]

And Sa'd bin Abi Waqqas narrated that the Prophet (peace be on him) said,

> If someone claims a person as his father with the knowledge that he is not his father, the Garden will be forbidden to him.[3]

---

[1] *Al-Fatwa (Islamic Legal Decisions)*, by Sheikh Shaltut, p. 300.
[2] Reported by al-Bukhari and Muslim.
[3] Reported by al-Bukhari and Muslim.

"Do Not Kill Your Children"

After safeguarding the lineage in this manner, Islam imposed certain mutual rights, which proceed naturally from the parent-child relationship, upon children and parents, making certain things *haram* for them in order to protect these rights.

The child has a right to life. Neither the father nor the mother have the right to take the life of the child, whether a boy or a girl, by killing it or burying it alive, as was done by some Arabs of *jahiliyyah*. Says Allah Ta'ala:

> And do not kill your children out of fear of poverty; We
> shall provide for them and for you. Truly, the killing of
> them is a great sin.   (17:31)

> ...When the female child who was buried alive is asked
> for what crime she was killed.   (81:8-9)

Whatever the motive for this crime may be, whether economical, such as fear of poverty and lack of provision, or non-economic, such as fear of disgrace in the case of a daughter, Islam absolutely prohibits this savage act which is nothing but premeditated murder and the oppression of a feeble, helpless human being. That is why, when the Prophet (peace be on him) was asked, "What is the greatest sin?" he replied,

> 'To ascribe divinity to someone other than Allah, when
> He is the One Who created you.' 'What next?' he was
> asked. 'To kill your child out of fear that it will share
> your food, he replied."[1]

The Prophet (peace be on him) took an oath of allegiance from both men and women at the time of their accepting Islam. This oath of allegiance included the condition that they would not kill their children and would consider it an absolutely prohibited crime:

> ...That they will not steal nor commit *zina* nor kill their
> children....(60:12)

It is the right of a child in relation to its parents that they should give it a good name, not one which will cause it embarrassment when it grows older. It is *haram* to give a name which denotes a

---

[1]Reported by al-Bukhari and Muslim.

slave or worshipper of someone other than Allah, as for example, 'Abd al-Nabi, 'Abd al-Masih, and the like.

A child has a right to sustenance, education, and proper care. The parents are not permitted to neglect the child's needs nor to abuse it. The Prophet (peace be on him) said:

> "Each one of you is a caretaker (*ra'iy*) and is responsible for those under his care." [1]

> "Wasting the sustenance of his dependents is sufficient sin for a man." [2]

> "Allah will ask every caretaker (*ra'iy*) about the people under his care, and the man will be asked concerning the people of his household." [3]

Equal Treatment of Children

It is obligatory for a father to treat all his children equally, especially in the matter of giving gifts. Accordingly, he is prohibited from bestowing more favors on some of his children than on others without any necessity or valid reason, since this will produce jealousy and may even arouse enmity and hatred among them. This applies equally to the mother. The Prophet (peace be on him) said,

> 'Do justice among your sons,' and repeated it thrice. [4]

The story behind this *hadith* is that the wife of Bashir bin Sa'd al-Ansari requested her husband to give a gift of a garden or a slave to her son, al-Nu'man bin Bashir. She asked Bashir to go to the Prophet (peace be on him) and request him to be a witness. Bashir went to him, saying, "The daughter of such and such — meaning his wife — has asked me to give a slave to her son." "Does he have brothers?" the Prophet (peace be on him) asked. "Yes," he replied. "Did you give the same to each of them?" inquired the Prophet (peace be on him). "No," said Bashir. The Prophet (peace be on him) then said,

---

[1] Reported by al-Bukhari and Muslim.
[2] Reported by Abu Daoud, al-Nisai, and al-Hakim.
[3] Reported by Ahmad, al-Nisai, and Abu Daoud.
[4] Reported by Muslim, Ahmad, and Abu Daoud.

"This is not correct, and I can never bear witness to other than what is just."[1]

Some other *ahadith* in this regard are as follows:

Do not ask me to be a witness to injustice. Your children have the right of receiving equal treatment, as you have the right that they should honor you.[2]

"Fear Allah and treat your children with equal justice."[3]

Imam Ahmad bin Hanbal said that preferential treatment of a child is permitted if he or she is handicapped while others are not.[4]

Observing the Limits of Allah Regarding Inheritance

It is *haram* for a father to deprive his children of inheritance, as for example, to deprive the females or the children of a wife who is not a favorite with him. Likewise, it is *haram* for one relative to deprive another eligible relative of his inheritance by means of a trick. It is Allah Subhanahu wa Ta'ala Himself, Who, out of His knowledge, wisdom and justice, has established the distribution of inheritance in order to give each eligible person his or her share, and He has commanded mankind to remain within the limits of His legislation; hence, anyone who deviates from His system in the distribution of shares offends his Lord.

Allah Ta'ala has mentioned matters of inheritance in three verses of the Qur'an. At the end of the first verse He says,

...Your fathers or your sons: you do not know which of them is nearer to you in benefit. This is an obligation ordained by Allah; indeed, Allah is Knower, Wise. (4:11)

After the second such verse He says,

...Which is not injurious (to the rightful heirs): a charge from Allah, and Allah is Knowing, Forbearing. Those

---

[1] Reported by Ibn Hibban in his *Sahih*.
[2] Reported by Abu Daoud.
[3] Reported by al-Bukhari and Muslim.
[4] In Al-Mughni, vol. 5, p. 605, it is stated that special treatment of a child is permissible due to a need, a handicap, blindness, his or her being from a large family, being engaged in studies, or something of the sort, as it is also permitted to withhold from a child who would spend what he is given on sinful or wicked things.

are the limits of Allah, and whoever obeys Allah and His Messenger, He will admit him to Gardens beneath which rivers flow, to abide therein, and that is the supreme achievement. But whoever disobeys Allah and His Messenger and transgresses His limits, He will admit him to Fire, to abide therein, and he shall have a humiliating punishment. (4:12-14)

And at the end of the third such verse He says,

...Allah makes clear to you (His laws) so that you do not err; and Allah has knowledge of all things. (4:176)

Accordingly, whoever disobeys Allah's laws of inheritance has deviated from the just course made plain by Him, transgressing His limits, and must expect the punishment promised him:

...the Fire, to abide therein, and his shall be a humiliating punishment. (4:14)

Disobedience to Parents: A Major Sin

It is the right of parents that their children should treat them with kindness, obedience, and honor. Devotion to parents is a natural instinct which must be strengthened by deliberate actions. The rights of the mother are stressed the more because of her suffering during pregnancy and childbirth, her suckling of the child, and her role in rearing it. In the words of Allah Ta'ala:

And We have enjoined on man kindness to his parents. His mother carries him in pain and she gives birth to him in pain, and (the period) of carryng him and weaning him is thirty months....(46:15)

Once a man came to the Prophet (peace be on him) and asked, 'Who is most deserving of my good companionship?' 'Your mother,' replied the Prophet (peace be on him). 'Who next?' the man asked. 'Your mother,' replied the Prophet (peace be on him). 'Who next?' he asked. 'Your mother,' replied the Prophet (peace be on him). 'Who next?' asked the man. 'Your father,' replied the Prophet. [1]

---

[1] Reported by al-Bukhari and Muslim.

The Prophet (peace be on him) declared disobedience to parents to be a major sin, second only to ascribing partners to Allah, as has been stated in the Qur'an. Al-Bukhari and Muslim report his saying,

'Shall I not inform you about the three major sins?' Those who were present replied, 'Yes, O Messenger of Allah.' He said 'Associating partners with Allah and disobedience to parents,' and sitting up from the reclining position, he continued, 'and telling lies and false testimony; beware of it.'

He also said,

"Three persons shall not enter the Garden: the one who is disobedient to his parents, the pimp, and the woman who imitates men."[1]

and,

"Allah defers (the punishment of) all sins to the Day of Resurrection excepting disobedience to parents, for which Allah punishes the sinner in this life before his death."[2]

Moreover, Islam emphasizes treating parents kindly, especially when they grow old. As their strength fails, they require more attention and care, and more consideration of their even more sensitive feelings. Concerning this the Qur'an says,

Thy Lord hath decreed that you worship none but Him and that you be kind to parents. If one or both of them attain old age with thee, do not say a word of annoyance[3] to them nor repulse them, but speak to them in gracious words and in mercy lower to them the wing of humility and say, My Lord, bestow Thy mercy on them, as they cherished me when I was little....(17:23-24)

In explaining this verse, a commentator says, "If a lesser thing than saying 'Uff!' to parents were known to Allah, He would have prohibited (even that)."

---

[1]Reported by al-Nisai, al-Bazzar on the authority of excellent transmitters, and al-Hakim.
[2]Reported by al-Hakim, on the uthority of sound transmitters.
[3]Literally, "Do not say *Uff!* (an expression of annoyance) to them." (Trans.)

Insulting Parents: A Major Sin

In addition to the foregoing, the Prophet (peace be on him) not only prohibited insulting or cursing one's parents but declared it to be a major sin. He said,

> 'Among the major sins is a man's cursing his parents.' The people who were present wondered how a sane and believing individual could curse his own parents, and enquired, 'How is it possible for a man to curse his own parents?' The Prophet (peace be on him) replied, 'He insults another man's father, and then the other insults his father, and he insults the other's mother, and the other returns the insult to his mother.'[1]

The Parent's Consent for Jihad

Pleasing one's parents is considered so important in Islam that the son is forbidden to volunteer for *jihad* without his parent's permission, in spite of the fact that fighting in the cause of Allah (*jihad fi sabeel Allah*) has such great merit in Islam that the merit of a person who spends his nights in prayer and his days in fasting falls short of it.

Narrated 'Abdullah bin 'Amr bin al-'As,

> A man came to the Prophet (peace be on him) and asked his permission to go for *jihad*. The Prophet (peace be on him) asked, 'Are your parents living?' 'Yes,' he replied. The Prophet (peace be on him) then said, 'Then strive in their service,'[2]

meaning that taking care of parents is a greater obligation than *jihad* in the cause of Allah.

'Abdullah also narrated,

> A man came to the Prophet (peace be on him) and said, 'I take the oath of allegiance to you for *hijrah* (emigration to Medinah) and *jihad*, seeking reward

---

[1]Reported by al-Bukhari and Muslim.
[2]Reported by al-Bukhari and Muslim.

from Allah.' The Prophet (peace be on him) enquired whether either of his parents were living. On his replying that both of them were, the Prophet (peace be on him) said, 'Are you (really) seeking reward from Allah?' 'Yes,' the man said. The Prophet (peace be on him) then said, 'Go back to your parents and be a good companion to them.'[1]

'Abdullah further narrated,

A man came to the Prophet (peace be on him) and said, 'I have come to swear allegiance to you for *hijrah,* and I have left my parents weeping.' The Prophet (peace be on him) said to him, 'Return to them and make them laugh as you made them weep.'[2]

Abu Sa'id reported that

A man from Yemen migrated to Madinah to be with the Prophet (peace be on him). The Prophet (peace be on him) asked him, 'Do you have any relatives in Yemen?' He answered, 'My parents.' 'Did you get their permission?' the Prophet (peace be on him) asked. On his replying that he did not, the Prophet (peace be on him) told him, 'Go back to them and ask their permission. If they agree to it, go on *jihad.* Otherwise stay and serve them.'[3]

Non-Muslim Parents

It is one of the beauties of Islam that, with respect to the treatment of parents, it forbids the Muslim to be disrespectful to them even if they should be non-Muslims who are fanatical to the point of arguing with him and putting pressure on him to renounce Islam. Says Allah Ta'ala:

...Be grateful to Me and to thy parents; to Me is (the final) goal. But if they strive to compel thee to associate with Me that of which thou hast no knowledge, do not

---

[1] Reported by Muslim.
[2] Reported by al-Bukhari and others.
[3] Reported by Abu Daoud.

obey them; but keep company with them in this life in a
kind manner and follow the way of those who turn to
Me. Then to Me will be your return and I will inform you
(of the meaning of) all that you did.   (31:14-15)

In these two verses the Muslim is commanded not to obey his
parents in what they try to tell him to do in this regard, since there
cannot be obedience to a creature in sin against the Creator — and
what sin could be greater than associating partners with Allah? At
the same time, he is commanded to treat them honorably in this
world, unaffected by their stand against his faith, and to follow the
path of those righteous Believers who turn to Allah and to leave the
judgement between himself and his parents to the Most Just of
Judges, on a Day when the parents will not be able to benefit the
child nor the child the parent. Indeed, such tolerant and beneficient
teachings are not to be found in any other religion.

CHAPTER FOUR
THE *HALAL* AND THE *HARAM* IN THE DAILY LIFE OF THE MUSLIM

Beliefs and Customs
Transactions
Play and Recreation
Social Relationships
Relation With Non-Muslims

1. *BELIEFS AND CUSTOMS*

Faith *(iman)* is the foundation of the Islamic society, and *tauheed* (the belief in the existence and unity of God) is the essence of this faith and the very core of Islam. The safeguarding of this *iman* and of this pure *tauheed* is the primary objective of all the Islamic teachings and legislation. In order to keep the Muslim society purified of all traces of *shirk* and remnants of error, a continuous war must be waged against all belief-systems which originate in man's ignorance of the divine guidance and in the errors of idol worship.

Respect for Allah's Laws in the Universe

One of the fundamental beliefs which Islam inculcates in the soul of Muslims is that this vast universe does not run itself without any control and guidance, nor does it follow the misguided, blind, conflicting, and contraditory desires of men or of any other creatures residing in it. The Qur'an says:

> If Reality had been in accord with their desires, the heavens and the earth, and whosoever is therein, would have been in corruption....(23:71)

Quite to the contrary, the universe is bound by permanent laws, as the Qur'an states elsewhere:

> Thou wilt not find any changes in the *sunnah* (practice or rule) of Allah, nor wilt thou find in the *sunnah* of Allah any turning aside.   (35:43)

Muslims have learned from the Book of their Lord and the practice of their Prophet (peace be on him) to respect these laws of the universe, to understand and to use the causes and relationships which Allah has established among things, and to reject the alleged esoteric causes propagated by priests, charlatans, and imposters.

The War Against Superstitions and Myths

A class of deceivers known as soothsayers or diviners existed in

238

Arab society during the Prophet's time; they pretended to know the events of the past and future through their contact with the *jinn* or through other secret sources. The Prophet (peace be on him) then declared war on this deception, which had no basis in knowledge, divine guidance, or a revealed scripture. He recited to them what Allah had revealed to him:

Say: No one in the heavens and the earth knows the Unseen except Allah....(27:65)

Accordingly, the Unseen is known neither to the angels, the *jinn* nor human beings. Acting on the command of his Lord, the Prophet (peace be on him) proclaimed,

...If I had knowledge of the Unseen, I should have had abundance of good and no evil should have touched me. Truly, I am but a warner and a bringer of good tidings to those who have faith.   (7:188)

Concerning the *jinn* who labored for Solomon, Allah Ta'ala says:

...It became clear to the *jinn* that if they had known the Unseen, they would not have continued in the humiliating punishment (of their task).   (34:14)

Accordingly, anyone who claims to know what pertains to the Unseen utters a falsehood against Allah and the truth, deceiving the people.

Once a delegation came to the Prophet (peace be on him) and, supposing him to be one of those who claimed to have knowledge of the Unseen, they concealed something in their hands, asking the Prophet (peace be on him) to tell them what it was. The Prophet (peace be on him) told them in plain words,

"I am not a diviner. The diviner, (what pertains to) the divination, and the soothsayers will all be in the Fire."

Believing in Those Who Fortell the Future Constitutes Kufr

Islam's campaign was not confined to the soothsayers and diviners but included all those who go to them, ask their help, and believe in their superstitions and errors. The Prophet (peace be on him) said,

The *salat* of one who goes to a soothsayer, asks him something and believes in what he says will not be accepted for forty days.[1]

He also said,

"Whoever goes to a soothsayer and believes in what he says has denied what was revealed to Muhammad,"[2]

for what was revealed to Muhammad (peace be on him) asserts that the knowledge of the Unseen belongs to Allah alone and that Muhammad (peace be on him) has no knowledge of it, much less anyone else:

Say: I do not tell you that the treasures of Allah are with me or that I know the Unseen, nor do I tell you that I am an angel; I follow only what is revealed to me....(6:50)

If, after being aware of this clear and explicit statement of the Qur'an, the Muslim believes that some people can fortell future events and know the secrets of the Unseen, he has indeed denied what was revealed to the Messenger of Allah (peace be on him).

Divination With Arrows

For the reason mentioned above, divination with arrows was prohibited by Islam. The Arabs of *jahiliyyah* used three arrows for divination; on one arrow was written, "My Lord commanded me," on another, "My Lord forbade me," and the third was left blank. If they planned to go on a journey, to marry, to carry out a raid, etc., they would go to the temple where these arrows were kept. One arrow would be selected randomly. If they selected the "commanding" arrow they would proceed with their plan; if they selected the "forbidding" arrow they would not proceed with it; while if the blank arrow was drawn they would replace it and repeat the process until they received a clear indication.

The practices in our society of making decisions on the basis of

---

[1]Reported by Musilm.
[2]Reported by al-Bazzar, from good and strong transmitters.

what is observed in sand, seashells, tea leaves, cards, palms, of opening a book at random, and the like are similar to this practice.[1] Islam has prohibited all such practices and considers them sinful. After mentioning the prohibited foods, Allah Subhanahu wa Ta'ala says:

> ...And (also forbidden) is predicting the future by means of divining arrows, for that is impiety....(5:4 (3))

And the Prophet (peace be on him) said,

> He who consults with soothsyers or divining arrows, or returns from a journey because of an ill omen, shall not attain the high rank (in Paradise).[2]

Magic

In like manner, Islam condemns magic and those who practice it. Concerning those who learn magic the Qur'an says:

> ...They learned (only) what harmed them and what did not benefit them....(2:103)

The Prophet (peace be on him) counted the practice of magic among those major deadly sins which destroy nations before destroying individuals and which degrade those who practice them in this world prior to the Hereafter. Said he,

> 'Avoid the seven destroyers.' The listeners asked, 'O Messenger of Allah, what are they?' He said, 'Associating (partners) with Allah (shirk), magic, taking a life which Allah has made sacred except in the course of justice, devouring usury, appropriating the property of the orphan, fleeing from the battlefield, and slandering virtuous believing women who are indiscreet.'[3]

---

[1]This also indicates the practice of astrology, belief in horoscopes, and related matters. The Prophet (peace be on him) said, "If anyone acquires any knowledge of astrology, he acquires a branch of magic." (Ahmad, Abu Daoud, and Ibn Majah) He also said, "The astrologer is a diviner, the diviner is a magician, and the magician is an unbeliever." (Razi)

[2]Reported by al-Nisai.

[3]Reported by al-Bukhari and Muslim.

Some jurists consider magic as unbelief (*kufr*) or as leading toward unbelief, and some have even advocated that those who practice it should be put to death in order to purify the society of their evil. The Qur'an has taught us to seek refuge in Allah from the evil of the practitioners of magic:[1]

...From the evil of those who blow on knots.... (113:4),

since blowing on knots is one of the methods which such people employ. The Prophet (peace be on him) said,

"Whoever blows on knots practices magic, and whoever practices magic is a *mushrik* (polytheist)."[2]

Just as it is *haram* for the Muslim to consult with diviners or fortune-tellers concerning the secrets of the Unseen, it is likewise *haram* for him to seek the help of magic, or those who practice it, to cure an illness or to remove a difficulty. The Messenger of Allah (peace be on him) disowned such persons, saying

He is not of us who seeks an omen or for whom an omen is sought, who divines or for whom divination is made, who practices magic or asks someone to practice magic for him.[3]

Says 'Abdullah bin Mas'ood,

Anyone who goes to a diviner, a practitioner of magic or a soothsayer, asking something and believing in what he says, denies what was revealed to Muhammad.[4]

And the Prophet (peace be on him) said,

"The alcoholic, the believer in magic, and the one who breaks the ties of kinship will not enter the Garden."[5]

The sin of such things is not limited to the practitioner of magic alone but includes those who believe in his magic, encourage him, and trust in what he says. The sin becomes greater and more flagrant if the magic is used for purposes which are *haram* in

---

[1] Magic should be understood to denote witchcraft, sorcery, and all related practices. (Trans.)
[2] Reported by al-Tabarani through two chains of transmitters, one of which is reliable.
[3] Reported by al-Bazzar on good authority.
[4] Reported by al-Bazzar and Abu Y'ala on good authority.
[5] Reported by Ibn Hibban in his *Sahih*.

themselves, such as sowing discord between a husband and wife, inflicting bodily injury, and other evil uses, which are popular among those who practice magic.

Charms and Amulets

In the same category is the hanging of charms, seashells and the like in the belief that they will bring about the cure of a disease or act as a protection from it. There are still some people in the twentieth century who hang a horseshoe on the door. Moreover, we still find today charlatans in various countries who exploit the ignorance of simple people by writing amulets and charms for them, drawing lines and talismans and reciting strange incantations, with the claim that these practices will protect the bearer from the aggression of evil spirits, the influence of demons, the evil eye, envy, and so on.

As far as the prevention and treatment of disease are concerned, Islam has prescribed measures which are well known, condemning those who turn away from them to the deceitful methods of swindlers. The Prophet (peace be on him) said,

"Seek the remedy, for He Who created illness also created its cure." [1]

He also said,

"There is a remedy in three things: a drink of honey, bleeding by a cupper, and cauterization by fire." [2]

In our time these three types of cures include, by analogy and extension, all medicines which are taken by mouth, surgical intervention, and therapies utilizing heat or electricity.

As for wearing beads, seashells, charms and amulets, or reciting certain incantations to treat or prevent illness, such practices are sheer ignorance and error, are contrary to the laws of Allah Ta'ala, and constitute a denial of *tauheed*.

'Uqba bin 'Amir narrated that he came to the Prophet (peace be on him) in a group of ten persons. The Prophet (peace be on him) accepted the oath of allegiance (*bay'ah*) from nine of them,

---

[1]Reported by Ahmad.
[2]Reported by al-Bukhari and Muslim.

withholding himself from the tenth. "What about him?" they asked. "There is an amulet on his arm," the Prophet (peace be on him) replied. The man tore off the amulet and the Prophet (peace be on him) then accepted his oath, saying,

"The one who wears it is a polytheist." [1]

The Prophet (peace be on him) also said,

May Allah not fulfill the hopes of the one who wears a charm; may Allah not protect the one who hangs seashells. [2]

'Umran bin Hasin narrated that the Prophet (peace be on him) saw a man wearing a brass bracelet on his arm and he said to him, "Woe to you, what is this?" He replied, "To protect me from weakness." The Prophet (peace be on him) said,

Indeed, this only increases your weakness. Throw it away, for if you die wearing it, you will never attain success. [3]

These teachings of the Prophet (peace be on him) penetrated the minds of his companions, and they rejected such erroneous and false practices, neither accepting nor believing in them. 'Isa bin Hamzah narrated, "I visited 'Abdullah bin Hakim who had a fever. I said, 'Why do you not wear a charm?' He replied, 'I seek refuge in Allah from that.' " In another version he said, "Death is preferable to that." The Messenger of Allah (peace be on him) said,

"Whoever wears a charm will be left to rely on it." [4]

'Abdullah bin Mas'ood once saw his wife wearing a knotted thread around her neck. He pulled at it and broke it, saying, "The family of 'Abdullah is free of associating anything with Allah for which He has sent no authority." Then he said, "I heard the Messenger of Allah (peace be on him) say,

'Incantations, amulets and spells are *shirk*.'

Someone once said to him, "Abu 'Abdur-Rahman (as he was

---

[1]Reported by Ahmad and al-Hakim; the words are from al-Hakim. Ahmad's transmitters are reliable.
[2]Reported by Ahmad, by Abu Y'ala with good transmitters, and by al-Hakim, who classified it as sound.
[3]Reported by Ahmad, by Ibn Hibban in his *Sahih*, and by Ibn Majah without "Throw it away..." to the end.
[4] Reported by al-Tirmidhi.

commonly called), we are familiar with incantations and amulets, but what are spells?" He said, "Something which women employ to make their husbands love them."[1] Accordingly, a spell denotes a kind of magical practice.

Scholars say that if incantations are in a foreign language so that one does not know what is being said, they are prohibited out of fear of their being mixed with unbelief and magic. However, if what is being said can be understood and there is mention of Allah in it, it is commendable because it is then a supplication to Allah and is not meant to be a cure or a medicine. The incantations of *jahiliyyah* were intermixed with magical formulae, polytheistic phrases, and nonsensical utterances.

It is reported that 'Abdullah bin Mas'ood forbade his wife to utter such *jahili* incantations. She told him, "I went out one day and saw such and such person. One of my eyes then began to water (meaning that it was the effect of his evil eye and envy). But when I recited an incantation it stoopped watering, and when I left off reciting it, the eye started watering again." Ibn Mas'ood said, "That is Satan. When you obey him he leaves you alone, but when you disobey him he stabs your eye with his finger. But if you do as the Prophet (peace be on him) did, it will be better for you and will most probably cure your eye. Bathe your eye with water and say,

Remove the hurt, O Lord of mankind. Heal me; Thou art the Healer. There is no cure except Thy cure which leaves behind no disease.[2]

Omens

Drawing evil omens from certain articles, places, times, individuals, and the like was, and still is, a current superstition. In antiquity, the people of the Prophet Salih (peace be on him) said to him,

---

[1]Reported by Ibn Hibban in his *Sahih*. Al-Hakim has a shorter version, and he says it has sound transmitters.
[2]This is Ibn Majah's wording; Abu Daoud has a shorter version of this *hadith*, and al-Hakim a shorter one than either of the preceding.

We augur an evil omen of thee and those with
thee....(27:47)

And whenever a calamity struck them, Pharoah and his people
...ascribed it to evil omens connected with Moses and
those with him. (7:31)

Many times, when Allah Ta'ala tried the unbelievers by sending a
calamity, they would say to the messengers of Allah (peace be on
them all),
...Indeed, we augur an evil omen from you. (36:18)

The reply of the messengers was,
Your auguring of evil omens is with yourselves, (36:19)

meaning, "The cause of your evil omens is in your own attitude,
stemming from your unbelief, stubborness, and arrogance in regard
to Allah and His messengers."

The Arabs of *jahiliyyah* had a long history of such practices
associated with a variety of beliefs which persisted until the coming
of Islam, which abolished all such notions and brought the people
back to the way of sound reason. The Prophet (peace be on him)
classified the auguring of evil omens with divination and magic in
his saying,
He is not of us who seeks for evil omens or for whom evil
omens are sought, who divines or for whom divination
is made, who practices magic or for whom magic is
practiced. [1]

The Prophet (peace be on him) also said,
"Augury from drawing lines in the sand, from the flight
of birds, and from throwing stones pertains to *shirk*." [2]

The auguring of omens has no basis in science or in reality but is a
weakness of the mind and a superstition. How can a sane human
being believe that a certain person or place, the cry of a bird, the flick
of an eyelid, or the hearing of a certain word can bode something
evil? Even if there is some weakness in human nature which is
conducive to the seeking of omens from certain things, one should
not surrender to this weakness, especially when a decision is to be
made or an action is to be taken. It is stated in a *hadith* that

---

[1] Reported by al-Tabarani on the authority of Ibn 'Abbas through good transmitters.
[2] Reported by Abu Daoud, al-Nisai, and Ibn Hibban in his *Sahih*.

No one is free of three things: suspicion, auguring evil
omens, and envy. Thus, if you have a suspicion, do not
pursue it; if you augur an evil omen, do not turn back;
and if you are envious, do not transgress.[1]

In this way these three things will remain mere thoughts which
cross the mind without affecting the actual behavior, and Allah
Ta'ala will forgive them. Ibn Mas'ood reported the Prophet (peace
be on him) as saying three times,

"Auguring evil omens is *shirk* (polytheism)."

And Ibn Mas'ood added, "None of us fails to be affected by this, but
Allah removes such influences through our trust in Him,"[2] meaning
that although there is no one among us who is not affected by this
weakness at one time or another, this weakness is removed from the
heart of the person who turns to Allah, trusting in Him and not
letting such ideas obsess him.

The War Against Jahili Customs

On the one hand Islam launched an attack on *jahili* beliefs and
superstitions which were a threat to reason, morals, and manners,
and on the other, on *jahili* customs, which were the product of
chauvinism: boastfulness, pride, and the glorification of the tribe.

No Chauvinism in Islam

Islam's first step in this direction was to reduce every kind of
group chauvinism to dust, forbidding the Muslim to revive any of
the disputes of such chauvinism or to summon others toward it. The
Prophet (peace be on him) declared himself free of responsibility for
anyone who practices it, saying,

He who calls others to group chauvinism does not
belong to us; he who fights for the sake of group

---

[1] Reported by al-Tabarani.
[2] Reported by Abu Daoud and al-Tirmidhi.

chauvinism does not belong to us; and he who dies upholding group chauvinism does not belong to us.[1]

There is no special distinction for a certain color of skin, a particular race of mankind, or a special region of the earth. The Muslim is forbidden to be a partisan of one race against another, one people against another, or one country against another. It is not permissible for a believer in Allah and the Last Day to support his people without regard for whether they are right or wrong, just or unjust.

Wathilah bin al-Asq'a narrated, "I asked, 'O Messenger of Allah, what is chauvinism?' and he replied,

That you should help your people in wrongdoing."[2]

And Allah Ta'ala says:

O you who believe, be steadfast in justice, as witnesses for Allah, even though it be against yourselves or parents or kindred.   (4:135)

...And do not let hatred of (other) people cause you to deviate from justice.   (5:9 (8))

"Help your brother, whether he is the opressor or the opressed," was a well-known proverb in pre-Islamic *jahiliyyah* which people used to take literally. The Prophet (peace be on him) changed its meaning in a subtle fashion. After the faith was firmly established in the hearts of his Companions, he once repeated this proverb to them. They were shocked, saying, "O Messenger of Allah, we know how to help the oppressed, but how can we help the oppressor?" He replied,

"Stop him from wrongdoing; that is helping him."[3]

We know from these statements that a call toward nationalism or racism is a call of *jahiliyyah*, and Islam, its Prophet (peace be on him), and its Book have totally rejected it. Islam does not recognize any loyalty other than to its belief, any relationship other than that of its brotherhood, or any differentiation among human beings other than on the basis of belief and unbelief. Even though he may

---

[1]Reported by Abu Daoud.
[2]Reported by Abu Daoud.
[3]Reported by al-Bukhari.

248

be a fellow countryman, a relative, or one's own blood brother, the unbeliever who shows hostility to Islam is an enemy to the Muslim. Says Allah Ta'ala:

Thou wilt not find any people who believe in Allah and the Last Day loving those who resist Allah and His Messenger, even if they are their fathers or their sons or their brothers or their kindred....(58:22)

O you who believe, do not take your fathers or your brothers as friends if they love unbelief more than faith....(9:23)

Lineage is Without Significance

Al-Bukhari reported that Abu Dharr and Bilal, the Abyssinian, both of whom were among the earliest Muslims, once quarreled and insulted each other. Carried away by his anger, Abu Dharr said to Bilal, "You son of a black woman!" Bilal complained about this to the Prophet (peace be on him), who turned to Abu Dharr, saying,

"Are you taunting him about his mother? There is still some influence of *jahiliyyah* in you!"[1]

Abu Dharr narrated that the Prophet (peace be on him) said to him,

"Look! You are no better than a white or black man unless you excel in the fear of Allah."[2]

The Prophet (peace be on him) also said,

"You are all children of Adam, and Adam was created of dust."[3]

Thus Islam made it *haram* for the Muslim to boast about his genealogy and kinship, mentioning his forefathers and saying, "I am the son of such and such," or "I am white and you are black, I am an Arab and you are a non-Arab." What is the value of kinships and genealogies when all people come from one single origin? And even

---

[1]Reported by al-Bukhari.
[2]Reported by al-Bukhari.
[3]Reported by Ahmad.

supposing that genealogy had value, how does it add to the credit or debit of a person to have been born to this or that father? Said the Prophet (peace be on him),

> These genealogies of yours are not a reason to revile anyone. You are all children of Adam. No one has superiority over another except in religion and *taqwa* (the fear of Allah).[1]

> Mankind is descended from Adam and Eve....On the Day of Resurrection Allah will not ask you about your kinships and genealogies. The most honorable among you in the sight of Allah is the one who is the most God-fearing (*mutaqqi*).[2]

The Prophet (peace be on him) launched a fierce atack on those who boast about their fathers and grandfathers, saying,

> Let people cease to boast about their ancestors who have died, who are merely fuel in hell, or they will certainly be of less account than the beetle which rolls dung with its nose. Allah has removed from you the pride of *jahiliyyah* and its boasting about ancestors. One is either a God-fearing Believer or a wicked sinner. All people are children of Adam, and Adam was created from dust.[3]

People who boast about their remote ancestors among the pharoahs or the choesroes (the rulers of ancient Persia) and the like should take note of this *hadith*. As the Messenger of Allah (peace be on him) has stated, these ancestors of theirs , whether Arab or non-Arab, or pre-Islamic *jahiliyyah*, are nothing but the fuel of hell.

During the Farewell Pilgrimage, while thousands of Muslims gathered in the sacred place, during the sacred month, the Prophet (peace be on him) delivered his last public address, emphasizing the basic principles:

> O people, your Lord is One. Know that there is no superiority of an Arab over a non-Arab or of non-Arab

---

[1]Reported by al-Bazzar.
[2]Reported by Ahmad.
[3]Reported by Abu Daoud and al-Tirmidhi; the wording is from the latter, who classifies it as good. It is also reported by al-Bayhaqi through good transmitters.

over an Arab, nor of a white over a black or of a black over a white, except through consciousness of Allah (*taqwa*). Verily, the most honorable among you in the sight of Allah is the one who has most *taqwa*.[1]

Mourning for the Dead

Among the customs of *jahiliyyah* which were denounced by Islam was the practice of wailing, lamenting, and showing excessive grief for the dead.

Islam's teaching concerning death is that it is not the annihilation of an individual, causing him to become non-existent, but that it is a journey from one world to another and that no amount of mourning will bring the dead back to life or change the decree of Allah Subhanahu wa Ta'ala. The Believer should receive death, as he receives any other calamity which may befall him, with patience and dignity, repeating the *ayah*, To Allah we belong and to Him do we return. (2:156)

The pre-Islamic manner of mourning for the dead is strictly forbidden to the Muslim. The Prophet (peace be on him) declared,

"He who slaps his cheeks, tears his clothes, and cries out in the manner of *jahiliyyah* is not of us."[2]

The Muslim is not permitted to wear a mourning band, discard his adornment, or change his usual attire to express his sorrow and grief.[3] However, a wife must observe a mourning period (*'iddah*) of four months and ten days for her deceased husband in loyalty to the sacred ties of marriage; in Islam this period is considered an extension of her previous marriage and she is not allowed to receive any new proposals of marriage during this period. Thus, she is required to refrain from adorning herself during that time both as a sign of mourning and in order to keep the thought of remarriage out of her own mind and that of her potential suitors. However, if the deceased is someone other than her husband, for example, her

---

[1]Reportred by Ahmad.
[2]Reported by al-Bukhari.
[3]The wearing of black as a sign of mourning is prohibited in Islam, even in the case of a widow in mourning for her husband. (Trans.)

father, brother or son, it is *haram* for her to mourn for more than three days. Al-Bukhari reported concerning Umm Habeebah and Zaynab bint Jahsh, both of whom were wives of the Prophet (peace be on him), that at the time of the deaths of Umm Habeebah's father, Abu Sufyan bin Harb, and Zaynab's brother, each of them perfumed herself, saying "By Allah, I am not in need of perfume, but I heard Allah's Messenger (peace be on him) say,

> It is *haram* for a woman who believes in Allah and the Last Day to mourn for a deceased person for more than three nights, except for the husband (for whom the period of mourning is) four months and ten days.[1]

The period of mourning fo the deceased husband is obligatory and should not be violated. A woman came to the Prophet (peace be on him) and said, "My daughter's husband has died, and her eye is infected. May she use kohl?"[2] The Prophet (peace be on him) said, "No," and repeated it twice or thrice.[3] This demonstrates that adorning or beautifying herself during the prescribed period of *iddah* is prohibited to the widow. As grief and the expression of it are natural, she may mourn and weep but without wailing and shouting. Upon the death of Khalid bin Walleed, 'Umar heard some women weeping. Some people wanted to stop them from it but 'Umar said, "Let them weep for Abu Sulayman (the name by which Khalid was called), as long as they do not throw dust on their heads or start crying out."

2. Business Transactions

Allah Subhanahu wa Ta'ala has created human beings in a state of dependence upon one another. Each individual does not own all the things he needs; one person has something which he can spare while at the same time he may need something which others have and which they can spare. Allah has directed people toward exchanging goods and utilities through buying and selling because

---

[1]Reported in the *Book of "Funerals"* in al-Bukhari's *Sahih.*
[2]In addition to being an adornment, kohl also possesses medicinal value for the eye. (Trans.)
[3]Reported in the *Book of Divorce* in al-Bukhari's *Sahih.* The narration here is that of Umm Habeebah, and Zainab's narrative is similar.

such transactions make social and economic life function smoothly and encourage people to be productive.

Various types of transactions and exchanges of property were current among the Arabs at the dawn of the Prophet's mission. He approved and confirmed such types of transactions which did not conflict with the principles of the *Shari'ah* and disapproved and prohibited those business practices which were against the purposes and aims of the *Shari'ah*. The prohibitions were due to specific reasons, as, for example, trading in *haram* goods, transactions involving fraud or exorbitant profits, or injustice to one of the contracting parties.

The Prohibition of Selling Haram Goods

Trading in goods which are normally used for commiting sin is *haram*. Examples of such things are swine, intoxicants, and other prohibited foods in general, as well as idols, crosses, statues, and the like. Permitting the sale or trade of such articles implies promoting and propagating them among people, and consequently encouraging them to do what is *haram*, while prohibiting their sale implies suppressing and ignoring them, thereby preventing people from coming into contact with them. The Prophet (peace be on him) said,

> "Surely, Allah and His Messenger have prohibited the sale of wine, the flesh of dead aniamls, swine and idols,"[1]

and also,

> "When Allah prohibits a thing, He prohibits (giving and receiving) the price of it as well."[2]

The Prohibition of a Sale Involving Uncertainty

The Prophet (peace be on him) forbade any kind of transaction

---

[1] Reported by al-Bukhari and Muslim.
[2] Reported by Ahmad and Abu Daoud.

which could lead to a quarrel or litigation due to some uncertainty[1] or which involved an unspecific quantity to be exchanged or delivered. This includes the sort of transaction in which there is no guarantee that the seller can deliver the goods for which he receives payment. Accordingly, the Prophet (peace be on him) forbade accepting money for a stallion's or male camel's covering, for fish in the water or birds in the air which one has not caught, or for the offspring of a camel still in the female's womb, since there is an element of uncertainty as to the outcome in all such transactions.

The Prophet (peace be on him) observed that people sold unripened fruits which were still in the fields or orchards; if the crop were destroyed by blight or some natural calamity, the buyer and seller would quarrel over who was to bear the loss. Hence, the Prophet (peace be on him) prohibited the sale of fruit until they were clearly in good condition,[2] unless they were to be picked on the spot. Similarly, he forbade selling ears of corn until they were white and safe from blight,[3] saying,

> "Tell me why, if Allah withholds the fruit, any of you should take his brother's property."[4]

However, not every sale involving what is unknown or uncertain is prohibited; for example, a person may buy a house without knowing the condition of its foundation or what is inside the walls. What is prohibited is selling something about which there is an obvious element of uncertainty which may lead to dispute and conflict, or may result in the unjust appropriation of other people's money. Again, if the risk of uncertainty is small — and this is determined by experience and custom — the sale is not prohibited. For example, one may sell root vegetables such as carrots, onions, and radishes while they are still in the ground, or fields of cucumbers, watermelons and the like. In the opinion of Imam Malik,

---

[1]See the chapter on "The Prohibition of *al-Gharar* (Transactions Involving Uncertainty)" in Muslim and others.
[2]Reported by al-Bukhari and Muslim.
[3]Reported by Muslim.
[4]Reported by al-Bukhari and others.

254

all such sales of needed items in which the margin of risk is bearable are permissible.[1]

Price Manipulation

In Islam the market is to be free and permitted to respond to the natural laws of supply and demand. Thus, when the prices became high in the Prophet's time and people asked him to fix prices for them, he replied,

> Allah is the One Who fixes prices, Who withholds, Who gives lavishly, and Who provides, and I hope that when I meet Him none of you will have a claim against me for any injustice with regard to blood or property.[2]

With these words the Prophet of Islam (peace be on him) declared that unnecessary interference in the freedom of individuals is injustice and that one should meet Allah free of blame for such a thing. If, however, any artificial forces, such as hoarding and manipulation of prices by certain merchants, interfere in the free market, public interest takes precedence over the freedom of such individuals. In such a situation price control becomes permissible in order to meet the needs of the society and to protect it from greedy opportunists by thwarting their schemes, for the above *hadith* does not mean that price control is prohibited regardless of the circumstances, even if it removes harm and prevents obvious injustice. Researchers among scholars have concluded that, depending on the nature of the circumstances, price control may at times be unjust and prohibited, and at other times may be just and permissible.

If price control compels people to sell their goods at a price which is not acceptable to them or denies them the reasonable profit permitted by Allah, it is *haram*. If, on the other hand, price control

---

[1]In *Al-qawa'id al-nuraniyyah*, p. 118, Ibn Taimiyyah says: "The principles laid down by (Imam) Malik concerning sales are superior to those of others, because he took them from Sa'id ibn al-Musayyib, who is the best authority on the *fiqh* (jurisprudence) of sales." Imam Ahmad bin Hanbal's opinion is close to that of Malik.
[2]Reported by Ahmad, Abu Daoud, al-Tirmidhi, Ibn Majah, al-Dari and Abu Y'ala.

establishes equity among people, for example, by forcing sellers to accept a price equal to that commanded by other comparable commodities and restraining them from taking more than this, it is allowed — indeed necessary.

The *hadith* cited above relates to the first type of situation. Accordingly, if merchants are selling a commodity in the customary fashion without any wrong-doing on their part and the price subsequently rises due to the scarcity of the commodity or due to an increase in population (indicating the operation of the law of supply and demand), this circumstance is from Allah, in which case to force them to sell the commodity at a fixed price would be unjust compulsion.

In relation to the second type of situation, should the dealers in a commodity refuse to sell it, despite the fact that people are in need of it, unless they secure a price higher than its known value, they must be compelled to sell it at a price equal to the price of an equivalent commodity. Price control here means nothing more than establishing comparable prices for equivalent commodities and it is therefore in conformity with the standard of justice demanded by Allah Ta'ala.[1]

The Condemnation of Hoarding

Freedom for individual and natural competition in the marketplace is guranteed by Islam. Nevertheless, Islam severely condemns those who, driven by ambition and greed, accumulate wealth at the expense of others and become rich by manipulating the prices of food and other necessities. This is why the Prophet (peace be on him) denounced hoarders in very strong words, saying,

> "If anyone withholds grain for forty days out of the desire for a high price, Allah will renounce him."[2]

He also said,

> "If anyone withholds goods until the price rises, he is a sinner."[3]

---

[1]Refer to *Risalat al-hisbah* by Ibn Taimiyyah, as well as to *Al-turuq al-hikmiyyah* by Ibn al-Qayyim, p. 214 ff.
[2]Reported by Ahmad, al-Hakim, Ibn Abu Shaybah, and al-Bazzar.
[3]Reported by Muslim.

And the term "sinner" here is not to be taken lightly. It is the same epithet which Allah Ta'ala has applied to some of the great tyrants in history, for example:

...Assuredly Pharoah and Haman and their hosts were sinners. (28:8)

The Prophet (peace be on him) also said,

"The man who hoards goods is evil. If prices fall he is grieved and if they rise he is happy,"[1]

thereby exposing the selfish and greedy mentality of hoarders. Again, he said,

"He who brings goods to the market is blessed with bounty, but he who withholds them is cursed."[2]

There are two ways of making a profit in a business. One is to withhold the commodity from the market until it becomes scarce and those who need it are unable to find it; then, compelled by their need, they come to the hoarder and pay him the price he demands, although it may be unreasonably high. The other way is to put the commodity on the market, sell it for a reasonable profit, buy more goods and sell them in like manner, and so on. Since this latter practice serves the public interest, a merchant who practices it is both blessed by Allah and well-provided for, as the foregoing *hadith* states.

A very important *hadith* concerning hoarding and manipulating prices has been narrated by M'aqal bin Yassar, a companion of the Prophet (peace be on him). The Umayyad governor, 'Ubaidullah bin Ziyad, came to visit M'aqal when he was bedridden due to a grave illness. After inquiring about his condition, 'Ubaidullah asked him, "Do you know of any instance of my having wrongfully shed someone's blood?" M'aqal replied tht he did not. "Do you know of any instance," 'Ubaidullah continued, "in which I interfered with the prices of the Muslims' goods?" Ma'aqal again replied that he did not know. Then M'aqal asked the people to help him to sit up, which they did. He then said, "Listen, O 'Ubaidullah, and I will tell you something which I heard from the Messenger of Allah (peace be on him). I heard the Messenger of Allah (peace be on him) say,

---

[1] Razi has mentioned this *hadith* in his *Jami'ah*.
[2] Reported by Ibn Majah and al-Hakim.

'Whoever interferes with the prices of the Muslims' goods in order to raise them deserves that Allah should make him sit in the Fire on the Day of Resurrection.'

"Did you hear this from Allah's Messenger (peace be on him)?" asked 'Ubaidullah, and Ma'qal replied, "More than once or twice."[1]

On the basis of the text and content of these foregoing *ahadith*, scholars have deduced that hoarding is prohibited under two conditions: one, that hoarding at a given time is injurious to the people of that country, and two, that the hoarder's aim is to force the price up in order to make more profit.

Interference in the Free Market

Another practice related to hoarding which was prohibited by the Prophet (peace be on him) was a townsman's selling on behalf of a man from the desert. Scholars have explained the situation in the following manner: a stranger would bring some goods to be sold in town at the current market price. A townsman would approach him, saying, "Leave them with me for a while. I will sell them for you when the price is better." Had the non-resident himself sold his goods, he would have done so for a lower price, thereby benefitting the people, while he himself would have made a reasonable profit.

This sort of practice was very common in Arab society when Islam came. Anas says, "Sale by a resident on behalf of a desert-dweller was prohibited to us, even though he might be a blood brother."[2] From this we learn that for the Muslim the public interest takes precedence over personal relationships. Said the Prophet (peace be on him),

A resident (of the town) must not sell for a man from the desert. If people are left alone, Allah will give them provision from one another.[3]

This significant expression of the Prophet's, "If people are left alone, Allah will give them provsion from one another," establishes

---

[1]Reported by Ahmad and al-Tabarani.
[2]Reported by al-Bukhari and Muslim.
[3]Reported by Muslim.

a basic principle in the field of commerce: that the market, its prices, and sales, should be left free to respond to internal economic forces and natural competition without manipulation. When Ibn 'Abbas was asked about the meaning of "A resident must not sell for a man from the desert," he replied, "The resident should not be a broker for him."[1] From this we understand that if someone were to inform the man from the desert about prices, proferring him good advice and telling him about prevailing market prices without charging him a commission, there would be no harm in it, for giving good advice is part of the religion; in fact, a sound *hadith* states,

"Religion is the giving of good advice,"[2]

and,

"If someone asks your advice, advise him."[3]

However, with regard to the broker, it is quite probable that, in a situation such as that described above, he might neglect the public interest for the sake of his own profit.

The Permissibility of Brokerage

With the exception of such cases, brokerage is permissible, since it is a sort of mediation and connection between the buyer and the seller, which in many cases facilitates a profitable transaction for at least one of them or for both.

In modern times, middlemen have become more necessary than at any time in the past because of the complexities of trade and commerce, which involve all types of exports and imports, and wholesale and retail sales and purchases; brokers play a very important role in keeping things moving. There is nothing wrong, therefore, with the broker's charging a commission for his services. The commission may be a fixed amount or proportional to the volume of sales, or whatever is agreed upon among the parties involved. Al-Bukhari states in his *Sahih*.

Ibn Sirin, 'Ata, Ibrahim, and Hassan saw nothing wrong with commissions charged by brokers. Ibn

---

[1]Reported by al-Bukhari.
[2]Reported by Muslim.
[3]Reported by Ahmad.

'Abbas said, 'There is no harm if one person says to another, "Sell this robe, and if you sell it for more than such and such a price, you may keep the extra amount."' Ibn Sirin said, 'There is nothing wrong if one person says to another, "Sell it for this price and keep the profit, or the profit will be shared between you and me."' The Prophet (peace be on him) said, 'The Muslims must abide by their terms.'[1]

Exploitation and Fraud

In order to prevent the manipulation of the market, the Prophet (peace be on him) also prohibited what is termed *najash*.[2] Ibn 'Umar explained that *najash* signifies someone's bidding for an item in excess of its price without having any intention of actually buying it, but merely in order to induce others to bid still higher. Many times this is pre-arranged for the purpose of deceiving others.

Among the variety of measures which the Prophet (peace be on him) took to keep business transactions as far removed as possible from all kinds of exploitation and fraud was that of prohibiting people from going out of town to buy merchandise which was on its way to the market, telling them to wait until it was brought to the marketplace.[3] The reason for this prohibition is that the market place, where the forces of demand and supply determine prices, is the best place for trading transactions. If someone goes out of town to buy from a trader who is bringing merchandise, there is a possibility that the seller, not knowing the current price of his merchandise, may be defrauded. If anyone does buy some of his merchandise in this manner, the seller has the option of canceling the transaction after arriving at the marketplace.[4]

---

[1]This *hadith* is reported by al-Bukhari with the chain of transmitters which does not reach back to the Prophet (peace be on him); however, Ahmad, Abu Daoud, al-Hakim, and others have a complete chain of transmitters.
[2]Reported by al-Bukhari and Muslim.
[3]Reported by Muslim, Ahmad, and Ibn Majah.
[4]Reported by Muslim.

Islam prohibits every type of fraud and deception, whether it be in buying and selling or in any other matter between people. In all situations the Muslim must be honest and truthful, holding his faith dearer than any worldly gain. The Prophet (peace be on him) said,

> Both parties to a business transaction have a right to cancel it as long as they have not separated. If they tell the truth and make everything clear, they will be blessed in their transaction, but if they lie and conceal anything, the blessing will be blotted out. [1]

He also said,

> It is not permissible to sell an article without making everything (about it) clear, nor is it permissible for anyone who knows (about its defects) to refrain from mentioning them. [2]

Once, when passing by a grain merchant, the Prophet's curiosity was aroused. He thrust his hand into the heap of grain and found it wet. "What is this, O merchant?" he asked. "It is because of rain," the man replied. The Prophet (peace be on him) then said to him,

> "Why did you not put it on top so that the people could see it? He who deceives us is not of us." [3]

In another report it is said that he passed by a heap of grain which was made to look good by the merchant. The Prophet (peace be on him) put his hand into it and found it to be bad. He told the merchant,

> "Sell the good and the bad separately. He who deceives us is not of us." [4]

The Muslims of earlier times strictly observed the practices of exposing the defects of what they sold, of telling the truth, and of giving good advice. When Ibn Sirin sold a sheep, he told the buyer, "I would like to tell you about a defect it has: it kicks the fodder." And

---

[1] Reported by al-Bukhari.
[2] Reported by al-Hakim and al-Bayhaqi.
[3] Reported by Muslim.
[4] Reported by Ahmad.

when al-Hassan bin Salih sold a slave girl he told the buyer, "Once she spat up blood." Although she had done this only once, al-Hassan's Muslim conscience required that he mention the fact, even if it resulted in his receiving a lower price.

Frequent Swearing

The sin of deceiving is the greater when the seller supports it by swearing[1] falsely. The Prophet (peace be on him) told the merchants to avoid swearing in general and, in particular, in support of a lie, saying,

> "Swearing produces a ready sale but blots out the blessing."[2]

He disapproved of frequent swearing in business transactions because first, it is probably done to deceive people, and second, because it reduces respect for the name of Allah.

Withholding Full Measure

One way of defrauding the customer is to measure or weigh incorrectly. The Qur'an emphasized this aspect of business transactions and included it among the ten obligations described in the last part of *Surah al-An'am:*

> ...And give full measure and (full) weight, in justice; We do not burden any soul beyond what it can bear....(6:152)

And elsewhere in the Qur'an Allah Ta'ala says,

> And give full measure when you measure and weigh with the straight balance; that is most fitting and best in the final determination.   (17:35)

He also says,

> Woe to the defrauders — those who, when they take the

---

[1] This means swearing that something is true in the name of Allah. (Trans.)
[2] Reported by al-Bukhari.

measure from people take it in full, but when they
measure for them or weigh for them give them short. Do
they not realize that they will be raised up again on a
mighty Day, a Day when mankind will stand before the
Lord of the worlds? (83:1-6)

The Muslim should try to do justice in measuring and weighing as
far as it is humanly possible, although absolute accuracy in this
regard is unattainable. This is why, following the command to give
full measure, the Qur'an adds, "We do not burden any soul beyond
what it can bear."

A story is narrated in the Qur'an concerning a people who were
dishonest in their business dealings, deviating from justice in
weighing and measuring, and being miserly with each other. Allah
Subhanahu wa Ta'ala sent a messenger to bring them back to
justice and honesty, as well as to the belief in His Unity. These were
the people of the prophet Shu'aib (peace be on him), who as a warner
and preacher, called on them to

Give full measure, and do not be of those who give less
(than what is due). And weigh with the straight
balance, and do not diminish people's goods nor do evil
on the earth, making mischief. (26:181-183)

What is correct in relation to weighing and measuring is correct in
relation to all other human affairs and relationships. The Muslim is
not permitted to have two standards, one for himself and one for
other people, this for the near and dear and that for the public,
demanding in full his rights and the rights of those who support
him, but when it concerns others, diminishing or depriving them of
their rights.

The Prohibition of Buying Stolen Property

In order to combat crime and to confine the criminal within a very
narrow sphere of activity, Islam has prohibited the Muslim to buy
any article which he knows to have been usurped, stolen, or taken
unjustly from its owner; anyone who does so abets the usurper, the
thief, or the one committing injustice in his respective crime. Said
the Prophet (peace be on him),

263

He who buys the stolen property, with the knowledge
that it was stolen, shares in the sin and shame of
stealing.[1]

The passage of time does not render a piece of stolen or
misappropriated property lawful, for in Islam the mere passage of
time does not transform the *haram* into the *halal* nor does it deprive
the original owner of his right to it.

The Prohibition of Interest

Islam permits increase in capital through trade. Allah
Subhanahu wa Ta'ala says,

O you who believe, do not consume your property
among yourselves wrongfully, but let there be trade by
mutual consent....(4:29)

At the same time, Islam blocks the way for anyone who tries to
increase his capital through lending on usury or interest (*riba*),
whether it is at a low or a high rate, reprimanding the Jews for
taking usury, even though they had been prohibited to do so. Among
the last revelations are the following verses of *Surah al-Baqarah:*

O you who believe, fear Allah and give up what remains
due to you of interest if you are indeed Believers. And if
you do not, then be warned of war (against you) by
Allah and His Messenger, while if you repent you shall
have your capital. Do not do wrong and you shall not be
wronged. (2:278-279)

The Prophet (peace be on him) declared war on usury and those
who deal in it; he pointed out its dangers to society, saying,

When usury and fornication appear in a community,
the people of that community render themselves
deserving of the punishment of Allah.[2]

Among the revealed religions,[3] Judaism, prior to Islam, had also
prohibited interest. In the Old Testament we read,

If you lend money to any of My people with you who is

---

[1]Reported by al-Bayhaqi.
[2]Reported by al-Hakim; Abu Y'ala has reported something similar on good authority.
[3]See footnote [1], page 5.

poor, you shall not be to him as a creditor, neither shall you require interest from him.   (Ex. 22:25)

As for Christianity, the Gospel according to Luke reads,

Give away to every one who begs of you, and of him who takes away from your goods, do not demand them back again.   (Luke 6:30)

It is, therefore, sad to see that the Old Testament has been subjected to such distortions that the meaning of "My people," which originally had a broader application, later became restricted to the Jews alone, as we read in Deuteronomy,

You may lend on interest to a foreigner, but to your brother you shall not lend on interst.   (Deut. 23:20)

The Wisdom of Prohibiting Interest

The strict prohibition of interest in Islam is a result of its deep concern for the moral, social, and economic welfare of mankind. Islamic scholars have given sound arguments explaining the wisdom of this prohibition, and recent studies have confirmed their opinions, with some additions and extensions of their arguments.

We confine ourselves to what Imam al-Razi says in his *Tafsir* of the Qur'an:

First: The taking of interest implies appropriating another person's property without giving him anything in exchange, because one who lends one *dirham* for two *dirhams* gets the extra *dirham* for nothing. Now, a man's property is for (the purpose of) fulfilling his needs and it has great sanctity, according to the *hadith,* 'A man's property is as sacred as his blood'[1] This means that taking it from him without giving him something in exchange is *haram.*

Second: Dependence on interest prevents people from

---

[1]Transmitted by Abu Na'eem in *Al-hilbah.*

working to earn money, since the person with *dirhams* can earn an extra *dirham* through interest, either in advance or at a later date, without working for it. The value of work will consequently be reduced in his estimation, and he will not bother to take the trouble of running a business or risking his money in trade or industry. This will lead to depriving people of benefits, and the business of the world cannot go on without industries, trade and commerce, building and construction, all of which need capital at risk. (This, from an economic point of view, is unquestionably a weighty argument.)

Third: Permitting the taking of interest discourages people from doing good to one another, as is required by Islam. If interest is prohibited in a society, people will lend to each other with good will, expecting back no more than what they have loaned, while if interest is made permissible the needy person will be required to pay back more on loans (than he has borrowed), weakening his feelings of good will and friendliness toward the lender. (This is the moral aspect of the prohibition of interest.)

Fourth: The lender is very likely to be wealthy and the borrower poor. If interest is allowed, the rich will exploit the poor, and this is against the spirit of mercy and charity. (This is the social aspect of the prohibtion of interest.)[1]

Thus, in a society in which interest is lawful, the strong benefit from the suffering of the weak. As a result, the rich become richer and the poor poorer, creating socio-economic classes in the society separated by wide gulfs. Naturally this generates envy and hatred among the poor toward the rich, and contempt and callousness among the rich toward the poor. Conflicts arise, the socio-economic fabric is rent, revolutions are born, and social order is threatened. Recent history amply illustrates the dangers to the peace and stability of nations inherent in interest-based economies.

---

[1] *Tafsir* by al-Fakhr al-Deen al-Razi, vol. 7, p. 4.

The Borrower on Interest and the Writer of the Deed

Unquestionably the money-lender who takes interest, getting more from the borrower than his capital, is accursed in the sight of Allah and the people. But Islam, with its characteristic method of dealing with the *haram*, does not confine the sin to the lender on interest alone; it considers the borrower who pays him interest, the writer of the promissory note, and the witness to it to be among his accomplices. A *hadith* says:

> Allah has cursed the one who takes interest, the one who pays it, the one who writes the contract, and the one who witnesses the contract.[1]

However, if a person is driven to borrowing money on interest due to some pressing need, the sin will be on the lender alone. Now, to establish such a pressing need certain conditions must be met:

1. The need must be real, not merely an extension of the scope of one's needs and the desire for luxury. It must be so basic that life is not possible without it, for example, food, clothing, and medical treatment.
2. This concession is limited to the exact amount needed. Thus, for example, if nine dollars is sufficient, borrowing ten dollars is not lawful.
3. The borrower must continue to search for ways to escape from his predicament, and his brother Muslims should help him in this. If no other means are found, he can resort to borrowing on interest with no intention of liking it or transgressing the limits, and hope for forgiveness from Allah, as indeed He is Forgiving and Merciful.
4. He must continue to hate it and regret doing it until Allah opens a way out for him.

---

[1]Reported by Ahmad, Abu Daoud, al-Nisai, Ibn Majah, and al-Tirmidhi, who calls it sound.

Concerning the Prophet's Seeking Refuge with Allah from Debt

The Muslim must be aware that his religion commands him to be moderate in his living habits and thrifty in his financial affairs:

> ...And do not be extravagant; indeed, He does not like those who are extravagant. (6:141)

> ...And do not squander your wealth wantonly; truly, those who squander are the brothers of the evil ones. (17:26-27)

When the Qur'an asked Muslims to spend in the way of Allah, it did not ask them to spend all but merely a part of their wealth. If a person spends only a part of what he earns, it is not likely that he will become destitute; thus, with moderation in his living habits and control of his spending, the Muslim will not be compelled to borrow. The Prophet (peace be on him) disliked the Muslim's being in debt because debt is a worry by night and a humiliation by day. He always asked Allah's protection from indebtedness, saying,

> "O Allah, I seek refuge in Thee from the burden of debt and from the anger of men."[1]

He also said,

> 'I seek refuge in Thee from unbelief and debt.' A man asked him, 'Do you equate debt with unbelief?' He replied, 'Yes.'[2]

In his prayers he would frequently say,

> 'O Allah, I seek refuge in Thee from sin and debt.' He was asked, 'Why do you so often seek the protection of Allah from debt?' He replied, 'One who is in debt tells lies and breaks promises.'[3]

From these statements it becomes clear that borrowing can endanger one's morals.

The Prophet (peace be on him) would not pray the funeral prayer for a person who had died in a state of indebtedness, not leaving

---

[1]Reported by Abu Daoud.
[2]Reported by al-Nisai and al-Hakim.
[3]Reported by al-Bukhari.

behind enough property to repay his loans; he did this in order to discourage others from such an end. In later years, when Allah had enriched him from the spoils of war, he paid the debts of such persons and led their funeral prayers.[1] He said,

"Everything will be forgiven to the *shaheed* (martyr in the cause of Allah) except debt."[2]

The Muslim who is informed of these *ahadith* will never resort to borrowing except in the case of dire need, and if he does borrow will always remain mindful of the obligation of repayment. A *hadith* states,

If a man borrows from people with the intention of repaying them, Allah will help him to repay, while if he borrows without intending to repay them, Allah will bring him to ruin.[3]

Accordingly, if a Muslim is not to resort to the kind of borrowing which is *halal* (that is, without interest) without a compelling need, what can we say concerning his borrowing money on interest?

Sale for Deferred Payment (Credit)

While it is best to buy an article by paying cash, it is also permissible to buy on credit by mutual consent. The Prophet (peace be on him) bought some grain from a Jew, to be paid for at specific time, pledging his coat of mail as security.[4]

A group of jurists are of the opinion that, should the seller increase his price if the buyer asks for deferred payments, as is common in installment buying, the price differential due to the time delay resembles interest, which is likewise a price for time; accordingly, they declare such sales to be *haram*. However, the majority of scholars permit it because the basic principle is the permissibility of things, and no clear text exists prohibiting such a transaction. Furthermore, there is, on the whole, no resemblance to interest in such a transaction, since the seller is free to increase the price as he

---

[1]This is from what is narrated by Jabir and Abu Hurairah.
[2]Reported by Muslim.
[3]Reported by al-Bukhari.
[4]Reported by al-Bukhari.

deems proper, as long as it is not to the extent of blatant exploitation or clear injustice, in which case it is *haram*. Al-Shawkani says, "On the basis of legal reasons, the followers of the Shafi'i and Hanafi schools, Zaid bin 'Ali, al-Muayyid Billah, and the majority of scholars consider it lawful."[1]

Payment in Advance

The Muslim is allowed to make an advance payment of a specified price for a specified quantity of merchandise to be delivered at a fixed time in the future. This type of transaction was prevalent in Madinah when the Prophet (peace be on him) arrived, and he introduced certain changes and conditions in this type of transaction in order to bring it into conformity with the Islamic *Shari'ah*. Ibn 'Abbas narrated, "When Allah's Messenger (peace be on him) came to Madinah, they were paying one and two years in advance for fruits, but he then said,

> Those who pay for anything in advance must do so for a specified measure and weight, with the fixing of a specified time.[2]

This limitation of specifying the measure or weight and time removes uncertainty and misunderstanding. Similar to this was the practice of paying in advance for the fruit of a certain number of palm trees, which the Prophet (peace be on him) prohibited because of the possibility of unforseen losses due to blight. The proper form of advance trade is therefore to specify the measure of weight, rather than selling the fruits of a certain number of trees or the crop of a certain acreage of sown field. However, such a transaction is *haram* if the owner of the trees or the farm land is clearly being exploited because he needs money.

---

[1] *Nayl al-awtar*, vol. 5, p. 153. Al-Shawkani said, "We have compiled a treatise on this subject and have called it *'Shifa al'ilal fi hukum ziyadat al-thamam li mujarrad al-ajal'* (The Reason for Increasing the Price Due to Lapse of Time), and have reseached it thoroughly."
[2] Reported by al-Bukhari, Muslim and others.

Partnership Between Capital and Labor

It may be said that Allah Subhanahu wa Ta'ala has distributed talents and wealth among human beings according to a wise plan of apportionment. We find many a talented and experienced individual who does not possess much wealth or none at all, while others have a great deal of money but little or no talent. Why, therefore, should not the wealthy person turn over to the one possessing talents some of his wealth to invest in a profitable business, so that the two may benefit from one another and share the profits according to some agreed-upon formula? In particular, business ventures on a large scale require the cooperation of many investors. Among the populace we find a large number of people who have savings and excess capital but who lack time or the capability of investing it. Why should not this money be pooled and placed under the management of capable people who will invest it in significant, large-scale projects?

We maintain that the Islamic *Shari'ah* did not prohibit cooperation between capital and management, or between capital and labor as these terms are understood in their Islamic legal sense. In fact, the *Shari'ah* established a firm and equitable basis for such cooperation: if the owner of capital wishes to become a partner with the working man, he must agree to share all the consequences of this partnership. The *Shari'ah* lays down the condition that in such a partnership, which is called *al-mudaribah* or *al-qirad*, the two parties should agree that they will share the profit if there is profit and loss if there is loss in a proportion agreed upon in advance. This proportion can be one-half, one-third, one-fourth, or any other proportion for one party and the remainder for the other party. Thus the partnership between capital and labor is that of two parties with joint responsibility, each having his share, whether of profit or loss, and whether much or little. If, in the balance, the losses exceed the profits, the difference is to be charged against the capital. This arrangement is not surprising, for while the owner of the capital has suffered a loss in his wealth, the working partner has lost his time and effort.

This is the law of Islam concerning partnership contracts. Conversely, were the owner of the capital to be guaranteed a fixed

271

profit on his capital regardless of the magnitude of the profit or loss, it would be a clear violation of justice and a bias in favor of capital against investment experience and labor; it would also be contrary to the realities of investment, which always contain elements of risk. To guarantee to the person who did not toil or take any risk is the very essence of abominable usury.

The Prophet (peace be on him) forbade the type of partnership on cultivable land which was known as *al-muzara'ah* (share-cropping),[1] in which the contract would give one partner the produce of a specified area of a farm or a fixed amount of grain such as one or two tons. He prohibited this because such a transaction is similar to usury or gambling; for if the farm produced less than the specific amount or nothing at all, one partner would still get his share, while the other would suffer a total loss, which is contrary to justice.

The explicit *hadith* invalidating share-cropping because of this condition is, in my opinion, the basis of consensus among jurists that no partnership is valid which specifies a fixed profit for one partner in every case, regardless of whether or not the investment was profitable. They say, "Suppose one of the partners makes a condition that he is to receive a specified amount of money. In case the profit does not exceed that amount, he would receive the entire profit, and even if there is no profit, he would receive that much; on the other hand, if the profit is large he will be hurt by the condition of getting only the specified amount."[2] This reasoning is in accordance with the spirit of Islam, which bases all human affairs on clearly defined principles of justice and fairness.

Partnership Among Owners of Capital

Just as it is lawful for the Muslim to use his own wealth for any permissible purpose or to give it to a capable, experienced person to

---

[1]Reported by Muslim.

[2]In his treatise, *Al-Islam wa mushkilatina al-mu'asirah (Islam and Contemporary Problems)*, Dr. Muhammad Yusuf Musa quotes Sheikh Muhmmad 'Abduh and Sheikh Abdul Wahhab as disagreeing with the jurists concerning partnership contracts. They argue that this has no basis in the Qur'an and the *Sunnah*. With due respect to their opinions, I maintain that the analogy to share-cropping is sufficient to apply it to other partnerships. But Allah knows best.

invest in a joint venture, it is also lawful for him to pool his capital with the capital of others for investment, trade, or any lawful business ventures.

There are all kinds of activities and projects, some requiring intensive labor, others intensive mental expenditure, and still others large capital. By themselves individuals may not be able to accomplish much, but when joined with others, they can achieve many things. Allah Ta'ala says,

> ...and help each other in righteousnesss and God-consciousness. (5:3 (2))

Any deed which produces good results for the individual or society, or which removes some evil, is righteousness, and a righteous deed becomes piety if a good intention is added to it. Islam is not content with merely allowing such joint endeavors but encourages and blesses them, promising Allah's help in this world and His reward in the Hereafter as long as these endeavors are within the sphere of what Allah has made *halal*, far removed from usury (interest) and from ambiguity, injustice, fraud, and cheating in any form. In this connection the Messenger of Allah (peace be on him) said,

> Allah's hand is over two partners as long as one of them does not cheat the other, but when he cheats his partner, He withdraws it from both.[1]

"Allah's hand" refers to His help, inspiration, and blessing. The Prophet (peace be on him) also stated in a *hadith qudsi* that Allah, the Great and Glorious says,

> I make a third with two partners as long as one of them does not cheat the other, but when he cheats him I depart from them.[2]

Razin's version adds,

> "and Satan comes."[3]

Insurance Companies

We now turn to the important questions relating to present-day

---

[1]Reported by al-Darqutni.
[2]Reported by Abu Daoud and by al-Hakim, who calls it sound.
[3]Reported by Razi in his *Jami'ah*.

companies which issue life insurance and insurance against hazards and accidents. What is the Islamic position and ruling concerning such companies?

Before answering this question we must first inquire into the nature of such companies and the nature of the relationship between the insured and the insurance firm; in other words, is the insured individual a partner of the firm's owners? If this is the case, every individual insured by the firm should have a share in its profits or losses since this is the meaning of a partnership in Islam.

With regard to insurance against hazards, the insured pays a specified premium during the year. If no accident of the type specified in the insurance policy occurs to the property (shop, factory, ship, etc.) during the year, the company keeps the premiums received and nothing is returned to the insured. If, on the other hand, some calamity occurs, the insured individual is paid the agreed-upon sum. This kind of transaction is far removed from either trade or partnership.

In relation to life insurance, supposing a person takes out insurance for twenty thousand dollars and dies soon after paying the first premium, his beneficiaries are then entitled to the entire sum of twenty thousand dollars. Had this been a business partnership, they would have been entitled only to the amount of the premium which was paid, plus the profit on it. Again, if the insured person fails to pay his premiums after having paid a few of them, according to the terms of insurance contracts he will lose all or a great part of what he has already paid. The least one can say about this is that it is, in the context of the Islamic legal system, an invalid condition.

The argument that the two parties, the insured and the insurance firm, enter into this contract willingly in accordance with their respective self-interest carries no weight; so do the lender and the borrower on interest and two gamblers. The mutual agreement of the two parties has no validity in a transaction which is not based on justice and equity, and which is not devoid of any trace of ambiguity or exploitation. Moreover, since justice, with no harm either to oneself or others, is the ultimate criterion here, a transaction is invalid if it stipulates that in certain situations one party is to take all, with no benefits guaranteed to the other.

274

Do Insurance Companies Constitute Cooperatives?

It is clear to us that the relationship between the insured and the insurer does not constitute a partnership. The question then is, What is the nature of this relationship? Is it a relationship of cooperation? Are insurance firms to be regarded as cooperatives which are organized by their members to help one another, each member paying a certain amount as his share?

In order to establish a cooperative system on a sound footing in any group which desires to help its members in the event of unforseen calamity, the following conditions must be met in regard to the money collected:

1. Every member who pays his allotted share of money pays it as a donation, in the spirit of brotherhood. From this pool of donations help is given to those who are in need.
2. If any part of this money is to be invested, it should be invested in *halal* businesses only.
3. It is not permitted to the member to donate his share on the condition that he will receive a pre-determined amount in the event of an unforseen calamity. Rather, he will be paid an amount which will compensate his loss or a part of it, depending on the resources of the group, from the pooled monies.
4. What has been donated is gift from the donor, and taking it back is *haram*.[1]

Apart from some of the Muslim cooperatives and associations in which the individual pays a certain sum monthly as a donation without any right to take it back and with no condition that he will receive a pre-determined amount in case of an unforseen calamity, these conditions are not met. As far as insurance companies — especially life insurance — are concerned, they do not satisfy these conditions in any respect because:

1. The insured individuals do not pay the premium as donations; such a thought never occurs to them.

---

[1]Taken from the book, *Al-Islam wal-manahij al-ishtirakiyyah (Islam and Socialism)*, by Muhammad al-Ghazzali, p. 131.

2. Insurance firms invest their monies in busineses which operate or lend their money on interest. All this is *haram* and the Muslim is prohibited to participate in such activities; the strictest and most permissive jurists alike all agree on this point.

3. In the event that the insured survives the term of the contract, he gets back all the premiums he paid plus some additional sum, which is nothing but interest.

Furthermore, insurance is contrary to the whole concept of cooperation among people. While the principle of cooperation requires that the poor and needy be paid more than the rich, the rich, who can afford higher premiums, get back much more in the event of death or an accident than the poor.[1]

A Modification

In my view insurance against hazards can be modified in a manner which would bring it closer to the Islamic principle by means of a contract of "donation with a condition of compensation." The insured would donate his payments to the company with the stipulation that the company would compensate him, in the event that he is struck by calamity, with an amount which would assist him and reduce the burden of his loss. Such a type of transaction is allowed in some Islamic schools of jurisprudence. If such a modification is effected, and if the company is free of usurious business, one may declare insurance against hazards to be a lawful contract. However, as far as life insurance is concerned, I see it as being very remote from Islamic business transactions.

The Islamic System of Insurance

Our observation that the modern form of insurance companies and their current practices are objectionable Islamically does not mean that Islam is against the concept of insurance itself; not in the least — it only opposes the means and methods. If other insurance

---

[1] In the 6th (1972) edition of the present volume, Dr. al-Qaradawi has cited three additional references about insurance published in the '40's and '50's. (Trans.)

practices are employed which do not conflict with Islamic forms of business transactions, Islam will welcome them.

In any case, the Islamic system has already insured the Muslims and others living under its governance in its characteristic fashion, the characteristic which permeates all its teachings and legislation. This provision is accomplished either through mutual help among individuals or through the government and its treasury, for the treasury, known as the *bait al-mal*, is the universal insurance company for all who reside within the Islamic domain.

In the Islamic *Shari'ah* we find insurance for individuals against hazards and provision for assisting them to overcome disasters which may befall them. Earlier we mentioned that a person who is rendered destitute due to a calamity is permitted to ask for financial help, particularly from the administrative authorities, until he is fully compensated or is able to stand on his own feet again. [1]

We also find the concept of insurnce for the heirs of a deceased person in the Prophet's saying,

> I am nearer to each Muslim than his very self. If he
> leaves behind some property it is for his heirs, and if he
> leaves behind a debt or a family with young children, he
> leaves them to me and they are my responsibility, [2]

meaning that they are the responsibility of the Islamic government.

The greatest form of insurance which Islam has legislated for its followers among those deserving to receive *zakat* funds relates to the category of *gharimeen* (those in debt). Some of the early interpeters of the word *gharim* say , "It denotes one whose house has burned down or whose property or trade has been destroyed by flood or other disasters." Some jurists hold that such a person may be given, from the *zakat* fund, an amount which would restore his previous financial position, even though the amount may reach thousands of dollars.

---

[1]See the *hadith* from Qubaisah on pp. 127 of this book in the section on "Work and Earning a Livelihood."
[2]Reported by al-Bukhari and Muslim.

277

The Use of Cultivable Land

If the Muslim owns a piece of cultivable land, he must make use of it by planting crops or trees. It is not consonant with Islam that such lands not be used for cultivation, as this is tantamount to rejecting the bounty of Allah and wasting wealth, which the Prophet (peace be on him) prohibited.

In this regard a number of options are available to the land owner:

1. *Cultivating the Land Himself*
    The first option available to the landowner is that he himself cultivate the land. This is commendable, and the owner will be rewarded by Allah for whatever men, beasts, and birds eat of the produce of his farm or garden. As we mentioned earlier, the *Ansar* among the Companions of the Prophet (may Allah be pleased with them) were farmers.

2. *Lending the Land to Others for Cultivation*
    If the land owner is unable to cultivate the land himself, he may lend it to another person who is able to cultivate it by employing the latter's own equipment, helpers, seeds, and animals. In such a case the land owner is very desirable in Islam. Abu Hurairah narrated that the Prophet (peace be on him) said,

    > "If anyone has land, he should cultivate it or lend it to his brother."[1]

    Said Jabir, "In the time of the Prophet (peace be on him) we used to do planting on a piece of land and in return would get what remained in the ears after they were threshed. In this way, as the Prophet (peace be on him) said,

    > If anyone has land, he should cultivate it or lend it to his brother for cultivation, or otherwise release it from his ownership.[2]

    Some early scholars, going by the apparent meaning of this *hadith*, held the opinion that cultivable land can be

---

[1]Reported by al-Bukhari and Muslim.
[2]Reported by Ahmad and Muslim. "Lending it to his brother for cultivation" means without receiving anything in return for it.

used in one of two ways: either the owner cultivates it himself or he lends it to someone else for cultivation, with no return for himself. In the latter case, the piece of land remains the property of the owner but the produce belongs to the one who cultivates it.

In the opinion of Ibn 'Abbas, the Prophet's order to lend the cultivable land to others if one does not farm it himself was not intended as command which must be obeyed but only as the recommendation of a laudable act. Al-Bukhari reported that 'Amr bin Dinar said, "I said to Taous (one of the closest companions of Ibn 'Abbas), 'I wish you would leave off share-cropping since people claim that the Prophet (peace be on him) prohibited it.' Taous replied, 'The most knowledgeable among them (that is, Ibn 'Abbas) informed me that the Prophet (peace be on him) did not prohibit it but said,

"Lending it free to your brother is better than asking a fixed sum from him."'[1]

3. *Taking a Proportion of the Crop*

The third alternative for the landowner is to let out his land to a person who will cultivate it, using the cultivator's own equipment, seeds, and animals on the condition that he is to get a specified percentage, such as half, a third, or whatever is agreed upon, of the total produce of the land; the owner may also make available to the cultivator his own seeds, equipment, animals, or other help. Such an arrangement is termed share-cropping.

Al-Bukhari and Muslim report on the authority of Ibn 'Umar, Ibn 'Abbas and Jabir bin 'Abdullah that the Prophet (peace be on him) gave the people of Khayber the land to work and cultivate, in return for which they were to get half of what it produced. `

In support of their position, scholars who consider share-cropping permissible say,

It is established and well-known that the Prophet (peace be on him) practiced it until his death and that after him the rightly-guided Caliphs practiced it until

[1]Reported by al-Bukhari.

279

their deaths, as likewise those who came after them. The wives of the prophet (may Allah be pleased with them) continued this practice after the death of the Prophet himself (peace be on him) until the last one of them had died, and so on. This practice cannot be considered to be abrogated because an abrogation is valid only if it was implemented by the Prophet himself (peace be on him)during his own lifetime. Now, if he practiced a thing until his death, and thereafter his successors and all the Companions (may Allah be pleased with them) acted on it and none of them opposed it, how then is anyone else entitled to invalidate it? And if it was (actually) abrogated during the lifetime of the Prophet (peace be on him), why then did he continue to practice it after abrogating it? And how was it possible that his closest Companions and successors should remain ignorant of its abrogtion while the story of Khayber was circulating widely and they were (themselves) acting according to it? And where was the narrator of (the report of) this abrogation, that none of them knew him or had heard about him?[1]

The Prohibited Form of Share-Cropping

The Prophet (peace be on him) prohibited his Companions to practice another form of share-cropping which was quite common at that time. The land owner would give out his land conditional to his getting the produce of one part of it and the cultivator the produce of the remaining part or perhaps half, or to the owner's getting a specified weight or measure of the grain produced and the cultivator the rest. But sometimes one part of the land produced a crop while the other did not, so that one of the two would receive nothing or very little, while the other took everything. Similarly, if the total produce did not exceed the specified weight or measure, the owner would get everything while the cultivator would get nothing.

Such a transaction clearly involves great uncertainty and risk, and is contrary to the spirit of justice. The Prophet (peace be on him) saw that justice demands that both should share the total produce,

---

[1] *Al-mughni* by Ibn Qudadmah, vol. 5, p. 384.

whether this total is much or little, according to the agreed-upon ratio. Proportions of the total produce must be specified so that if the crop is bountiful, it is bountiful for both; if it is meager it is meager for both, and if nothing is produced, neither of them receives anything. This is the fair distribution for both parties.

Al-Bukhari reported that Rafi' bin Khadij said, "We had the most agricultural land in Madinah, and one of us would rent out his land, designating a part of it for himself. Sometimes a calamity would hit that part while the rest of the land was safe, and sometimes the other way around. Consequently, the Prophet (peace be on him) prohibited us from doing so."

Muslim reported Rafi' bin Khadij as saying, "People used to let out land in the time of the Prophet (peace be on him) in exchange for what they grew by the streamlets or at the borders of the fields, or for a fixed quantity of produce. Sometimes it would happen that the part so set aside was destroyed while the other was safe and sometimes the opposite, and the people had no investments other than this. Hence the Prophet (peace be on him) forbade this practice.

Again, Al-Bukhari reported from Rafi' bin Khadij that the Prophet (peace be on him) asked, "What do you do with your agricultural lands?" The people replied, "We let them out for (the produce of) the quarter of their area or for a measure of barley or dates." He said "Do not do that." What is meant here is that the land owner would take this fixed quantity as "overhead" and would also share in some proportion of the remainder, for example, the entire produce of the specified one-fourth of the area, plus one-half of the produce of the remaining three-fourths of the area.

We observe from this that the Prophet (peace be on him) was eager to establish perfect justice in his society and to remove every source of conflict and discord from the community of Believers. Zaid bin Thabit narrated that two people came to the Prophet (peace be on him) disputing about some land, and he said,

"If this is what happens among you, then do not let out your farms." [1]

The landowner and the cultivator must therefore be magnanimous and generous to one another; the landowner should not demand too high a share of the yield and the worker should take

---

[1]Reported by Abu Daoud.

281

proper care of the land. Ibn 'Abbas said that the Prophet (peace be on him) did not prohibit share-cropping but advised the owner and the cultivator to be considerate of each other. [1] And when someone said to Taous, "O Abu 'Abdur Rahman, why do you not give up share-cropping, since they claim that the Prophet (peace be on him) forbade it?" he replied, "I help them (the cultivators) and provide for them."[2] His concern was not simply that he should earn something from his land regardless of whether those who were employed on it got something or suffered hunger; rather, he helped them and took care of them. That was the true Muslim society.

There may be a landowner who prefers to keep his land idle, not planting any crops or fruit trees on it, rather than renting it to a farmer for a small proprtion of the yield, since he may consider the return too little. With this in mind, the caliph 'Umar bin 'Abdul-Aziz issued a decree to all concerned saying, "Let out your land for one-third, one-fourth, one-fifth and up to one-tenth of the yield, but do not leave the land uncultivated."

4. *Renting the Land for Money*

The fourth option available to the Muslim landowner is to lease the land to the cultivator for a fixed amount of money, gold, or silver. Some well-known jurists have declared this to be permissible, while others consider it *haram* on the basis of sound *ahadith* of the Prophet (peace be on him) which prohibit renting out land for money. Among the narrators of these *ahadith* are two Companions who participated in the Battle of Badr, as well as Raf'i bin Khadij, Jabir, Abu Sa'id, Abu Huraiah, and Ibn 'Umar; all of them report that the Prophet (peace be on him) absolutely prohibited the renting of agricultural land for money.[3]

Exempted from this prohibition is share-cropping for a specified proportion of the total yield, as is demonstrated by the Prophet's transaction with the people of Khayber. He turned land over to them to cultivate for one-half the total yield and continued to do this until his death; after his death, the rightly-

---

[1] Reported by al-Tirmidhi, who calls it sound.
[2] Reported by Ibn Majah.
[3] See *Al-muhallah*, vol. 8, p. 212.

guided Caliphs continued to practice share-cropping on a proportionate basis.

The student of the legislative development of this problem comes across a clear exposition by Ibn Hazm, who stated:

When the Prophet (peace be on him) arrived (in Madinah), the people used to lease their farms, as is reported by Raf'i and others. This practice had undoubtedly been common among them before the time of the Prophet (peace be on him), and it continued after he became the Messenger; it is not permissible for any sane person to doubt this fact. Then, as is authentically transmitted by Jabir, Abu Huraiah, Abu Sa'id, Zahir al-Badri, and Ibn 'Umar, the Prophet (peace be on him) totally prohibited the leasing of land, thus nullifying this practice; this is certainly correct and there is no doubt concerning the matter. He who asserts that what was nullified (i.e., the leasing of land) has been restored and that the certainty of nullification is not established is a liar and denies the veracity of others saying what he does not know. According to the Qur'an, making such an assertion is *haram* unless one brings proof for it. And he can never find a proof for it except in the instance in which the land is let for a given proportion (such as one third or one-fourth) of the total yield, as it is authentically reported that the Prophet (peace be on him) did this with the people of Khayber after prohibiting it for several years, and he continued to give them land on a share-cropping basis until his death.[1]

A group of early jurists hold the same opinion. Taous, the jurist of Yemen and one of the greatest of the second generation Muslim scholars, disliked renting land for silver or gold but saw no harm in renting it for one-third or one-fourth of the yield. When someone disputed with him, saying that the Prophet (peace be on him) had prohibited this, he replied, "Mu'ad bin Jabal, the governor of Yemen appointed by the Prophet (peace be on him), arrived here

---

[1]*Al-muhallah,* vol. 8, p. 224.

and gave out the land for one-third or one-fourth (of its yield), and we continue this practice to this day." Thus, in his opinion, renting land for gold or silver was disapproved but share-cropping was permissible.

Reasoning by Analogy Implies No Leasing for Money

Correct reasoning by analogy (*qiyas*) based on Islamic principles and sound and clear texts leads to the conclusion that the leasing of cultivable land for money is *haram*:

(A)   The Prophet (peace be on him) prohibited the leasing of land for a fixed amount of the yield such as one or two tons, and permitted share-cropping only on the basis of a proportion such as one-half, one-third, or one-fourth — that is to say, on a percentage basis. Such a basis is just and equitable, as both partners share in the profit if the land is productive and in the loss if blight strikes the crop. However, if one party is guaranteed a profit while the other has to take the risk of ending up with nothing for his effort and toil, the whole transaction resembles gambling or a usurious contract. If we reflect on the matter of leasing land for money in this light, what difference do we find between the last-mentioned practice and the type of share-cropping which is prohibited? In both the owner of the land is guaranteed his share in the form of money regardless of what happens to the land, while the lessee must gamble his effort and labor, not knowing whether he will gain or lose.

(B)   When the owner of an article lends it to another person and charges rent for the use of it, he is rightfully entitled to this rent in consideration of the fact that he prepared the article in question for the renter's use; as the article becomes worn out by usage and depreciates over time, the owner deserves compensation. But as far as land is concerned, in what way has the owner made it ready for the lessee's use, since indeed, it is Allah and not the owner who makes the land ready for cultivation. Again, how does land become worn out or depreciate by cultivation, since land is not like buildings or

284

machinery which depreciate over a period of time or get worn out by being used?

(C) The person who rents a house lives in it, thus receiving an immediate benefit, while the man who rents a piece of machinery uses it and thus derives an immediate benefit. But the man who rents a piece of land does not benefit from it at once, nor are his benefits assured. When he rents it he receives no direct benefit from it, as in the case of renting a house, but works hard, plowing and planting, in the hope of benefitting from it at a later date. His hope may be fulfilled or it may not; consequently, any analogy between renting land and renting a house and the like is a false one.

(D) In the two *Sahihs* of al-Bukhari and Muslim it is reported that the Messenger of Allah (peace be on him) forbade the sale of fruits until they were obviously in good condition and of ears of grain until they were ripe and safe from blight. He gave the reason for this prohibition by saying,

> "Tell me why, if Allah withholds the fruit, any of you should take his brother's property."

If this is the position relative to selling fruits which have appeared, but the safety of which is not assured, so that if they are ruined by some calamity their sale would be nullified, how is it possible for a person to take money for the use of a piece of cultivable land which has not yet been plowed or planted? Is it not more appropriate that he be told, "Tell me why, if Allah withholds the fruit, you should take your brother's property?"

I myself have witnessed how certain cotton fields were struck by an infestation of caterpillars known as *doodah* until nothing was left of them except dry stalks. Nevertheless, the owners of the land demanded the rent, and the lessees had no choice except to pay it, obliged by the conditions of the contracts which they had signed under grave necessity. Where then is the equality and justice so eagerly sought by Islam?

Consequently, there is no denying the fact that justice cannot be achieved except through share-cropping on a proportionate basis, according to which the gain or loss accrues to both parties alike.[1]

Although Shaikh al-Islam Ibn Taymiyyah considers the leasing of land to be *halal*, he nevertheless remarks that share-cropping is more akin to the justice of the *Shari'ah* and its principles, saying "Share-cropping is preferable to renting and closer to justice and to the principles of the *Shari'ah*, since in this case both parties share in the profit or loss, in contrast to leasing for rent, under which the land owner takes his rent, while the lessee may or may not receive the harvest.[2]

Another great thinker, Ibn al-Qayyim, commenting on the oppression perpetrated by the rulers and military personnel on farmers during his time, says:

> Had the soldiers and the rulers relied on what Allah and His Messenger (peace be on him) have legislated and followed the practice of the Messenger (peace be on him) and of the rightly-guided Caliphs in their dealings with the farmers, Allah would have showered His blessings on them from the sky and the earth; they would have been given to eat from above their heads and from beneath their feet, and from that one-fourth of share-cropping would have received many times more than they receive by oppression and tyranny. But their ignorance and greed prevented them from doing anything but committing oppression and injustice, and thus Allah withheld His blessings and His provision from them. In addition to being deprived of Allah's blessing in this world, they will receive His punishment in the Hereafter. If it is asked, What is the legislation of Allah and His Messenger (peace be on him) and the practice of the Companions in this regard so that one may follow it? the reply is this: The equitable form of share-cropping is that in which both the landowner and the cultivator are on equal footing, neither of them enjoying any of those privileges for which Allah has

---

[1]Concerning this subject, refer to what has been said by Ibn Hazm in *Al-muhallah*, vol. 8, Ibn Taymiyyah in *Al-qawaid al-nuraniyyah;* Abul 'Ala Maududi in *Milkiyyat al-ard fil-Islam;* and Professor Mahmoud Abu Sa'ud in his article, *"Istighlal al-ard fil-Islam,"* published in *Al-Muslimoon.*

[2]From Ibn Taymiyyah's treatise, *Al-hasbah fi al-Islam*, p. 21.

sent down no authority. These customs which they (the soldiers and rulers) have introduced are ruining the country, corrupting the people, and have kept away Allah's help and blessings. Many of the rulers and soldiers are consuming what is *haram*, and if the body is nourished by what is *haram*, the Fire is its fitting abode. Such equitable share-cropping was the practice of the Muslims during the time of the Prophet (peace be on him) and during the time of the rightly-guided Caliphs. Such was the practice of the families and descendants of Abu Bakr, 'Umar, 'Uthman, 'Ali and of the families of other emigrants (*muhajireen*). Great Companions of the Prophet (peace be on him) such as Ibn Mas'ood, Ubay bin K'ab, Zaid bin Thabit, and others expressed their opinions favorbly concerning it, and this was also the opinion of the jurists who rely on the *hadith*, such as Ahmad bin Hanbal, Ishaq bin Rahawait, Muhammad ibn Isma'il al-Bukhari, Daoud bin 'Ali, Muhammad bin Ishaq bin Khazimah, and Abu Bakr bin Nasr al-Maruzi. Other great Muslim scholars, such as al-Laith bin Sa'd, Ibn Abu Laila, Abu Yusuf, Muhammad bin al-Hasan and others, have all expressed the same opinion. The Prophet (peace be on him) made an agreement with the people of Khayber that they would work the land for half of the produce of fruit and crops, spending their own money for the preparation of the land and the seed. This agreement remained in effect during his lifetime and thereafter until 'Umar exiled them from Khayber. Accordingly, the scholars who say that the seed may be provided either by the worker alone or by both the partners are entirely correct. Al-Bukhari in his *Sahih* mentions that 'Umar ibn al-Khattab employed people with the stipulation that if he ('Umar) provided the seed, his share would be half and if they brought the seed their share would be more than half. [1]

In all the reports which have reached us from the time of the

---

[1] *Al-turuq al-hikmiyyah fil-Islam* by Ibn Qayyim, pp. 248-250.

Prophet (peace be on him) and his Companions, we find that the cultivator's share was never less than one-half, and in some cases it was more. This division, according to which the cultivator's share would not be less than half, as was alloted by the Prophet (peace be on him) to the Jews of Khayber,[1] appeals to the mind, for it is not appropriate that the share of the land, which is an inanimate thing, should be greater than the share of the human, the cultivator.

Partnership in Raising Animals

Partnership in raising animals is quite common in Muslim countries, especially in villages. One of the partners puts up all or a part of the price of the livestock and cattle, while the other partner raises them; the two then share the yield and the profits of this joint venture.

In order to form an opinion concerning this partnership, we should first look at its various forms:

1. In the first form of such a business, the partnership is entered into for purely commercial purposes, for example, raising calves for beef or cows and water buffalo for milk production.

    It is supposed here that one partner contributes the price of the animals and the other contributes the effort, that is to say, the management and supervision; the expenses of feeding, watering, and the like are borne by the joint partnership and not by one partner alone. After a sale is made, the feeding expenses are deducted from the proceeds before dividing up the profits in the agreed-upon proportions. It is not just that one partner alone be required to bear all the feeding expenses without receiving any commensurate return, while the profits are divided between the two; this point is quite clear.

2. The second form of such a business is the same as the first except that the partner who manages the business also bears the feeding expenses and in return benefits from the milk or makes

---

[1] Refer to what is said by Ibn Hazm in *Al-muhallah*, vol. 8; Abul 'Ala Maududi in *Milkiyyat al-ard fil-Islam;* and Mahmoud Abu Sa'ud in his article, *"Istighlal al-ard fil-Islam,"* published in *Al-Muslimoon.*

use of the animals in the field for plowing, irrigating, or planting; this is the situation when large animals are involved. We see no harm in such a contract. Although one may not be able to balance exactly the cost of feed with the benefits derived from milking or working the animal, so that there is an element of uncertainty about it, we still prefer to consider this arrangement *halal*. The element of risk is negligible, and there are other examples of such contracts which are permitted by the *Shari'ah*. In the sound *ahadith* concerning mortgages, the Prophet (peace be on him) stated the permissibility of using an animal which is mortgaged for riding or milking, saying,

"A mortgaged animal may be used for riding or milking by the person who bears the expenses of feeding it."[1]

In this *hadith* the Prophet (peace be on him) equated spending on feeding the animal with using it for riding or milking. Accordingly, if this type of mortgage is allowed for people's mutual benefit, with the possibility that the expenses of feeding may be more or less than the benefit derived from the animal by using it for riding or milking, we see no harm in allowing a similar arrangement in the case of partnerships in raising animals, as the needs of people are better served in this manner. This is my own deduction from this *hadith*, and I hope it is correct.

However, if the partnership is in raising young calves which cannot be used for work or for milk with the stipulation that the price is to be paid by one partner and the feeding expenses by the other, the rules of Islam do not permit such an arrangement. The partner who bears the cost of feeding is the only loser, receiving no return in the form of work or milk, while the other partner has the clear advantage. Such an arrangement is contrary to the justice which Islam seeks to establish in every transaction. However, if the two partners share the cost of feeding and raising the animal until it reaches the age of usefulness, such an arrangement is, in our view, *halal*.

---

[1] Reported by al-Bukhari on the authority of Abu Hurairah.

3. RECREATION AND PLAY

Islam is a practical religion, it does not float in the stratosphere of imaginary ideals but remains with the human being on the ground of realities and day-to-day concerns. It does not regard people as angels but accepts them as mortals who eat food and walk in the marketplace. Islam does not require of Muslims that their speech should consist entirely of pious utterances, that their silence should be a meditation, that they should listen to nothing except the recitation of the Qur'an, nor that they should spend all their leisure time in the mosque. Rather, it recognizes that Allah has created human beings with needs and desires, so that, as they need to eat and drink, they also need to relax, and to enjoy themselves.

"A Time for This and a Time for That"

Some of the Companions of the Prophet (peace be on him) attained great spiritual heights. They believed that in order to remain at such a spiritual level they should always be serious, engaged in constant worship, turning their backs on all the enjoyments of life and the good things of the world, neither playing nor relaxing but keeping their eyes and their minds fixed on the Hereafter and its concerns, away from common life and its amusements.

Let us listen to what this great Companion and scribe of the Prophet (peace be jon him), Hanzalah al-Usaidi, has to say about himself:

> Abu Bakr met me and asked, 'How are you, Hanzalah?' I replied, 'Hanzalah has become a hypocrite.' He said, '*Subhanallah!* What are you saying?' I replied, 'When we are with Allah's Messenger (peace be on him), he mentions the Fire and the Garden until it is as if we can see them. But when we leave the Prophet's company and play with our wives and children or busy ourselves with our properties, we forget much.' Abu Bakr said, 'By Allah, I have experienced the same thing.' He and I then went to visit the Messenger of Allah (peace be on him), and I said, 'O Messenger of Allah, Hanzalah has

become a hypocrite.' He asked, 'And how is that?' I replied, 'O Messenger of Allah, when we are with you, you talk about the Fire and the Garden until it is as if we can see them. Then we go out and play with our wives and children and deal with our properties, and we forget much.' The Messenger of Allah (peace be on him) then said, 'By Him in Whose hand is my soul, if you were to continue at the same level at which you were when with me and in remembering Allah, the angels would shake hands with you when you are resting and when you walk about, but, O Hanzalah, there is a time (for this) and a time (for that).' He repeated this phrase three times.[1]

The Humanness of the Messenger of Allah

The life-pattern of the Messenger of Allah (peace be on him) is a perfect example for every human being. When he was in private he would worship his Lord with such intense devotion, standing for long hours in *salat*, that his feet would become swollen; in matters pertaining to truth or justice he did not care about anyone's opinion, seeking only the pleasure of Allah. But in his living habits and dealings with people he was a human being, enjoying good things, participating in small talk, smiling and joking, yet never departing from the truth. The Prophet (peace be on him) liked happiness and disliked grief; he sought refuge with Allah from difficulties and troubles which result in sorrow, supplicating,

"O Allah, I seek refuge in Thee from distress and grief."[2]

Concerning his sense of humor, it is reported that once an old woman came to him, saying, "O Messenger of Allah, pray to Allah that He admit me to the Garden." The Prophet (peace be on him) said, "O mother of such a person, no old woman will enter the Garden." The woman broke down and wept, supposing that she would not enter Paradise. The Prophet (peace be on him) then

---

[1]Reported by Muslim.
[2]Reported by Abu Daoud.

explained to her that no old woman would enter the Garden as an old woman, for Allah would restore her youth and admit her to the Garden as a young virgin. He then recited to her the verse,

We created them as a (new) creation, and made them virgins, lovers, friends.[1] (56: 35-37)

Relaxing the Mind

Following the Prophet's example, his noble and pure Companions also enjoyed humor and laughter, play and sport, which relaxed their bodies and minds and prepared them the better to travel on the long, arduous path of striving in the cause of truth and justice. 'Ali bin Abu Talib said, "Minds get tired, as do bodies, so treat them with humor," and "Refresh your minds from time to time, for a tired mind becomes blind." And Abu al-Darda said, "I entertain my heart with something trivial in order to make it stronger in the service of the truth."

Accordingly, there is no harm in the Muslim's entertaining himself in order to relax his mind or refreshing himself with some permissible sport or play with his friends. However, the pursuit of pleasure should not become the goal of his life so that he devotes himself to it, forgetting his religious obligations. Nor should he joke about serious matters. It has been aptly said, "Season your conversation with humor in the same proportion as you season your food with salt."

The Musim is forbidden to joke and laugh about other people's values and honor. Allah Ta'ala says:

O you who believe, let not some people mock at other people; it may be that they are better than thee...(49:11)

Nor is it appropriate for the Muslim to tell jokes based on what is untrue in order to make people laugh. The Prophet (peace be on him) warned against this, saying,

"Woe to the one who says something which is false in order to make people laugh! Woe to him, woe to him!"[2]

---

[1]Reported by 'Abd bin Humaid and al-Tirmidhi.
[2]Reported by al-Tirmidhi.

Permissible Sports

There are many kinds of games and sports which the Prophet (peace be on him) recommended to the Muslims as a source of enjoyment and recreation which, at the same time, prepare them for worship and other obligations. These sports, which require skill and determination, and which also involve physical exercise and body-building activity, are related to the martial arts, training Muslims for the battlefields of *jihad* in the cause of Allah. Among them are the following:

Foot Racing

The Companions of the Prophet (may Allah be pleased with them) used to race on foot and the Prophet (peace be on him) encouraged them in this. It is reported that 'Ali was a fast runner. The Prophet (peace be on him) himself raced with his wife 'Aishah in order to please her, to enjoy himself, and to set an example for his Companions. 'Aishah said,

> I raced with the Prophet (peace be on him) and beat him in the race. Later, when I had put on some weight, we raced again and he won. Then he said, 'This cancels that,'[1] referring to the previous occasion.

Wrestling

The Prophet (peace be on him) once wrestled with a man called Rukanah who was well-known for his strength, throwing him down more than once.[2] In another report of this incident, the Prophet (peace be on him) started wrestling with him. As the fight was hard, Rukanah said, "A sheep for a sheep."[3] The Prophet (peace be on him) then threw him. The man said, "The same again." The Prophet (peace be on him) threw him again, and the man said, "The same again." The Prophet (peace be on him) threw him a third time. The man then said, "What shall I tell my wife? One sheep was eaten by

---

[1] Reported by Ahmad and Abu Daoud.
[2] Reported by Abu Daoud.
[3] This must have occured before the prohibiton of gambling, or perhaps the Prophet (peace be on him) did not accept the bet and hence did not enforce its terms.

the wolf, one ran away, but what about the third" Then the Prophet (peace be on him) said,

"We are not going to defeat you and take something
from you as well. Take your sheep!"

From these reports concerning the Prophet (peace be on him), jurists have deduced the permissibility of foot racing, whether it be between men against each other or between men and women who are their *muharammat* or wives. They have also concluded that foot racing, wrestling, and sports of this type do not compromise the dignity of scholarship, piety, or age. The Prophet (peace be on him) was more than fifty years old when he raced with 'Aishah.

Archery

Among the permissible sports is competition in archery or with other weapons.

The Prophet (peace be on him) once passed by a group of his Companions who were competing in archery. He encouraged them, saying,

Shoot, and I am with you.[1]

He realized that archery was not just a hobby or a sport but, more importantly, constituted that kind of force which Allah has commanded to be mustered :

And make ready for them all thou art able of (armed)
force....(8:60)

The Prophet (peace be on him) said,

"The missiles (arrows) are the force,"

repeating it three times.[2]

He also said,

"Practice archery; that is good for you."[3]

However, the Prophet (peace be on him) warned archers against using chickens and the like as targets for practice, as the Arabs of *jahiliyyah* used to do. Once 'Abdullah bin 'Umar saw a group of

---

[1]Reported by al-Bukhari
[2]Reported by Muslim.
[3]Reported by al-Bazzar and by al-Tabarani on good authority.

294

people doing this and he told them, "The Prophet (peace be on him) cursed the one who takes anything possessing life as a target."[1]

He cursed such an individual because this sort of act involves the torturing and unnecessary killing of an animal, and a human being has no right to have fun and sport at the expense of a living creature. For the same reason the Prophet (peace be on him) forbade making animals fight each other.[2] Some Arabs used to laugh and find it amusing to see two rams or bulls fight each other until one of them was gored to death. Scholars have said that the prohibtion of making animals fight recognizes that such a practice causes them unnecessary suffering merely for the fun of it, without any benefit.

Spear Play

Spear play is similar to archery. The Prophet (peace be on him) allowed some Abyssinians to display their skill with spears in his mosque; he let his wife 'Aishah watch their show and encouraged them by saying, "Carry on, O Bani Arfidah," (as the Abyssinians were known to among the Arabs). 'Umar, with his serious disposition, wanted to stop them but the Prophet (peace be on him) prevented him from it. It is reported in the two *Sahihs* of al-Bukhari and Muslim from Abu Hurairah that while the Abyssinians were performing their show with spears in the presence of the Prophet (peace be on him), 'Umar entered. He picked up some pebbles and started throwing them at them but the Prophet (peace be on him) said, "Leave them alone, O 'Umar."

This indulgence on the part of the Prophet (peace be on him) in permitting and encouraging such a sport in his mosque was to demonstrate that the mosque serves both worldy and religious purposes. Muslims congregate in the mosque not only to worship but also to play. However, this play is not to be merely for fun but should involve physical exercise and some sort of training. Commenting on this *hadith*, scholars have said that the mosque is the center of the Muslim's community affairs, and any activity which combines benefits for religion and for the Muslims may be carried out in it. Muslims of the present time should note how devoid mosques today

---

[1]Reported by al-Bukhari and Muslim
[2]Reported by Abu Daoud and al-Tirmidhi.

295

are of vitality and strength, often having become havens for the elderly and the lazy.

The above incidents also provide an example of the Prophet's concern for his wife's amusement and recreation. 'Aishah, his wife, said, "The Messenger of Allah (peace be on him) covered me with his cloak while I watched the Abyssinians play in the mosque. He then stood (in his place) for my sake until I was the one who got tired, so estimate the time a young girl eager for amusement would wait." [1]

She also said, "I used to play with dolls in the house of the Messenger of Allah (peace be on him) and my friends would come over to play with me. They would hide when they saw the Messenger of Allah (peace be on him) approaching but in fact he was very happy to see them with me, so we played together." [2]

Horseback Riding

Allah Ta'ala says,

> And (He created) horses, mules, and donkeys for you to ride and as adornment....(16:8)

and the Prophet (peace be on him) said,

> "There is blessing in the forelocks of horses." [3]

He also said,

> "Practice archery and horseback riding." [4]

And again,

> Any action without the remembrance of Allah is either a diversion or heedlesness excepting four acts: walking from target to target (during archery practice), training a horse, playing with one's family, and learning to swim. [5]

Said 'Umar, "Teach your children swimming and archery, and tell them to jump on the horse's back." Ibn 'Umar reported that the Prophet (peace be on him) organized horse races and gave a prize to the winner. [6] All this was done by the Prophet (peace be on him) to

---

[1] Reported by al-Bukhari and Muslim.
[2] Reported by al-Bukhari and Muslim.
[3] Reported by Ahmad.
[4] Reported by Muslim.
[5] Reported by al-Tabarani on good authority.
[6] Reported by Ahmad.

encourage competition in sports involving physical exercise and discipline.

Anas was asked, "Did you bet during the time of the Prophet (peace be on him)? Did the Prophet (peace be on him) bet?" "Yes," Anas replied. "By Allah, he bet on a horse called Subhah. The horse won the race and the Prophet (peace be on him) was very pleased about it."[1]

Betting on horses is permissible if the one who is paying the money is not one of the competitors or if it is paid by one of the competitors; however, if each person bets an amount on the condition that the winner is to take all, this is gambling and is consequently prohibited. The Prophet (peace be on him) termed racing a horse on which bets are laid "the horse of Satan" and considered the price of it, its fodder, and riding it as sinful,[2] saying,

> Horses are of three kinds: the horse of *al-Rahman* (the Most Merciful, i.e., Allah), the horse of man, and the horse of Satan. As for the horse of the Most Merciful, it is dedicated to *jihad* in the cause of Allah, so feeding it, cleaning its urine and dung, and everything related to it are counted as good deeds. As for the horse of Satan, it is that on which people bet and gamble. As for the horse of man, it is that which is for breeding, and it is a protection against poverty.[3]

Hunting

Hunting is among the beneficial sports which are encouraged by Islam. It is a sport, an exercise, and also a means of livelihood, regardless of whether it is done with weapons or with hunting animals such as dogs and hawks. We have already discussed the Islamic conditions and rules for hunting in an earlier chapter.

However, Islam prohibits hunting in two situations. The first is when a person is in the sacred state of consecration (*ihram*) for the performance of *hajj* or *'umrah*, because this is a state of total peace in which one is not permited to kill or shed blood, as commanded by Allah:

---

[1]Reported by Ahmad.
[2]Reported by Ahmad.
[3]Reported by al-Bukhari and Musim.

O you who believe, do not kill game while you are in
ihram....(5:98(95)

...But to hunt on land is forbidden to you as long as you
are in *ihram*....(5:99(96)

The second situation exists when a person is within the limits of the
sacred territory of Makkah. Islam has declared this to be a region of
peace and security, a sanctuary for every living creature, whether
beast, bird, or plant, since the Prophet (peace be on him) prohibited
hunting its game, cutting its trees, or disturbing its airspace.[1]

Playing with Dice: Backgammon

Any sort of game played with money which has an element of
gambling is *haram*. The Qur'an classifies gambling in the same
category as drinking, idolatry, and divining with arrows. The
Prophet (peace be on him) said,

"He who says to his friend, 'Come, let us gamble,' must
give charity *(sadaqah)*",[2]

meaning that merely to invite someone to gamble is a sin requiring
penance.

Playing backgammon while betting with money is clearly *haram*.
Some scholars consider it *haram* even if no betting is involved, while
others consider it *makruh* rather than *haram*. Those who consider it
haram base their judgement on the *hadith* transmitted by Baraidah
in which the Prophet (peace be on him) said,

"He who plays with dice is like the one who handles the
flesh and blood of swine."[3]

The same scholars cite the *hadith* from Abu Musa al-Ashari in
which the Prophet (peace be on him) said,

"He who plays with dice disobeys Allah and His
Messenger."[4]

---

[1]Reported by al-Bukhari and Muslim.
[2]Reported by al-Bukhari and Muslim.
[3]Reported by Muslim, Ahmad and Abu Daoud.
[4]Reported by Ahmad, Abu Daoud, Ibn Majah, and Malik in his *Al -muwatta.*

298

These two sayings of the Prophet (peace be on him) are clearly applicable to all players of backgammon, whether they gamble in playing or not.

Al-Shawkani says that Ibn Mughaffal and Ibn al-Musayyib allowed playing with dice if it did not involve gambling, apparently interpreting the above *ahadith* to refer to those who played for money.

Playing Chess

Chess is a very popular game, and the opinion of jurists concerning it varies. Some consider it *halal*, others *makruh*, and still others *haram*. Those who consider it *haram* cite some *ahadith* in support of their position, but researchers have proved that chess did not appear until after the death of the Prophet (peace be on him), thus all such *ahadith* must have been fabricated.

The Companions of the Prophet (may Allah be pleased with them) themselves held differing views about playing chess. Ibn 'Umar said that it is worse than backgammon and 'Ali regarded it as gambling (perhaps meaning when it is played for money), while some others merely expressed disapproval of it.

However, some Companions and some of the second generation scholars allowed it. Among these were Ibn 'Abbas, Abu Hurairah, Ibn Sirin, Hisham bin 'Umrah, and Sa'id bin al-Musayyib. We agree with these great jurists, since the original principle is the permissibility of acts and no text is to be found prohibiting it. Moreover, in addition to being a game and a recreation, chess is also a mental exercise which requires thought and planning. In this respect it is the opposite of backgammon, for while backgammon is a game of chance and therefore comparable to divining with arrows, chess is a game of skill and strategy which may be compared to archery.

However, playing chess is permissible only if the following three conditions are met:

1. One should not get so absorbed in it that he delays his *salat*; chess is well-known to be a stealer of time.
2. There should be no gambling involved.

3. The players should not utter obscenities or vulgarities.

If any of these conditions are not met it should be considered as *haram*.

Singing and Music

Among the entertainments which may comfort the soul, please the heart, and refresh the ear is singing. Islam permits singing under the condition that it not be in any way obscene or harmful to Islamic morals. There is no harm in its being accompanied by music which is not exciting.

In order to create an atmosphere of joy and happiness, singing is recommended on festive occasions such as the days of 'Eid, weddings and wedding feasts, births, *'aqiqat* (the celebration of the birth of a baby by the slaughter of sheep), and on the return of a traveler.

'Aishah narrated that when a woman was married to an Ansari man, the Prophet (peace be on him) said,

> " 'Aishah, did they have any enertainment? The *Ansar* are fond of entertainment."[1]

Ibn 'Abbas said, " 'Aishah gave a girl relative of hers in marriage to a man of the *Ansar*. The Prophet (peace be on him) came and asked, 'Did you send a singer along with her?' 'No,' said 'Aishah. The Messenger of Allah (peace be on him) then said,

> The *Ansar* are a people who love poetry. You should have sent along someone who would sing, 'Here we come, to you we come, greet us as we greet you.' "[2]

'Aishah narrated that during the days of Mina, on the day of 'Eid al-Adha, two girls were with her, singing and playing on a hand drum. The Prophet (peace be on him) was present, listening to them with his head under a shawl. Abu Bakr then entered and scolded the girls. The Prophet (peace be on him), uncovering his face, told him,

> "Let them be, Abu Bakr. These are the days of 'Eid."[3]

---

[1]Reported by al-Bukhari.
[2]Reported by Ibn Majah.
[3]Reported by al-Bukhari and Muslim.

In his book, *Ihya ulum al-deen*,[1] Imam al-Ghazzali mentions the *ahadith* about the singing girls, the Abyssinians playing with spears in the Prophet's Mosque, the Prophet's encouraging them by saying, "Carry on, O Bani Arfidah," his asking his wife, 'Aishah, "Would you like to watch?" and standing there with her until she herself became tired and went away, and 'Aishah's playing with dolls with her friends. He then says:

All these *ahadith* are reported by al-Bukhari and Muslim in the two *Sahihs*, and they clearly prove that singing and playing are not *haram*. From them we may deduce the following:

First: The permissibility of playing; the Abyssinians were in the habit of dancing and playing.

Second: Doing this in the mosque.

Third: The Prophet's saying, 'Carry on, O Bani Arfidah,' was a command and a request that they should play; then how can their play be considered *haram?*

Fourth: The Prophet (peace be on him) prevented Abu Bakr and 'Umar from interrupting and scolding the players and singers. He told Abu Bakr that 'Eid was a joyous occasion and that singing was a means of enjoyment.

Fifth: On both occasions he stayed for a long time with 'Aishah, letting her watch the show of the Abyssinians and listening with her to the singing of the girls. This proves that it is far better to be good-humored in pleasing women and children with games than to express such disapproval of such amusements out of a sense of harsh piety and asceticism.

Sixth: The Prophet (peace be on him) himself encouraged 'Aishah by asking her, "Would you like to watch?"[2]

Seventh: The permissibility of singing and playing on the drum...

---

[1]In the quarter on "Habits", in the book *Listening to Singing*.
[2]Reported by al-Bukhari and Muslim.

and what follows, to the end of al-Ghazzali's discussion on singing.

It is reported that many Companions of the Prophet (may Allah be pleased with them) as well as second generation Muslim scholars used to listen to singing and did not see anything wrong with it. As for the *ahadith* which have been reported against singing, they are all weak and have been shown by researchers to be unsound. The jurist Abu Bakr al-'Arabi says, "No sound *hadith* is available concerning the prohibition of singing," while Ibn Hazm says, "All that is reported on this subject is false and fabricated."

However, since singing is in many cases associated with drinking parties and night clubs, many scholars have declared it to be *haram* or at least *makruh*. They state that singing constitutes that kind of idle talk which is mentioned in the *ayah*,

> And among the people is the one who buys idle talk (at the expense of his soul) in order to lead (people) astray from the path of Allah without knowledge, holding it in mockery; for such there will be a humilaiting punishment. (31:6)

Says Ibn Hazm:

> This verse condemns a particular behavior, that of doing something to mock the path of Allah. Anyone who does this is an unbeliever; if he even should buy a copy of the Qur'an, doing so in order to make it the object of his mockery and thereby leading people astray, he would be an unbeliever. It is this type of behavior which is condemned by Allah and not the idle talk in which one may indulge for mere relaxation, without intending to lead people astray from the path of Allah.

Ibn Hazm also refutes the argument of those who say that since singing is not of "the truth" it must be of "error," referring to the verse, "And what is beyond the truth except error?" (10:32). He comments,

> The Messenger of Allah (peace be on him) said, 'Deeds will be judged according to intentions, and everyone will get what he intended.'[1] Accordingly, the one who listens to singing with the intention of using it in

---

[1] Reported by al-Bukhari and Muslim.

support of a sin is a sinner, and this holds true of anything other than singing (as well), while one who listens to singing with the intention of refreshing his soul in order to gain strength to do his duty toward Allah Ta'ala and to do good deeds, is a good and obedient servant of Allah, and his action is of the truth. And he who listens to singing intending neither obedience nor disobedience is doing something neutral and harmless, which is similar to going to the park and walking around, standing by a window and looking at the sky, wearing blue or green cloths, and so on.

However, there are some limitations to be observed in the matter of singing:

1. The subject matter of songs should not be against the teachings of Islam. For example, if the song is in praise of wine, and it invites people to drink, singing or listening to it is *haram*.

2. Although the subject matter itself may not be against the Islamic teachings, the manner of singing may render it *haram*; this would be the case, for example, if the singing were accompanied by suggestive sexual movement.

3. Islam fights against excess and extravagance in anything, even in worship; how, then, can it tolerate excessive involvement with entertainment? Too much time should not be wasted in such activities; after all, what is time but life itself? One cannot dispute the fact that spending time in permissible activities consumes time which ought to be reseverd for carrying out religious obligations and doing good deeds. It is aptly said, "There is no excess except at the expense of a neglected duty."

4. Each individual is the best judge of himself. If a certain type of singing arouses one's passions, leads him towards sin, excites the animal instincts, and dulls spirituality, he must avoid it, thus closing the door to temptations.

5. There is unanimous agreement that if singing is done in conjunctin with *haram* activities — for example, at a drinking party, or if it is mixed with obscenity and sin — it is *haram*. The Prophet (peace be on him) warned of a severe punishment for people who sing or listen to singing in such a situation when he said,

> Some people of my *ummah* will drink wine, calling it by
> another name, while they listen to singers
> accompanied by musical instruments. Allah will cause
> the earth to swallow them and will turn some of them
> into monkeys and swine.[1]

This does not mean that they will be physically transformed into the
bodies and outward form of monkeys and swine but rather in heart
and soul, carrying the heart of a monkey and the soul of a pig in their
human bodies.

Gambling, the Companion of Drinking

While permitting a variety of games and sports, Islam prohibits
any game which involves betting, that is, which has an element of
gambling in it. We have alrady quoted the saying of the Prophet,

> "He who says to his friend, 'Come, let us gamble,' must
> give charity."

It is not lawful for the Muslim to seek relaxation and recreation in
gambling, nor is it lawful for him to acquire money through it.

There are sound and noble objectives behind this strict
prohibition of gambling:

1. The Islamic teachings urge the Muslim to follow Allah's
   directives for earning a living, to use natural laws and direct
   means for the attainment of his objectives, and to employ such
   causes as produce the desired effects. Gambling, which includes
   raffling or the lottery, on the other hand, makes a person
   dependent on chance, "luck" and empty wishes, taking him
   away from honest labor, serious work and productive effort. The
   person who depends on gambling loses respect for the laws of
   causation which Allah has established and commanded people
   to use.

2. In Islam, an individual's property is sacred; it may not be taken
   from him except through lawful exchange or unless he gives it
   freely as a gift or in charity. Accordingly, taking it from him by
   gambling is unlawful.

---

[1]Reported by Ibn Majah.

3. It is therefore not surprising that gamblers develop hatred and enmity toward one another, although they may claim that losing does not trouble them. There is always a winner and a loser. The loser may seem composed but behind his composure is frustration, anger, and regret: frustration due to disappointment, anger at the loss of money, and regret for not having played a winning game.

4. Gambling has its own compulsion. The loser plays again in hope of winning the next game in order to regain his earlier losses, while the winner plays again to enjoy the pleasure of winning, impelled by greed for more. Naturally, luck changes hands, the loser becomes the winner and the winner the loser, and the joy of winning changes into the bitterness of loss. Thus the gamblers may persist at playing the game, unable to bring themselves to leave it; this is the secret of the addiction to gambling.

5. Because of this addiction, gambling is a danger to the society as well as to the individual. This habit consumes gamblers' time and energy, making them non-productive idlers and parasites on society, who take but do not give, who consume but do not produce. Moreover, due to his absorption with gambling, the gambler neglects his obligations toward his Creator and his duties toward his community. It often happens that a gambling addict sells his honor, religion, and country for the sake of the gaming table, since his devotion to this table dulls his sense of values and kills all other devotions.

How correct the Qur'an is in mentioning drinking and gambling together in its verses, since their harmful effects on the individual, the family, and society are very similar. What is more like alcoholism than addiction to gambling? This is why one usually is not found without the other. Again, how correct the Qur'an is when it teaches us that both of these, drinking and gambling, are inspired by Satan, that they are akin to idolatry and divining by arrows, and that they are filthy and abominable habits which must be shunned:

> O you who believe, truly intoxicants and gambling and divination by arrows are an abomination of Satan's doing; avoid them in order that you may be successful. Assuredly Satan desires to sow enmity and hatred

among you by means of intoxicants and gambling, and to hinder you from the remembrance of Allah and from *salat*. Will you not then desist? (5:93-94 (90-91))

The Lottery, a Form of Gambling

What is known as the lottery or raffle is likewise a form of gambling. There should be no laxity or permissiveness toward it in the name of "charitable institutions" or "humanitarian causes." Those who consider it permissible in relation to such causes are similar to people who raise funds for the same causes by means of *haram* dances or "artistic" shows. To both such groups we say, "Allah is pure and does not accept anything except what is pure."

People who resort to such means of raising money assume that members of society have become devoid of goodness of heart and feelings of charity, compassion and mercy, as a result of which there is no other way of getting money from them except through gambling and sensuous entertaiment. But Islam does not assume this for its society. It believes in the basic goodness of man and appeals to that goodness, seeking nothing but pure means for noble causes. The Islamic means of raising money are to invite toward righteousness, to appeal to human sympathy, and to recall to peoples' minds the implications of the belief in Allah Subhanahu wa Ta'ala and the Hereafter.

Movies

Many Muslims ask about Islam's stand concerning the watching of movies, dramatic performances and the like. Is it permissible or not?

No doubt movies are important tools of instruction and recreation. Their situation is like that of any other tool which in itself is neutral and harmless, and any ruling concerning it will depend on how it is used.

Consequently, movies may be regarded as permissible and good — in fact, desirable — if the following conditions are met:

306

First: The content must be free of sin and immorality — indeed, of anything which is against the Islamic beliefs, morals, and manners. Portrayals which excite sexual desire or greed, glorify crime, or propagate deviant ideas, false beliefs, and the like are *haram*, and it is not permissible for the Muslim to watch or to encourage them.

Second: The watching of movies should not result in the neglect of religious obligations or worldly responsibilities. The five daily prayers constitute the foremost of the religious obligations; hence it is *haram* for the Muslim to miss any prayer — for example *salat al-Maghrib* — in order to watch a movie. Allah Ta'ala says,

> Then woe to the worshipers who are neglectful of their
> prayers, (107:4-5)

referring to those who postpone a prayer until its time is past. Again, one of the most important reasons mentioned in the Qur'an for the prohibition of drinking and gambling is that they keep people away from the remembrance of Allah and from *salat*.

Third: Physical intermingling and free mixing among men and women in movie theatres must be avoided in order to prevent sexual undertones and temptation, particularly because showing a film requires a darkened hall. We have already mentioned the *hadith*,

> It is better for one of you to be pricked in the head with
> an iron pick than to touch a woman whom it is unlawful
> to touch.[1]

4. Social Relations

The relations among the members of the Islamic society are based on two fundamental principles: first, awareness of the strong bond of brotherhood which links one individual to another, and second, the protection of the rights of the individual and the sanctity of his life, honor, and property, as guaranteed by the *Shari'ah* of Islam.

Any words, deed, or behavior which contravene or threaten these two principles is prohibited by Islam, the degree of prohibition depending on the magnitude of material or moral injury which might result from it. In the following *ayat* we find some examples of those prohibited acts which are injurious to the brotherhod and sanctity of human beings. Allah Subhanahu wa Ta'ala says:

---

[1]Reported by al-Bayhaqi and al-Tabarani on sound authority.

Verily, the Believers are brothers. Then set matters right between your brothers and be conscious of Allah in order that you may obtain mercy. O you who believe, let not some people mock at other people, for they may be better than themselves, nor (let) women (mock) at women who may be better than themselves. And do not slander yourselves, nor revile by (offensive) nicknames; evil is a name connoting wickedness after believing; and whoever does not turn away (from doing this), those are wrongdoers. O you who believe, avoid (indulging in) much suspicion; truly, some suspicion is a sin. And do not spy or backbite one another; would any of you like to eat the flesh of his dead brother? You would abhor that. And be conscious of Allah; indeed, Allah is Relenting, Merciful. (49:10-12)

Here Allah proclaims that the Believers are indeed brothers to one another united through the brotherhood of Islam in addition to their brotherhood in humanity. This brotherly relationship requires that they get to know each other and do not avoid each other, that they establish ties and do not break them, that they love and do not hate, that they be sincere and not superficial, and that they come together and do not separate from one another. And the Prophet (peace be on him) says,

Do not be envious of each other, nor backbite nor hate one another, but become brothers in the service of Allah.[1]

The Unlawfulness of Severing Ties with a Fellow Muslim

It is *haram* for the Muslim to shun a brother Muslim, to break ties with him, or to turn away from him. If two Muslims quarrel with each other, they are allowed a cooling-off period of three days, after which they must seek out means of reconciliation and peace, overcoming their pride, anger and hatred. One of the charcteristics of the believers praised in the Qur'an is that they are "humble

---

[1]Reported by al-Bukhari and others.

toward the Believers." (5:57 (54)). The Prophet (peace be on him) said,

> It is not permissible for a Muslim to keep apart from his brother for more than three days. If three days pass, he should meet him and greet him, and if he replies to it, they will both have shared in the reward, while if he does not reply, he will bear his sin while the Muslim (who offered him the greeting) will have been freed from the sin of keeping apart.[1]

The prohibition of severing ties is even more emphatic in the case of blood relatives. Islam has made it obligatory upon Muslims to strengthen the ties of relationship,[2] holding them sacred. Says Allah Ta'ala:

> ...And be conscious of Allah, in Whom you claim your rights of one another, and of the wombs (that bore you); indeed, Allah is Watcher over you. (4:1)

Using picturesque language, the Prophet (peace be on him) emphasized the value of this relationship in the sight of Allah by saying,

> The womb is tied to the Throne (of Allah) and it says, 'With him who keeps me united, Allah will keep connection, but with him who severs me, Allah will sever connection.'[3]

He also said,

> "One who cuts will not enter Paradise."[4]

In explaining the meaning of this, some scholars say it means "one who cuts the ties of relationship," while others say that it means "one who cuts the road," that is, the highway robber. The Prophet's *ahadith* imply that both pertain to the same category.

Joining the ties of relationship does not merely mean returning a visit for a visit or one good turn for another, since this much is quite natural and to be expected; rather, it means to persist in friendly relations even with those relatives who shun you. The Prophet (peace be on him) said,

---

[1] Reported by Abu Daoud.
[2] Literally, "the ties of the womb." (Trans.)
[3] Reported by al-Bukhari and Muslim.
[4] Reported by al-Bukhari.

The one who joins the ties of relationship is not the one who merely requites others, but he is the one who joins such ties (even) when they are severed by others.[1]

This applies as long as such shunning or boycotting is not for the sake of Allah, while if it is for the sake of Allah and in the cause of justice these injunctions do not apply. The strongest bond among the believers is established through loving for the sake of Allah and hating for the sake of Allah.

For fifty days the Prophet (peace be on him) and his Companions boycotted three men who stayed behind from the Battle of Tabuk. This boycott was so total that the three did not know what to do or where to turn, and felt that the earth, in spite of its vastness had become a prison to them. No one visited them, spoke to them, or greeted them. This boycott continued until Allah accepted their repentance and revealed to the Prophet (peace be on him) that He had pardoned them.[2] On another occasion, the Prophet (peace be on him) stayed away from some of his wives for forty days.

'Abdullah bin 'Umar boycotted one of his sons for the remainder of his life because his son did not abide by the *hadith*, narrated to him by his father, in which the Prophet (peace be on him) prohibited men to prevent their women from going to the mosque.[3]

Estrangement and enmity between Muslims must never be for any worldly reason, for in the sight of Allah and the Muslim, the whole world is of such little value that it is not worth abandoning and breaking the relationship with a brother Muslim. How can it be otherwise, when the penalty of such rancour is the deprivation of the forgiveness and mercy of Allah Subhanahu wa Ta'ala? The Prophet (peace be on him) said:

> The gates of the Garden are opened on Mondays and Thursdays, and Allah forgives every person who does not associate anything with Allah excepting a man between whom and his brother there is enmity. Thrice the command will be given: 'Leave the two of them until they are reconciled.'[4]

---

[1] Reported by al-Bukhari.
[2] Reported by al-Bukhari and Muslim.
[3] Reported by Ahmad. Al-Suyuti wrote an article entitled, *"Al-zajar lei al-hajar,"* *("Punishment by Boycott"),* justifying it on the basis of several *ahadith* and actions of the Prophet's Companions.
[4] Reported by Muslim.

It should suffice for the aggrieved person that his brother come to him and apologize; he must then accept the apology and be reconciled. It is *haram* for him to rebuff his brother by not accepting his apology. The Prophet (peace be on him) warned against this by saying that the one who does so will not meet him, the Prophet, at the Fountain in Paradise on the Day of Resurrection.[1]

Settling Disputes

While it is incumbent upon the disputants to settle their differenes in a brotherly fashion, the Muslim community also has a responsibility in this regard. As the Muslim society is based upon mutual caring and cooperation, it cannot stand passively by watching its members disputing and quarreling, permitting the conflict to grow larger. It is the responsibility of those who command respect and authority in the community to come forward in order to set things right, with absolute impartiality and without allowing themselves to become emotionally involved with one side or the other. Allah Ta'ala says,

Verily, the Believers are brothers. Then set matters right between your brothers and be conscious of Allah in order that you may obtain mercy. (49:10)

The Prophet (peace be on him), explaining the merit of such mediation and the danger of conflict and hostility, said,

'Shall I not inform you of something more excellent in degree than fasting, charity and *salat*?' On receiving the reply, 'Certainly,' he said, 'It is putting things right between people, for to incite people to dispute is like a razor. And I do not mean that is shaves off the hair but that is shears the religion.[2]

"Let Not Some People Mock at Other People"

In verses 49:10-12, Allah has prescribed a number of things

---

[1]Reported by al-Tabarani.
[2]Reported by al-Tirmidhi and others.

related to the preservation of brotherhood and what this implies with regard to what is to be held sacred among human beings. The first among these is the prohibition of mocking, deriding, and scoffing at others. The Believer who fears Allah and hopes to attain the Garden in the Hereafter will not scoff at any individual nor make people the object of his jokes, scorn, sarcasm or mockery, because this is nothing but pride, arrogance, and contempt for others, as well as ignorance of the scale by which Allah measures goodness. Says Allah Subhanahu wa Ta'ala:

Let not some people mock at other people, for they may be better than themselves, nor (let) women (mock) at women who may better than themselves. (49:11)

In the scale of Allah, goodness is measured by faith, sincerity, and the quality of the relationship with Allah Ta'ala, not by physical appearance, wealth, or power. Said the Prophet (peace be on him).

Allah does not look at your physical features or your wealth, but He looks at your hearts and your deeds.[1]

How, then, can it be permissible for a person to laugh at someone's physical handicap, deformity, or poverty? It is reported that 'Abdullah bin Mas'ood had thin, weak legs. Once, upon seeing his leg uncovered, some people laughed, whereupon the Prophet (peace be on him) said,

Are you laughing at the frailty of his legs? By Him in Whose hand is my soul, in the scale of Allah they are weightier than Mount Uhud.[2]

The Qur'an speaks of how the criminal idolators used to laugh at the faithful Muslims, especially at the weak and oppressed ones like Bilal and 'Ammar, and how the tables will be turned on the Day of Reckoning, when the mockers will become the mocked:

Verily, the criminals used to laugh at those who believed and wink at one another when they passed them, and when they returned to their families they would return joking (about them). And when they saw them they would say, 'Surely these people are astray.'

[1]Reported by Muslim.
[2]Reported by al-Tiyalisi and Ahmad.

But they had not been sent as watchers over them. Then on this day those who believe will laugh at the disbelievers. (83:29-34)

Although it has already been implied in the first part of the verse 49:11, nevertheless this *ayah* goes on to state explicitly that women should not mock at other women. This emphasis is due to the fact that mocking at others is quite common among women.

"Do Not Slander"

The second of these prohibitions is against *lamz*, which literally means "piercing and stabbing." Here it is used to mean finding faults, as the person who finds faults in others is doing something similar to piercing them with a sword or stabbing them with a dagger — and perhaps the wound inflicted by the tongue is more lasting. A poet has said,

The wounds of blades may heal one day,
But the wounds of the tongue? They never may.

The form of prohibition expressed in this verse is very subtle, saying, "Do not slander yourselves," that is, one another. For the Qur'an regards the community of Muslims as one body in its mutual concerns and responsibilities, so that whoever slanders his brother in effect slanders himself.

"Do Not Revile by Nicknames"

One form of slandering is calling others by derogatory nicknames of the sort which highlight some defect and are used to mock and deride a person. A Muslim should not call his brother by a name which is offensive to him, thereby causing him pain and thus trampling on the feelings of Islamic brotherliness.

Suspicion

Islam aims at establishing its society on clearness of conscience and mutual trust, not on doubts, suspicions, accusations and mistrust. Hence this *ayah* mentions the fourth prohibition by which what is to be held sacred among people is safeguarded:

O you who believe, avoid (indulging in) much suspicion;
truly some suspicion is a sin.   (49:12)

The kind of suspicion which is a sin is the ascribing of evil motives, and it is not permissible for a Muslim to impute such motives to his brother Muslim without justification and clear evidence. Because the basic assumption concerning people is that they are innocent, a mere suspicion should not be allowed to result in the accusation of an innocent person. Regarding this the Prophet (peace be on him) said,

"Avoid suspicion, for airing suspicion is the most lying
form of speech." [1]

Human weakness is such that no one is free of suspicion and wrong thoughts especially concerning those with whom relationships are not good. However, one must not give in to such thoughts nor go beyond thoughts to action, as stated in the *hadith*,

"If you have a suspicion, do not pursue it." [2]

Spying

Inwardly, mistrust of others produces evil thoughts in the mind while outwardly it leads a person toward spying. But Islam establishes its society on the purity of both what is inner and what is outer. Therefore, just as spying follows suspicion, the prohibition of spying comes immediately after that of suspicion.

Prying into other peoples' private affairs and spying on their secrets is not permitted, even if they are engaged in sin, as long as they do it privately and not openly.

---

[1]Reported by al-Bukhari and others.
[2]Reported by al-Tabarani.

Abu Haitham, the scribe of 'Uqbah bin 'Amir, a Companion of the Prophet (peace be on him) narrated, "I said to 'Uqbah bin 'Amir, 'Some of our neighbors drink wine, and I am going to call the police and have them arrested.' He said, 'Do not do so, but advise them and warn them.' I said, 'I told them to stop it but they do not listen to me. I am therefore going to inform the police and have them arrested.' 'Uqbah then said, 'Woe to you! Do not do that, for I heard the Mesenger of Allah (peace be on him) say,

> If one conceals the private affairs (of others), it is like reviving a girl who has been buried alive from her grave.[1]

The Prophet (peace be on him) classified those who search out other peoples' faults as being among the hypocrites, who proclaim their belief with their tongues while their hearts do not confirm what they say. He denounced such people publicly. Ibn 'Umar narrated, "Allah's Messenger (peace be on him) mounted the pulpit and called out in a loud voice,

> O you who declare Islam with your tongues but whose hearts have not been reached by faith, do not annoy the Muslims nor seek out their faults, for he who seeks out the faults of his brother Muslim will have his faults sought out by Allah, and when Allah seeks out someone's faults, He exposes them, even though he should be in the interior of his house.[2]

In order to safeguard peoples' privacy, the Prophet (peace be on him) strictly forbade that anyone should look into other peoples' houses without their permission and absolved the residents for any injury they might inflict upon one who so looks. He said,

> If someone peeps into the house of a people without their permission, it becomes allowable to them to gouge out his eye.[3]

Likewise, he prohibited listening clandestinely to peoples' conversation without their knowledge or approval, saying,

> He who listens clandestinely to peoples' conversation

---

[1] Reported by Abu Daoud, al-Nisai, Ibn Hibban in his *Sahih*, and al-Hakim. The wording is from Ibn Hibban.
[2] Reported by al-Tirmidhi, and Ibn Majah has reported something similar.
[3] Reported by al-Bukhari and Muslim.

against their wishes will have molten lead poured into his ears on the Day of Resurrection.[1]

Allah Subhanahu wa Ta'ala has made it obligatory on the person who wants to visit someone at his home not to enter the house until permission is given and he has greeted its inhabitants:

> O you who believe, do not enter houses other than your own until you have asked permission and offered *salam* (greeting) to its people; that is best for you in order that you may be heedful. And if you do not find anyone therein, do not enter until permission is given to you. And if you are told, 'Withdraw,' then do so; that is purer for you; and Allah knows what you do. (24: 27-28)

Said the Prophet (peace be on him),

> He who pulls the curtain and looks into a house before he is granted permission to enter has committed an offense.[2]

The texts prohibiting spying and searching out peoples' faults apply equally to the government and to individuals. Mu'awiyah reported the Prophet (peace be on him) as saying,

> "If you seek out peoples' faults, you will corrupt them, or bring them very near to corruption,"[3]

and Abu Imamah reported that the Prophet (peace be on him) said,

> The ruler who sows suspicion among the people corrupts them.[4]

Backbiting

The sixth evil prohibited in the verses cited above is backbiting (*gheeba*):

> And do not...backbite one another. (49:12)

The Prophet (peace be on him) wanted to drive home the meaning of backbiting to his Companions through questions and answers. He asked them,

---

[1]Reported by al-Bukhari and Muslim.
[2]Reported by Ahmad and al-Tirmidhi.
[3]Reported by Abu Daoud and by Ibn Hibban in his *Sahih*.
[4]Reported by Abu Daoud.

'Do you know what backbiting is?' They replied, 'Allah and His Messenger know best'. He said, 'It is saying something about your brother which he would dislike'. Someone asked 'What if I say something about my brother which is true?' The Prophet (peace be on him) replied, 'If what you say of him is true, it is backbiting and if it is not true you have slandered him.'[1]

When a person dislikes someone, he is likely to find faults in his appearance, behavior, lineage, and anything else which pertains to him. 'Aishah narrated that she said to the Prophet (pece be on him), "Do you see that Safiyyah (another wife of the Prophet) is such and such?" meaning that she was short. The Prophet (peace be on him) replied,

"You have spoken a word such that, if it were mixed in the water of the ocean, it would darken it."[2]

Backbiting is nothing but a desire to belittle people, to slander their honor, and to deride their accomplishments in their absence. Since this is stabbing in the back, it is an expression of narrow-mindedness and cowardice. Backbiting is a negative trait, and only those engage in it who themselves are not achievers. It is a tool of destruction, for one who is addicted to it leaves no one without throwing a dart at him and wounding him.

It is no wonder then, that the Qur'an paints such a repulsive picture of this vile habit as would make people shrink from it in horror:

And do not...backbite one anther; would any of you like to eat the flesh of his dead brother? You would abhor that. (49:12)

Since one feels sick at the very thought of eating human flesh, how much more revolting it is to think of eating the flesh of one's dead brother!

Whenever an opportunity arose, the Prophet (peace be on him) stressed this Qur'anic imagery in order to imprint it on peoples' hearts and minds. Ibn Mas'ood narrated, "We were sitting with the Prophet (peace be on him). Then a man got up and left, whereupon

---

[1]Reported by Muslim, Abu Daoud, al-Tirmidhi, and al-Nisai.
[2]Reported by Abu Daoud, al-Tirmidhi, and al-Bayhaqi.

another person spoke ill of him. The Prophet (peace be on him) told him, 'Pick your teeth.' The man replied, 'Why? I haven't eaten any meat.' The Prophet (peace be on him) replied,

'You have eaten your brother's flesh. ' "[1]

Jabir narrated, "While we were with the Prophet (peace be on him) the wind brought a foul odor in our direction, whereupon the Prophet (peace be on him) said,

'Do you know what this odor is? It it he odor of those who backbite the Believers.' "[2]

All these textual quotations demonstrate the sanctity and dignity which is accorded to one in Islam. However, scholars have listed some exceptions, necessarily limited to certain circumstances, when talking about a person in his absence is permitted. Among these exceptions is the instance of a person who has been wronged and who complains about the wrongdoer. While he must then speak about what the other dislikes, it is his right to do so in order to secure justice; consequently, he is given permission to describe the wrong he has suffered. Allah Ta'ala says:

Allah does not like the announcing of evil in public speech except by one who has been wronged; and Allah is Hearing, Knowing. (4:148)

If someone wants to investigate the character or suitability of a person with whom he wants to enter into partnership, who has asked for his daughter in marriage, or who is seeking employment with him, it is permissible for those who have been asked to give their frank and honest opinion. Here there is a conflict between two obligations: one, to give good advice to the person who seeks the information, and two, to protect the honor of the person about whom the opinion is sought. But the first obligation takes precedence over the second, as it is more important and more sacred. Fatimah bint Qais asked the Prophet (peace be on him) about two men who had asked for her hand in marriage. The Prophet (peace be on him) told her about one of them, "He is good for nothing and has no property," and about the other, "He does not put his stick down from his shoulder," meaning that he frequently beat the women of his household.

---

[1] Reported by al-Tabarani on sound authority.
[2] Reported by Ahmad on reliable authority.

318

It is also permissible to speak about a person without his knowledge if a legal opinion or religious ruling is rerquired concerning him or if help is needed to combat some evil he may be causing, or to refer to him by a name, title, or characteristic which he dislikes but without which he cannot be identified, as for example, "the lame person" or "the person with one eye." Likewise, cross-questioning a witness or criticizing the reproters of *ahadith* and news is permissible.[1]

The general rule concerning the permissibility of speaking about someone in his absence is governed by two considerations: (1) the need and (2) the intention.

(1) When there is no compelling need to mention the third person in a manner in which he would dislike, one must refrain from violating the sanctity of his personality and honor. If there is a need to mention him but the need can be met by an indirect reference, one must not be explicit. If a general discussion is sufficient, the mentioning of specific persons must be avoided. For example, in seeking a juristic opinion, one can phrase the question as, "What would your opinion be if someone did such and such a thing?" rather than, "This person is doing such and such. What do you think about it?" Again, if one must identify the person, he must mention only what is true, since ascribing anything false to him is *haram*.

(2) In any event, the intention is the decisive factor. The speaker knows his own motives better than anyone else — whether it constitutes a genuine complaint against wrongdoing or mere spite, an inquiry concerning an issue or a slander, a scholarly criticism or envious backbiting, a piece of good advice or the spreading of a rumor. It is said in this connection that the Believer is a sterner judge of himself than a tyrannical ruler or a greedy partner could be.

Islam has decreed that the listener is the partner of the one who is absent, and he must defend his absent brother by repudiating the slander being spoken.

The Prophet (peace be on him) said,

> If anyone defends his brother who is slandered in his absence, it will be (his) due from Allah to set him free from the Fire.[2]

---

[1] See al-Ghazzali's discussion of the uses and abuses of speech in his *Ihya;* al-Nawawi's *Commentary on the Sahih of Muslim;* and al-Shawkani's treatise on what is permissible and what is prohibited in talking behind the backs of others.

[2] Reported by Ahmad on good authority.

And again,

> If anyone defends his brother's honor in this world,
> Allah will shield his face from the Fire on the Day of
> Resurrection.[1]

If a person does not have the courage to speak out in defense of his brother against malicious tongues, the least he can do is to withdraw from such company until they turn to some other topic; otherwise, the verse, "Truly, you would then be like them" (4:140) would apply to him.

Spreading Gossip

Another bad habit, which usually accompanies backbiting and is strictly prohibited by Islam, is gossiping. This means passing on to others what you hear from someone in such a manner that will cause dissension among people, sour their relationships, or increase already-existing bitterness between them.

From the very early Makkan period of revelation, the Qur'an condemned this trait saying,

> And do not obey any despicable man, ready with oaths,
> a slanderer, going among the people with calumnies.
> (68:10-11)

And the Prophet (peace be on him) said,

> "The one who spreads gossip which he has overheard
> will not enter the Garden, "[2]

and,

> The most evil among Allah's slaves are those who go
> about spreading gossip dividing those who love each
> other and desiring to defame those who are innocent.[3]

In order to foster peace and reconcilliation, Islam permits a mediator to conceal the bad words said by one person against another and permits him to add some good words which, in fact, neither of them has said. This is not considered to be lying, for the Prophet (peace be on him) said,

---

[1] Reported by al-Tirmidhi on sound authority.
[2] Reported by al-Bukhari and Muslim.
[3] Reported by Ahmad.

"He is not a liar who makes peace between two persons,
saying what is good or adding something good."[1]

Islam's anger is particularly directed against those people who, as soon as they hear something bad, hasten to recount it for the sake of currying favor or merely out of love of causing trouble and dissension. Indeed, many such people are not satisfied to simply repeat what they have heard but add to it or invent something of their own. As a poet has said,

If they hear a good word they hide it,
And if a bad word they shout it,
And if nothing is heard they make up a lie.

A man came to 'Umar bin 'Abd al-'Aziz and told him something about another person which the latter would have disliked being mentioned. Thereupon 'Umar said to him, "Let us examine your case: If you are lying, you are one of those who is mentioned in the *ayah*, 'If a wicked person brings you some news, investigate it' (49:6) and if you are telling the truth, you are one of those mentioned in the *ayah*, 'A slanderer, going among the people with calumnies.' (68:11) But if you wish we may forgive you." The man replied, "Please forgive me, O Ameer al-Mu'mineen (Leader of the Believers). I shall never do it again.

The Sacredness of Honor

We have already noted that the Islamic teachings safeguard human dignity and honor, regarding them, in fact, as inviolable and sacred. Once, while looking at the Ka'aba, 'Abdullah bin 'Umar remarked, "How great and sacred you are! But the sanctity of the Believer is greater than yours" — and the sanctity of the Muslim includes the sanctity of his life, his honor, and his property.

During the Farewell Pilgrimage the Prophet (peace be on him) addressed the asembly of Muslims, saying,

Your lives, your honor, and your property are as sacred
to each other as the sacredness of this your day, in this
your month, and in this your city.[2]

---

[1] Reported by al-Bukhari and Musilm.
[2] Reported by Muslim.

Islam safeguards the sanctity of a person's honor against backbiting even if what is said about him is true. How much more abhorrent it is, then,if what is said is false and baseless; this is a sheer wrong and a great sin. The Prophet (peace be on him) said,

If anyone says something about a person which is not true in order to defame him, Allah will confine him in the fire of Hell until it extinguishes his utterance.[1]

'Aishah reported that the Prophet (peace be on him) said to his Companions,

'Do you know what the worst form of usury is in the sight of Allah?' They said, 'Allah and His Messenger know best.' The Prophet (peace be on him) replied, 'The worst form of usury is the violation of the personal honor of a Muslim.' He then recited, 'Those who harm believing men and believing women undeservedly have laid upon themselves a calumny and a manifest sin.'[2] (33:58)

The vilest kind of attack on personal honor is that of accusing a virtuous believing woman of immorality. Such an accusation not only ruins her reputation and that of her family, destroying her future, but also broadcasts scandals within the Muslim society. This is why the Prophet Muhammad (peace be on him) listed it among the seven most heinous sins and the Qur'an threatened its perpetrators with dire punishments:

Those who accuse chaste but careless (or indiscreet) believing women shall be accursed in this world and in the Hereafter, and theirs will be a grevious punishment on the Day when their tongues, their hands, and their feet will bear witness against them concerning what they did. On that Day Allah will pay them in full their just due, and they will show that Allah is indeed the manifest Truth. (24:23-25)

Indeed, those who love that a scandal should be spread concerning those who believe will have a painful punishment in this world and in the Hereafter; and Allah knows and you do not know. (24:19)

---

[1]Reported by al-Tabarani.
[2]Reported by Ibn Abu Hatim, Ibn Murdawai and al-Bayhaqi.

The Sacredness of Life

Islam has made human life sacred and has safeguarded its preservation. According to its teachings, aggression against human life is the second greatest sin in the sight of Allah, second only to denial of Him. The Qur'an declares,

> ...If anyone kills a person for any reason other than for (the killing of) a person or for sowing corruption in the land, it will be as if he had killed the whole of mankind....(5:35 (32))

Because the human race constitutes a single family, an offense against one of its members is in fact an offense against the whole of humanity. The crime is more serious if the slain is a believer in Allah.

> And for the one who kills a Believer intentionally, his recompense is Hell, to abide therein; and the wrath of Allah is upon him and His curse, and a tremendous punishment has been prepared for him.   (4:93)

The Prophet (peace be on him) said,

> "The passing away of the world would mean less to Allah than the murder of a Muslim man."[1]

He also said,

> "A Believer remains within the scope of his religion as long as he does not kill anyone unlawfully."[2]

And again,

> Allah may forgive every sin except in the case of one who dies a *mushrik* or one who kills a Believer intentionally.[3]

On the basis of these verses and *ahadith*, Ibn 'Abbas deduced that the repentance of the murder will not be accepted by Allah. For, he argued, since in the case of an offense against another individual, the wrongdoer's repentance is not accepted unless the wrong done to others is righted or their satisfction secured, the question is how, in

---

[1] Reported by Muslim, al-Nisai, and al-Tirmidhi.
[2] Reported by al-Bukhari.
[3] Reported by Abu Daoud, Ibn Hibban, and al-Hakim.

the case of murder, one can restore the murdered person to life or secure his satisfaction. Others say that sincere repentance is accepted by Allah; if it erases even the greatest sin, that of *shirk* or ascribing partners to Allah, why not lesser sins? Allah Ta'ala says:

...Those who do not invoke, together with Allah, any other deity, nor take the life which Allah has made sacred except in (the course of) justice, nor commit *zina*. And whoever does that shall pay the price (of his sin). The punishment shall be doubled for him on the Day of Resurrection and he will abide in it in disgrace, except for him who repents and belives and does righteous deeds. As for them, Allah will change their evil deeds to good deeds, and Allah is Forgiving, Merciful. (25:68-70)

"The Murderer and the Murdered Will Be in Hell"

The Prophet (peace be on him) considered a Muslim's fighting another Muslim to be a door to unbelief and a deed pertaining to pre-Islamic *jahiliyyah*, during which people used to wage wars and shed blood over a camel or a horse. He said,

"Insulting the Muslim is wickedness and fighting him is unbelief."[1]

"Do not become unbelievers after I pass away, killing one another."[2]

He further said,

'When two Muslims draw weapons against each other, they are at the brink of Hell. If one of them kills the other, they both enter it together.' Someone asked, 'O Messenger of Allah, this one was the murderer, but what was the fault of the murdered?' He replied, 'He was eager to kill the other.'[3]

Because of this the Prophet (peace be on him) forbade any act which might lead to murder or to a fight, even pointing a weapon, saying,

None of you should point a weapon at his brother.

[1]Reported by al-Bukhari and Muslim.
[2]Reported by al-Bukhari and Muslim.
[3]Reported by al-Bukhari and Muslim.

324

Perhaps Satan may make his hand slip and then he will fall into the pit of Fire.[1]

He also said,

If anyone points a piece of iron at his brother, the angels curse him until he stops doing it, even if he is his real brother.[2]

He even went so far as to say,

"It is not permissible for the Muslim to frighten his brother."[3]

The sin of murder is not limited to the murderer alone. Each individual who participated in this crime, by deed, or by word, will be the recipient of Allah's punishmet in proportion to his share in it; even a person who happened to be at the scene of the murder will receive a share of the sin. A *hadith* states,

None of you should remain in a place where a man is being killed unjustly, for the curse (of Allah) descends on anyone who was present and did not defend him.[4]

The Sanctity of the Lives of Allies and Non-Muslim Residents

Thus far we have quoted those texts which warn Muslims against killing or fighting fellow Muslims. But let no one get the impression that the life of a non-Muslim is not safe in a Muslim society, for Allah has declared the life of every human being to be sacred, and He has safeguarded it.

This applies as long as the non-Muslim does not fight against the Muslims; if he does so, shedding blood is permissible. However, if the non-Muslim is of a people with whom there is a treaty or if he is a *dhimmi* (a non-Muslim resident of an Islamic state), his life is sacred, and it is unlawful for the Muslim to attack him. In this regard the Prophet (peace be on him) has said,

---

[1] Reported by al-Bukhari.
[2] Reported by Muslim.
[3] Reported by Abu Daoud as well as by al-Tabarani on reliable authority.
[4] Reported by al-Tabarani and by al-Bayhaqi on good authority.

Anyone who kills a person from among the people with whom there is a treaty will not smell the fragrance of the Garden, although its fragrance reaches to a walking distance of forty years.[1]

"Anyone who kills a *dhimmi* will not smell the fragrance of the Garden."[2]

Capital Punishment

Allah Subhanahu wa Ta'ala says,

...Do not take the life which Allah has made sacred except in (the course of) justice....(6:151)

Allah has mentioned three crimes for which the death penalty is justified:

1. Unjust murder. Murder which has been proved demands retaliation by taking the life of the murderer — a life for a life, a like return for an evil committed, as the initiator of the killing is the initiator of the wrongdoing. As the Qur'an states,

    In the law of *qisas* (retaliation) there is life for you, O people of understanding....(2:179)

2. Publicly committing *zina* with a person who is not one's spouse if at least four upright people have actually witnessed intercourse taking place and testified before the court that they saw it. The death penalty applies to either of the two who is married. Confession, repeated four times before the court by the adulterer or adulteress, is equivalent to the testimony of four witnesses.

3. Apostacy from Islam after willingly accepting it and subsequently declaring an open revolt against it in such a manner which threatens the solidarity of the Muslim community is a crime punishable by death. No one is compelled to accept Islam, but at the same time no one is permitted to play tricks with it, as some Jews did during the Prophet's time:

    A party of the People of the Book say, 'Believe in what has been revealed to the Believers' at the beginning of

---

[1]Reported by al-Bukhari and others.
[2]Reported by al-Nisai.

326

the day and reject it at the end of it, in order that they may turn back (from Islam). (3:72)

The Prophet (peace be on him) limited capital punishment to these three crimes only, saying,

The shedding of the blood of a Muslim is not lawful except for one of three reasons: a life for a life, a married person who commits *zina*, and one who turns aside from his religion and abandons the community.[1]

In any of these instances, the death penalty can be implemented only by the proper authority after due process of law prescribed by the *Shari'ah*; individuals cannot take the law into their own hands, becoming judges and executioners, since this would result in absolute chaos and disorder. However, the judge may turn the murderer over to the victim's next-of-kin to be executed in his presence so that their hearts may be eased and the desire for revenge extinguished. This is in obedience to the saying of Allah Ta'ala,

...And whoever is killed wrongfully, We have given authority to the heir; but let him not go to excess in killing (by way of retaliation), for indeed he will be helped. (17:33)

Suicide

Whatever applies to the crime of murder likewise applies to committing suicide. Whoever takes his life by any means whatsoever has unjustly taken a life which Allah has made sacred. For since he did not create himself, nor even so much as a single cell of his body, the life of an individual does not belong to him; it is a trust given to him by Allah Subhanahu wa Ta'ala. He is not allowed to diminish it, let alone to harm or destroy it. Allah Ta'ala says:

...Do not kill yourselves; indeed, Allah is merciful to you. (4:29)

The Islamic teachings require the Muslim to be resolute in facing hardships; he is not permitted to give up and to run away from the

---

[1]Reported by al-Bukhari and Muslim.

vicissitudes of life when a tragedy befalls or some of his hopes are dashed. Indeed, the believer is created for striving, not for sitting idle; for combat, not for escape. His faith and character do not permit him to run away from the battlefield of life, and he posesses a weapon which never fails and ammunition which is never exhausted: the weapon of his unshakable faith and the ammunition of his moral steadfastness.

The Prophet (peace be on him) warned that anyone who commits the crime of suicide will be deprived of the mercy of Allah and will not enter the Garden; he will deserve Allah's wrath and be cast into the Fire. The Prophet (peace be on him) said,

> 'In the time before you, a man was wounded. His wounds troubled him so much that he took a knife and cut his wrist and bled himself to death. Thereupon Allah said, 'My slave hurried in the matter of his life.' therefore, he is deprived of the Garden.'[1]

If a person is deprived of the Garden because he cannot bear the pain of his wounds and so kills himself, what about the one who takes his life because he has suffered a loss, whether great or small, in his business, has failed an examination, or has been rejected by a woman. Let those people who are weak of will pay careful attention to the following *hadith*.

> He who throws himself down from a rock and commits suicide will be throwing himself into the fire of Hell; he who drinks poison and kills himself will have the poison in his hand, drinking it forever in the fire of Hell; and he who kills himself with a weapon will have that weapon in his hand, stabbing himself forever in the fire of Hell.[2]

The Sanctity of Property

The Muslim is permitted to acquire wealth, as much as he desires, as long as he acquires it through lawful means and increases it through lawful investments. While in another religion it is said, "It

[1]Reported by al-Bukhari and Muslim.
[2]Reported by al-Bukhari and Muslim.

is easier for a camel to pass through the eye of a needle than for a rich man to enter the kingdom of God,"[1] in Islam it is said,

"What an excellent thing is lawfully earned wealth in the hands of a good man."[2]

Since the Islamic *Shari'ah* sanctions the right to personal property, it protects it, both by means of moral exhortation and legislation, from robbery, theft, and fraud. The Prophet (peace be on him) mentioned the sanctity of property in the same sentence with the sanctity of life and honor and considered stealing as contradictory to faith, saying,

"A thief is not a Believer while he is engaged in stealing."[3]

Says Allah Ta'ala:

As for the male and female thief, cut off their hands, a recompense for what they earned, punishment from Allah; and Allah is Mighty, Wise. (5:41 (38))

And the Prophet (peace be on him) said,

"It is *haram* for the Muslim to take (so much as) a stick without the consent of its owner,"[4]

thus emphasizing what Allah has prohibited to the Muslim in respect of other peoples' property.

Allah the Great and Glorious says:

O you who believe, do not consume your property among yourselves wrongfully, but let there be trade by mutual consent....(4:29)

The Prohibition of Bribery

Taking a bribe is one way of consuming someone else's wealth wrongfully. A bribe refers to any kind of property which is offered to a judge or public servant in order to obtain a decision in favor of oneself or against a rival, to expedite one's own affair, or to delay that of one's competition, and so on.

---

[1]The author refers here to a quotation that the New Testament attributes to Jesus (pbuh). This does not imply that there is sufficient evidence that he actually said it. See footnote [1], page 5.

[2]Reported by Ahmad.
[3]Reported by al-Bukhari and Muslim
[4]Reported by Ibn Hibban in his *Sahih.*

Islam has prohibited the Muslim to approach the officials of a government or their subordinates for the purpose of offering them a bribe; it has prohibited the latter to accept it; and it has prohibited that any third person should arrange matters between the givers and the takers of the bribe. Allah Ta'ala says:

> And do not consume your property among yourselves wrongfully, nor seek access to judges by means of it in order that you may sinfully consume a portion of peoples' wealth, while you know (what you do). (2:188)

The Prophet (peace be on him) said,

> "Allah's curse is on the one who offers the bribe and on the judge who accepts it."[1]

Thawban said,

> The Messenger of Allah (peace be on him) cursed the one who offers the bribe, the one who receives it, and the one who arranges it.[2]

If the recipient of the bribe accepts it in order to do injustice, his sin is the greater, while if he intended to do justice, it was his simple duty for which no payment was needed.

The Prophet (peace be on him) sent 'Abdullah bin Rawahah to the Jews to estimate what they owed as taxes on their palm trees. The Jews offered him some money as a gift. He told them, "What you have offered as a bribe is *haram* and we do not accept it."[3]

It is not surprising that Islam has prohibited bribery and that it is severe against all those who participate in it. The proliferation of bribery in a society leads to corruption and oppression: unjust decisions are made and just ones are blocked, undeserving persons are given chances and deserving ones are passed over, and the spirit of greed permeates the society in place of the spirit of dutifulness.

Gifts to Officials

The intention of the Islamic *Shari'ah* is to prohibit bribery in any shape or form. Thus, referring to a bribe as a "gift" does not transfer

---

[1] Reported by Ahmad, al-Tirmidhi, and Ibn Hibban in his *Sahih*.
[2] Reported by Ahmad and al-Hakim.
[3] Reported by Malik

it from the realm of the *haram* to that of the *halal*. A *hadith* states,

> When we (the Prophet) appoint a person to a position, we take care of his provision. If he takes anything beyond that, it is an illegal gain.[1]

Caliph 'Umar bin 'Abd al-'Aziz was given a gift which he refused. On being told that the Prophet (peace be on him) had accepted gifts, he said, "To him it was a gift, but to us it is a bribe."

The Prophet (peace be on him) sent a man to collect *zakat* from the Azd tribe. On returning to the Prophet (peace be on him) he kept something for himself, telling the Prophet (peace be on him), "That is for you and this is for me as a gift." Thereupon the Prophet (peace be on him) became angry and said,

> If what you say is right, would these gifts have reached you if you had remained in your father's or your mother's house? He then continued, Why should a person employed by me say, 'That is for you and this is for me as a gift?' Did gifts reach him while he lived in his mother's house? By Him in Whose hand is my soul, no one takes something wrongfully without Allah's making him carry it on the Day of Resurrection. So let none of you come on the day of Resurrection carrying a braying camel, a mooing cow, or a bleating goat (which he received in this manner). He then raised his hands high in supplication and said, O Allah, have I conveyed the message?[2]

Said Imam al-Ghazzali,

> In view of these admonitions, the judge or the governor or anyone in a position of authority should imagine himself sitting in his father's or mother's house. If he thinks that even after leaving the job he will still have received this gift while sitting in his mother's house, he may accept the gift offered to him. If, on the other hand, this gift is offered to him because of his position of authority, he must not accept it. If he finds it difficult to

---

[1] Reported by Abu Daoud.
[2] Reported by al-Bukhari and Muslim.

decide, concerning gifts from his friends, whether they would still have given them to him if he were not in that position, it is a doubtful situation and it is preferable to avoid accepting them. [1]

Bribery to Redress a Wrong

If someone finds himself in a situation in which all avenues of redressing a wrong done him, or recovering a right which has been forfeited, are blocked except through the payment of a bribe, it is preferable that he wait patiently until Allah opens to him a better way of redressing the wrong or recovering his rights. Still, should he resort to bribery, the sin of it will not be on him provided he has tried all other lawful avenues and that in so doing he regains his own rights without infringing upon the rights of others; in such a case the burden of the sin will fall entirely on the recipient of the bribe.

Some scholars have deduced this from *ahadith* reporting that the Prophet (peace be on him) gave charity to some people who were persistent in begging although, in fact, they did not deserve to receive charity. 'Umar reported that the Prophet (peace be on him) said,

> 'One of you takes charity from me and carries it away under his arm, and it is (Hell)-fire for him.' 'Umar asked, 'O Messenger of Allah, how can you give it to him, knowing that it is fire for him?' The Prophet (peace be on him) replied, 'What am I to do? They ask from me persistently, and Allah has forbidden me to be closed-handed.' [2]

If when the pressure of insistent begging induced the Prophet (peace be on him) to give a beggar what he knew to be Hell-fire for him, what can we say about the pressure of the need to defend oneself against injustice or to regain one's right?

---

[1] *Ihya 'ulum al-deen,* the book of *"Al-halal wa al-haram,"* in the section entitled *"Al-adat" (Customs),* p. 137.
[2] Reported by Abu Y'ala on good authority; Ahmad reported something similar on sound authority.

Wasteful Spending

Just as the wealth of others is sacred and any violation of it, whether secret or open, is prohibited, in like manner a person's own wealth is sacred with respect to himself; he should not waste it by extravagant spending, scattering it to the right and left. This is because the Muslim *ummah*, which constitutes an owner in addition to every other owner, has a right to the wealth of individuals. For this reason Islam has given the *ummah* the right to manage the properties of the weak-minded who squander their wealth. The Qur'an says,

> Do not give your wealth, which Allah has made a means of support for you, to the weak-minded, but feed and clothe them from it and speak to them words of kindness. (4:5)

In this *ayah* Allah Subhanahu wa Ta'ala refers to the wealth of the weak-minded as "your wealth," since the wealth of the individual is also the wealth of the *ummah*.

Islam is the religion of justice and moderation, and the *ummah* of Islam is the "middle nation." The Muslim must be just in all his affairs. This is why Allah has prohibited to the Believers wastefulness and extravagant spending, as He has likewise prohibited them from greed and miserliness. Allah Ta'ala says:

> O children of Adam, wear your beautiful apparel at every place of worship, and eat and drink but do not be wasteful; indeed, He does not like the wasteful. (7:31)

Wasting wealth means to spend it, in large or small amounts, on what Allah has prohibited, for example, alcoholic beverages, drugs, gold and silver utensils, and the like, or to squander it on things which are of no benefit either to oneself or others, since the Prophet (peace be on him) prohibited the squandering of wealth.[1] Giving away so much in charity that one has nothing left for the necessities of life also constitutes wasting of wealth.

In explaining the *ayah*,

---

[1] Reported by al-Bukhari.

...They ask thee what they should spend (in charity). Say (Spend) what is beyond your needs....(2:219)

Imam al-Razi comments,

> Allah Ta'ala taught people how to spend their wealth. He told His Prophet (peace be on him), 'Give to the relative his right, and to the needy and the wayfarer, but do not squander (your wealth) wantonly; truly, the squanderers are brothers of the evil ones.' (17:26) He also says, 'Let not thy hand be tied to thy neck (in miserliness), nor extend it to its utmost reach,' (17:29) and He said, 'And those who, when they spend, are neither extravagant nor miserly.' (25:67) The Prophet (peace be on him) said, 'If one of you has something to spend, he should start with himself, then with those whom he supports, and so on.[1] He also said, 'The best charity is that which leaves you self-sufficient.'[2] Jabir bin 'Abdullah narrated, 'Once when we were with the Messenger of Allah (peace be on him), a man came with a lump of gold as large as an egg and said, "O Messenger of Allah, take it as charity; by Allah, this is all I possess." The Prophet (peace be on him) turned away from him. The man came around in front of the Prophet (peace be on him), whereupon the Prophet (peace be on him) said angrily, "Give it to me," and taking the piece of gold from him threw it toward him in such a way that, had it hit him, it would have been painful to him. He then said, "One of you brings me his wealth while he possesses nothing else, and then he sits down and begs from people. Charity is that which leaves you self-sufficient. Take this back; we have no need of it." '[3]

The Prophet (peace be on him) reported that he used to store food for his family sufficient for one year.[4] Men of wisdom have said, 'The optimum course is between the two extremes. Spending much is

---

[1] Reported by Muslim.
[2] Reported by al-Tabarani on good authority.
[3] Reported by Abu Daoud and al-Hakim.
[4] Reported by al-Bukhari.

squandering, while spending little is greed, and moderation is best.' This is the meaning of the words of Allah, 'Say: (Spend) What is beyond your needs,' (2:219) and moderation is the foundation of the *Shari'ah* brought by Muhammad (peace be on him). The foundation of the Jewish law is extreme harshness and that of Christian law extreme laxity, while the *Shari'ah* of Muhammad (peace be on him) is in the middle of all such matters. That is why it is the most perfect of all systems of law.[1]

5. Relationship of the Muslim With Non-Muslims

When we contemplate summarizing the Islamic teachings concerning dealings with non-Muslims in relation to the *halal* and the *haram*, we find that the following two verses of the Qur'an are sufficient, for they provide comprehensive guidelines in this matter. Says Allah Subhanahu wa Ta'ala:

> Allah does not forbid you, with regard to those who do not fight you on account of your religion nor drive you out of your homes, to treat them with goodness and to be just to them; truly, Allah loves those who are just. Indeed, Allah forbids you (only) with regard to those who fight you on account of religion and drive you out of your homes, and assist (others) in driving you out, that you turn to them (in friendship); and whoever turns to them (in friendship), they are wrongdoers. (60:8-9)

The first of these two verses not only calls for justice and fairness in dealing with non-Muslims who neither fight Muslims on religious grounds nor drive them out of their homes — that is, those who are neither at war with, nor hostile to, Muslims — but also urges Muslims to be kind to them. The word *Birr* or "goodness" which is used in this verse is a very comprehensive term signifying that kindness and generosity which is over and above justice; it is the same word which is used to describe the Muslim's duty to his parents.

---

[1] *Tafsir* by al-Fakhr al-Deen al-Razi, vol. 6, p. 51, with some condensation.

We have said that this verse calls for justice; as Allah says, "Allah loves those who are just," (60:8) and the Believer always tries his best to do what Allah loves. Now, there is no contradiction between Allah's saying, "Allah does not forbid you," (60:8) which is rather mild, and our interpretation of "calling for" and "urging" justice above. By the use of this expression, Allah Ta'ala wanted to remove from peoples' minds the erroneous ideas that all non-Muslims are alike and that they do not deserve good treatment and kindness from Muslims. Thus Allah made clear the fact that He did not prohibit kindness to non-Muslims in general but only to those who are at war with, and hostile to, the Muslims. This is similar to what Allah said concerning al-Safa and al-Marwah[1] when some people refrained from going between them due to some customs of *jahiliyyah*:

> ...For one who makes *hajj* or *'umrah* to the (Sacred) House, there is no fault in going between them....(2:158)

Since going between the two hills - the rite of *sa'i* - is actually obligatory as it is a part of *hajj* and *'umrah*, the denial of fault occurs in order to remove the misconception of *jahiliyyah*.

Special Consideration for the People of the Book

While Islam does not prohibit Muslims to be kind and generous to peoples of other religions, even if they are idolators and polytheists, as for example, the polytheists of Arabia, concerning whom the above verses were revealed, it looks upon the People of the Book, that is, Jews and Christians, with special regard, whether they reside in a Muslim society or outside it.

The Qur'an never addresses them without saying, "O People of the Book" or "O You who have been given the Book," indicating that they were originally people of a revealed religion. For this reason there exists a relationship of mercy and spiritual kinship between them and the Muslims, all having in common the principles of the one true religion sent by Allah through his prophets (peace be on them all):

[1]The two small hills in Makkah, adjacent to the Sacred Mosque containing the Ka'aba, between which Muslims walk seven times as a part of the rites of *hajj* and *'umrah*. (Trans.)

He has ordained for (the Muslims) the same religion which He enjoined on Noah, and that which We have revealed to thee (Muhammad) and that which We enjoined on Abraham, Moses, and Jesus: that you should establish the faith and make no division in it....(42:13)

Muslims are required to believe in all the Books revealed by Allah and in all the prophets sent by Him; otherwise they are not Believers.

Say: We (Muslims) believe in Allah and in what He has revealed to us, and in what He revealed to Abraham and Ishmael and Isaac and Jacob and the tribes (of Israel), and in what was given to Moses and Jesus, and in what was given to (all) the prophets by their Lord. We make no distinction between any of them, and to Him do we submit. (2:136)

Consequently, if the People of the Book read the Qur'an, they will find in it praise for their Books, messengers, and prophets.

If Muslims hold discussions with the People of the Book, they should avoid such approaches as cause bitterness or arouse hostility:

And do not dispute with the People of the Book except by (the way) which is best, unless it be with such of them as transgress, and say, 'We believe in what has been sent down to us and sent down to you, and our God and your God is one, and to Him do we submit.' (29:46)

We have already seen how Islam permits eating with the People of the Book, sharing the meat they slaughter, and marrying their women, marriage being a relationship of mutual love and mercy. As Allah Ta'ala says:

...The food of those who were given the Scripture (before you) is permitted to you and your food is permitted to them. And (lawful to you in marriage are) chaste women from among the Believers and chaste women from among those who were given the Scripture before you....(5:6 (5))

This relates to the People of the Book in general. However,

Christians in particular have been given special status by the Qur'an and are considered much closer to the hearts of the Believers.

Non-Muslim Residents of an Islamic State

The above injunctions include all People of the Book wherever they may be. However, those people who live under the protection of an Islamic government enjoy special priviliges. They are referred to as "the Protected People" *(ahl al-dhimmah* or *dhimmies)*, meaning that Allah, His Messenger (peace be on him), and the community of Muslims have made a covenant with them that they may live in safety and security under the Islamic government.

In modern terminology, *dhimmies* are "citizens" of the Islamic state. From the earliest period of Islam to the present day, Muslims are in unanimous agreement that they enjoy the same rights and carry the same responsibilities as Muslims themselves, while being free to practice their own faiths.

The Prophet (peace be on him) emphasized the duties of Muslims toward *dhimmies*, threatening anyone who violates them with the wrath and punishment of Allah. He said,

"He who hurts a *dhimmi* hurts me, and he who hurts me annoys Allah."[1]

Whoever hurts a *dhimmi*, I am his adversary, and I shall be an adversary to him on the Day of Resurrection.[2]

On the Day of Resurrection I shall dispute with anyone who oppresses a person from among the People of the Covenant, or infringes on his right, or puts a responsibility on him which is beyond his strength, or takes something from him against his will.[3]

The successors of the Prophet, the caliphs, safeguarded these rights and sanctities of non-Muslim citizens, and the jurists of Islam, in spite of the variation of their opinions regarding many

[1]Reported by al-Tabarani in *Al-awsat* on good authority.
[2]Reported by al-Khatib on good authority.
[3]Reported by Abu Daoud.

338

other matters, are unanimous in emphasizing these rights and sanctities.

Says the Maliki jurist, Shaha al-Deen al-Qarafi:

The covenant of protection imposes upon us certain obligations toward the *ahl al-dhimmah*. They are our neighbors, under our shelter and protection upon the guarantee of Allah, His Messenger (peace be on him), and the religion of Islam. Whoever violates these obligations against any one of them by so much as an abusive word, by slandering his reputation, or by doing him some injury or assisting in it, has breached the guarantee of Allah, His Messenger (peace be on him), and the religion of Islam.[1]

And the Zahiri jurist, Ibn Hazm, says:

If one is a *dhimmi,* and the enemy comes with his forces to take him, it is our obligation to fight the enemy with soldiers and weapons and to give our lives for him, thus honoring the guarantee of Allah and His Messenger (peace be on him). To hand him over to the enemy would mean to dishonor this guarantee.[2]

Meaning of Friendship with Non-Muslims

A question which troubles some people and which is sometimes discussed openly is the following: How can we show kindness, affection, and good treatment to non-Muslims since Allah Ta'ala Himself prohibits Muslims to take non-believers as friends, allies, and supporters in such verses as the following:

O you who believe, do not take the Jews and Christians as friends; they are the friends (only) of each other. And whoever among you turns to them (for friendship) is certainly one of them; indeed, Allah does not guide the people who do wrong. Yet thou seest those in whose hearts is a disease racing toward them...(5:54-55(51-52))

---

[1]From the book, *Al-furuq,* by al-Qarafi.
[2]From the book, *Maratib al-ijma',* by Ibn Hazm.

The answer to this is that these verses are not unconditional, to be applied to every Jew, Christian, or non-Muslim. Interpreting them in this manner contradicts the injunctions of the Qur'an which enjoin affection and kindness to the good and peace-loving peoples of every religion, as well as the verses which permit marriage to the women of the People of the Book, with all that Allah says concerning marriage—"and He has put love and mercy between you" (30:21)—and the verse concerning the Christians:

...And thou wilt find those who say, 'Surely we are Christians,' to be nearest to them (the Muslims) in affection....(5:85 (82))[1]

The verses cited above were revealed in connection with those people who were hostile to Islam and made war upon the Muslims. Accordingly, it is not permissible for the Muslim to support or assist them—that is, to be their ally—nor to entrust them with secrets at the expense of his own religion and community. This point is explained in other verses, in which Allah Ta'ala says:

They will spare nothing to ruin you; they yearn for what makes you suffer. Hatred has been expressed by their mouths, but what their hearts conceal is still greater. Thus have We made clear to you the revelations (or signs), if you possess understanding. Ah! You love them, but they do not love you....(3:118-119)

This *ayah* throws light on the character of such people, who conceal great enmity and hatred against the Muslims in their hearts and whose tongues express some of the effects of such hostility.

Allah Ta'ala also says,

Thou wilt not find a people who believe in Allah and the Last Day loving those who oppose Allah and His Messenger, even though they may be their fathers or their sons or their brothers or their kin....(58:22)

Opposition to Allah is not simply belief but includes hostility toward Islam and Muslims.

Allah also says,

O you who believe, do not take My enemy and your

---

[1] The terms Christian and Christianity do not appear in the Christian scriptures nor can they be attributed to Jesus (pbuh) himself. The followers of Jesus were known as *Nasara* (helpers) and this is the word used in the Arabic text of the Qur'an; the name "Christian" was originally used by those who held the followers in contempt.

340

enemy as friends, offering them affection, even though they have disbelieved in what has come to you of the truth, driving out the Messenger and yourselves because you believe in Allah, your Lord....(60:1)

This verse was revealed in connection with the pagans of Makkah, who declared war on Allah and His Messenger (peace be on him), driving the Muslims out of their homes simply because they said, "Our Lord is Allah." With this type of people, friendship and alliance cannot be permitted. Yet in spite of this, the Qur'an did not dismiss the hope that some day there might be a reconciliation; it did not declare utter disappointment in them but encouraged the Muslims to entertain the hope of better circumstanes and improved relationships, for in the same *surah* Allah says:

It may be that Allah will bring about affection between you and those who are your enemies from among them. And Allah is All-Powerful, and Allah is Forgiving, Merciful. (60:7)

This Qur'anic statement gives the assurance that this bitter hostility and deep hatred will pass way, as it is also stated in the *hadith*,

"Hate your enemy mildly; he may become your friend one day." [1]

The prohibition against befriending the enemies of Islam is even more emphatic when they are stronger than the Muslims, crushing hopes and generating fear in the minds of people. In such a situation, only hypocrites and those in whose hearts there is a disease hasten to befriend them, giving them help today in order to benefit from them tomorrow. Allah Ta'ala describes this situation as follows:

Yet thou seest those in whose hearts is a disease racing toward them (the enemies of Islam), saying, 'We are afraid that a change of fortune may befall us.' But it may be that Allah will give (thee) the victory or some decision from Himself, and then they will become

---

[1] Reported by al-Tirmidhi. Al-Bayhaqi reported it in *Shi'ab al-iman* from Abu Hurairah. Al-Suyuti called it "good," transmitting the first part as "Love your friend mildly; he may become your enemy one day."

regretful for what they thought secretly within themselves. (5:55 (52))

And again,

Give to the hypocrites the tidings that they will have a grievous punishment. Do those who take the unbelievers as friends instead of the Believers seek honor among them? For indeed all honor belongs to Allah alone. (4:138-139)

Seeking Help From Non-Muslims

There is no harm done if Muslims, at either the private or governmental level, seek help from non-Muslims in technical matters which have no connection with the religion — for example, in medicine, industry, or agriculture. At the same time it is of course extremely desirable that Muslims become self-sufficient in all such fields.

We see from the life of the Prophet (peace be on him) that he employed 'Abdullah bin 'Uraiqit, a polytheist, to be his guide on his flight (hijrah) from Makkah to Madinah. Scholars have concluded from this that a person's unbelief does not mean that he is basically untrustworthy, for what could be more risky than depending on a guide to show the route, particularly in fleeing from Makkah to Madinah?

Going considerably beyond this, scholars say that it is permissible for the leader of the Muslims to seek help from non-Muslims, especially the People of the Book, in military matters, and to give them an equal share of spoils with the Muslims. Al-Zuhri reported that the Messenger of Allah (peace be on him) sought help from some of the Jews in a war and gave them a share of the spoils, and that Safwan bin Umayyah fought on the side of the Prophet (peace be on him) while still an idolator.[1] The condition for seeking help from a non-Muslim is that he be trusted by the Muslims; otherwise, help may not be sought from him. Since it is prohibited to seek help from unreliable Muslims, such as those who spread

---

[1] Reported by Sa'id in his *Sunan*.

342

rumors and anxieties, this is the more true in the case of non-believers.[1]

The Muslim is permitted to give gifts to non-Muslims and to accept gifts from them. It is sufficient here to mention that the Prophet (peace be on him) accepted gifts from non-Muslim kings.[2] Scholars of *ahadith* state that there are many *ahadith* which report that the Prophet (peace be on him) accepted gifts from non-Muslims, and Umm Salmah, a wife of the Prophet, narrated that the Prophet (peace be on him) told her,

> "I have sent al-Najashi[3] a robe and some silk."[4]

Indeed, Islam respects a human being only because he is human; how much the more then, if he is from the People of the Book and still more if he is a *dhimmi*? Once a funeral procession passed by the Prophet (peace be on him) and he stood up. Thereupon someone remarked, "O Messenger of Allah, it is the funeral of a Jew."

The Prophet (peace be on him) replied,

> "Was he not a soul?"[5]

Thus, truly, in Islam every human being has a dignity and a place.

The Extension of Islam's Universal Mercy to Animals

The universal mercy of Islam embraces not only human beings, whether unbelievers, People of the Book, or Muslims, but all other living creatures of Allah as well. Accordingly, Islam prohibits cruelty to animals. Thirteen hundred years before any societies for the prevention of cruelty to animals were established, Islam had made kindness to animals a part of its faith and cruelty to them a sufficient reason for a person to be thrown into the Fire.

The Prophet (peace be on him) related to his Companions the story of a man who found a dog panting with thirst. The man went down into a well, filled his shoes with water which he gave to the dog, and

---

[1] *Al-mughni*, vol. 8, p. 41.
[2] Reported by Ahmad and al-Tirmidhi.
[3] The Christian ruler of Abyssinia who secretly embraced Islam. (Trans.)
[4] Reported by Ahmad and al-Tabarani.
[5] Reported by al-Bukhari.

continued to do so until the dog's thirst was quenched. The Prophet (peace be on him) said,

'Then Allah was grateful to him and forgave him his sins.' The Companions asked, 'Is there a reward for us in relation to animals, O Messenger of Allah?' He replied 'There is a reward in (relation to) every living creature.'[1]

Side by side with this radiant picture of Allah's forgiveness and pleasure, the Prophet (peace be on him) drew another picture depicting Allah's anger and punishment. He said,

A woman was sent to the Fire because of a cat. She imprisoned her and neither fed her nor set her free to feed upon the rodents of the earth.[2]

Respect for Allah's living creatures reached such an extent that when the Prophet (peace be on him) saw a donkey with a branded face, he denounced such a practice saying,

"I would not brand an animal except on the part of its body farthest from its face."[3]

In another report, he passed by a donkey with a branded face and said,

"Have you not heard that I have cursed anyone who brands an animal on its face or who hits it on its face?"[4]

We have already mentioned that when Ibn 'Umar saw some people practicing archery using a hen as a target, he said,

"The Prophet (peace be on him) cursed anyone who made a living thing into a target."

And Ibn 'Abbas said, The Prophet (peace be on him) forbade that animals be made to fight each other, since people would goad animals into fighting each other until one of them was pecked or gored to death, or close to it. Ibn 'Abbas also reported that the Prophet (peace be on him) strongly condemned the castration of animals.[5]

The Qur'an condemned the Arabs of *jahiliyyah* for their slitting the ears of cattle, calling this a practice inspired by Satan. (4:119)

---

[1] Reported by al-Bukhari.
[2] Reported by al-Bukhari.
[3] Reported by Muslim.
[4] Reported by Abu Daoud and al-Tirmidhi.
[5] Reported by al-Bazzar on sound authority.

In relation to the method of slaughtering an animal, we have already pointed out that Islam insists that the manner of slaughter should be that which is least painful to the victim and its requiring that the knife be sharpened but not in front of the animal. Islam also prohibits the slaughtering of one animal in front of another. Never, prior to Islam, had the world witnessed such concern for animals, a concern which was beyond its imagination.

CONCLUDING REMARKS

The purpose of writing this book did not extend beyond discussing what is *halal* and *haram* in actions and outward behavior. As for the *halal* and *haram* in the actions of the mind and the movements of the soul, it was not our intention to deal with them in this volume, even though such diseases of the soul as envy and covetousness, pride and arrogance, hypocrisy and ostentation, greed and lust, are among the major sins. Islam declares unrelenting war on them, and the Prophet (peace be on him) has warned of their evil consequences, charcterizing some of them as "the diseases of earlier nations" and calling them "the razor" which shaves not hair but religion.

Anyone who studies the Qur'an and the *Sunnah* of the Prophet (peace be on him) knows that soundness of heart and integrity of soul are considered as the basis of success, both for the individual and for the society, in this world and in the Hereafter:

> Indeed, Allah does not change the condition of a people until they change what is in themselves....(13:11)

> The Day on which (neither) wealth nor sons will be of no avail except to the one who brings to Allah a sound heart. (26:88-89)

Hence, the Prophet (peace be on him) has said,

> The *halal* is clear and the *haram* is clear. Between the two there are doubtful matters concerning which people do not know whether they are *halal* or *haram*. One who avoids them in order to safeguard his religion and honor is safe, while if someone engages in a part of them he may be doing something *haram*, like one who grazes his animals near the *hima* (the grounds reserved for animals belonging to the king which are out of bounds for others' animals); it is thus quite likely that some of his animals will stray into it. Truly, every king has a *hima*, and the *hima* of Allah is what He has prohibited.[1]

---

[1]Reported by al-Bukhari, Muslim, and others; the narration is taken from al-Tirmidhi.

He then explained the value of the heart, the source of the emotions, inclinations, and intentions which are the basis of all human behavior, saying,

> In the body there is a piece of flesh such that if it is good the whole body is good, while if it is corrupted the whole body is corrupted, and that is the heart.

For the heart is the chief organ of the body and rules it. If the ruler is good, the subjects are good, but if the ruler becomes corrupt, the subjects become corrupt.

In the scale of Allah it is the heart and the intentions which have weight, not the face and the tongue:

> Allah does not look at your physical features, but He looks at your hearts.

> Deeds are judged by their intentions, and everyone will be judged according to what he intended.

Such is the place of the actions of the heart and the affairs of the soul in Islam. However, because they relate to the character of the individual rather than to what is lawful and what is prohibited, we have not dealt with them in this volume. These inner aspects of Islam have been discussed by other scholars and by Muslim Sufis in great depth and detail. They have referred to the moral and spiritual sins as "diseases of the heart," have diagnosed their causes , and have prescribed remedies for them in the light of the Book of Allah and the noble *Sunnah* of the Prophet (peace be on him). Imam al-Ghazzali has devoted one-fourth of his encyclopedic work about Islam, *Ihya 'ulum al-deen*, to this topic, terming them "fatal diseases," since they lead a person to degradation in this world and to the Fire in the Hereafter.

Another point to be noted is that we have dealt here only with sins of "commission" and not those of "omission," although sins are of two kinds: doing something which is forbidden and not doing something which is obligatory. The second type of sin was not the subject matter of this book, although we have touched upon it here and there in the course of discussion. Had we aimed at describing the sins of omission, we would have been discussing an entirely different subject; we would then have been describing all the obligations which Allah has laid upon the Muslim, for unquestionably not doing them or neglecting them is *haram*. For example, seeking knowledge is an obligation on every Muslim man and woman. If the Muslim keeps himself in the darkness of ignorance, he will commit sins through lack of knowledge and consequently will not carry out his religious obligations such as *salat, zakat*, fasting, and *hajj* , which are pillars of Islam. It is not permissible for the Muslim to abandon them without a legitimate excuse since not to carry them out is a major sin, while to downgrade their value and ignore them is to abandon Islam.

To give another example, it is an obligation on the Muslim *ummah* to muster military power to the utmost extent of its capacity in order to defend itself and to keep the enemy of Allah and of Islam at bay. This is a general obligation on the entire community of Islam and, in particular, on those who are at the helm of affairs; accordingly, the neglect of such an important obligation is a major sin and a great shame. We could go on multiplying examples, since the case of all the other obligations, whether individual or collective, is similar.

We do not claim to have covered the whole range of what is *halal* and what is *haram*. In these pages we have only highlighted the most important matters which are permissible or prohibited in the personal, family, and social life of the Muslim, especially those matters which people neglect or consider insignificant due to their ignorance of the reasons behind a prohibition or permission. We have attempted to show the deep wisdom of the Islamic *Shari'ah* in its legislations concerning the *halal* and *haram*, so that anyone who possesses two eyes can observe that Allah Ta'ala is not arbitrary in His commandments, neither permitting things in order to be indulgent to people nor prohibiting them in order to make their lives miserable. Rather, He has legislated for them what is in their own best interest, safeguarding their lives, intellect, property, morals and honor, and guiding them toward success in this world and in the Hereafter.

All man-made laws are inherently defective and incomplete, since the law-makers, whether they be individuals, governments, or legislatures, limit themselves to dealing with material considerations, neglecting the demands of religion and morality. They are forever confined within the narrow bounds of nationalism and the interests of a sector of mankind, paying little attention to the world at large and to the wider concerns of humanity; they legislate for the present, not knowing what lies in their future, nor what the effects of their laws will be. Over and above all this, legislators are human beings subject to their own weaknesses, desires, and prejudices ("Indeed, he (man) is unjust, ignorant.") (33:72) It is therefore not strange that man-made laws are short-sighted, shallow, biased toward the material interests of the society, and that they provide only temporary remedies. It should not be surprising if human legislation concerning what is legal or illegal is to a great extent influenced by public opinion, by lobbyists, and by what is popular or unpopular; accordingly, things are often made legal even if it is known that they are extremely dangerous and evil in their consequences.

One example of this may be sufficient. The government of the United States legalized drinking, repealing the earlier legislation which had banned it. The repeal of prohibition was enacted despite full knowledge of the evil and harm which the consumption of alcohol causes to individuals, families, and society. In contrast to this, the *Shari'ah* of Islam is free of all such defects. How can it be otherwise when it was legislated by the All-Knowing Creator Who is aware of His creation, what is suitable for it, and of what it is capable?

> ...Allah knows the one who makes corruption from him
> who sets things right....(2:220)
> Should He not know Who created (all things)? And He
> is the Subtle, the Aware. (67:14)

This is the legislation of the All-Wise God. He did not prohibit anything unnecessarily nor permit anything randomly. His creation is measured and His laws are harmonious.

It is the legislation of the All-Merciful Lord. He desires ease for human beings and does not desire hardship for them. How can it be otherwise, when He is more compassionate to His servants than the mothers who bore them?

It is the legislation of the All-Powerful King. He is independent of His servants and is not partial to one race or one generation, permitting to some what He prohibits to others. How could this be, when He is the Lord of all being?

This is what the Muslim believes concerning what Allah has made *halal* or *haram* and what He has legislated in relation to other aspects. He therefore accepts it with a convinced mind, a contented

349

heart, and with a strong determination to implement it. Indeed, he believes that his happiness in this world and his success in the Hereafter depend entirely upon his observing the limits set by Allah, following His injunctions, and observing His prohibtions. In order to secure his happiness and success in both worlds, therefore, he must restrain himself from transgresing these limits.

In order to illustrate how observant the first generation of Muslims was with regard to the limits set by Allah and how hard they strove to implement His commands, we cite two examples from their lives.

The First Example

In our discussion concerning the prohibition of alcohol, we mentioned how deeply the Arabs loved drinking wine and how greatly they enjoyed drinking parties. Then Allah Ta'ala gradually turned them away from drinking until He revealed the decisive verse prohibiting it totally and forever, calling it "an abomination of Satan's doing." (5:93 (90)) Thereupon the Prophet (peace be on him) forbade Muslims to drink alcohol, to sell it, or to give it as a gift to non-Muslims.

When the Muslims heard about the prohibition of *khamr*, they at once brought out their stocks of wine and poured them into the streets of Madinah as a declaration that they had abandoned drinking. Even more remarkable in expressing their total submission to what Allah had legislated was the action of those who were engaged in drinking wine when the verse, "Will you not then desist?" (5:94 (91)) reached them. Without hesitating for a moment, they threw whatever drinks were left in their glasses upon the ground, exclaiming, "O Lord, we have desisted!"

When we compare this manifest success in combatting and eradicating alcohol from the Islamic society with the disastrous failure of the government of the United States,[1] which decided one day to combat this evil by means of laws and force, we cannot escape the obvious conclusion that human beings do not reform themselves except by means of the *Shari'ah* of Allah, which relies on the faith

---

[1] A more detailed discussion of this comparison is given in our book, *Al-'aqidah dururat li al-hayat (The Role of Belief in Life),* under the heading of "Belief and Morals."

and the consciences of the people before endeavoring to apply authority and force.

The Second Example

This concerns the response of the first generation of Muslim women to Allah's prohibitng women the display of their adornment and enjoining modesty and the covering of their *'awrah*. During the period of *jahiliyyah* women used to go about with their hair, neck and breasts uncovered, displaying the ornaments they wore such as earrings and necklaces. Allah Ta'ala then prohibited Muslim women this wanton display of the period of Ignorance, commanding them to be different and distinguishable from the women of *jahiliyyah* by observing modesty and by drawing their head-coverings over their hair, neck and bosoms in order to conceal them.

The following are narrations from the Mother of the Believers, 'Aishah (may Allah be pleased with her), concerning the manner in which the *Muhajir* and *Ansar* women received the divine injunction which required a major change in their life-styles, affecting their appearance, dress, and ornamentation. She said, "May Allah shower His mercy on the early *Muhajir* women. When the verse, 'That they should draw their head-coverings over their bosoms' (24:31) was revealed, they tore up their garments to cover themselves."[1]

Once when some women were in the company of 'Aishah, they mentioned the women of the Quraish and their merits. 'Aishah remarked,

> The Quraish women were indeed good, but, by Allah, I have seen no one better than the women of the *Ansar* in applying the Book of Allah and believing in the revelation. When the *ayah* of *Surah al-Noor*, 'That they should draw their head-coverings over their bosoms,' was revealed, their men returned to their homes and recited it to their women. No sooner did the man recite it to his wife, his daughter, his sister, or any other female relative, then she tied any piece of cloth available to her, perhaps from a curtain having pictures on it (on her head), so that when they came to pray behind the

---

[1]Reported by al-Bukhari.

351

Prophet (peace be on him), it looked as if crows were sitting on their heads. [1]

This was the response of the believing women to what Allah had legislated for them. They hastened to implement what He had commanded and to abandon what He had prohibited without hesitating, stopping to think about it, or waiting. They did not even delay a day or two so that they could get a suitable, soft piece of cloth and sew it to fit their heads and cover their bosoms, rather, any cloth which was available, whether rough, brightly-colored, or having pictures on it, was sufficiently soft and befitting. If no other cloth was found, they simply tore up the garments they were wearing and tied the strips to their heads, not caring about their appearance, which, as the Mother of the believers has described it, resembled that of crows sitting on their heads.

The point we wish to stress here is that mere academic knowledge of the *halal* and *haram*, and of the limits of these is not sufficient. Although the major sins and principal obligations are known to every Muslim, nonetheless we find a great many of them indulging in these sins and neglecting those obligations, and rushing toward the Fire with their eyes wide open.

If the Muslim is well-versed in the knowledge of his religion and its *Shari'ah*, and at the same time possesses a fully alert conscience which safeguards the limits so that they cannot be overstepped, he is indeed rich in all goodness. The Prophet (peace be on him) spoke the truth when he said,

"When Allah intends good for a person, He makes his own soul a watcher over him." [2]

We end our book with the following supplication which has come to us from the early Muslims:

O Allah, make us independent of Thy *haram* with Thy *halal*, of disobedience to Thee with obedience to Thee, and of any other than Thee with Thy bounty.

All praise is for Allah Subhanahu wa Ta'ala, Who guided us to this; had He not given us guidance, we would not have been guided.

---

[1] Ibn Kathir mentions this in his discussion of this *ayah*, on the authority of Ibn Abi Hatim.
[2] Al-Iraqi said, "Al-Dailami reported it in *Musnad al-firdaus* on good authority."

INDEX

CPSIA information can be obtained at www.ICGtesting.com
Printed in the USA
BVOW081126120513

320504BV00001B/201/P